Ceridwen Spark is a l
and Governance in
National University.
Gender Studies at M_
held two part-time postdoctoral fellowships, one at
Monash University and the other at Victoria University.
During these fellowships, she researched cross-cultural interaction in
PNG; the medical investigation of kuru; gender and education in PNG;
and international adoption. In recent years, Ceridwen has focused on
investigating the experiences of women leaders and educated, urban-
dwelling women in PNG. She has published articles about this work
in various refereed journals. In 2011–12, Ceridwen sought and gained
AusAID funding for the Pawa Meri project, which involves making six
films about leading women in PNG. These films will be released in
PNG and elsewhere in the Pacific.

Seumas Spark is an historian attached to Monash
University. His PhD, undertaken at the University
of Edinburgh, focused on the collection and burial
of the Second World War British military dead and
the profound social consequences of that treatment.
Battlefield to Grave, a monograph based on his thesis,
will be published by Manchester University Press. Seumas is interested
in the social history of war, and PNG history.

Christina Twomey is Professor of History at Monash
University and an Australian Research Council Future
Fellow. She is the author of three books, including
*Australia's Forgotten Prisoners: Civilians Interned by
the Japanese in World War Two* (Cambridge University
Press, 2007) and, with co-author Mark Peel, *A History
of Australia* (Palgrave Macmillan, 2011). Christina has also published
widely on the cultural history of war and humanitarianism, and has been
particularly interested in issues of imprisonment, captivity, witnessing
and photography. In 2012, Christina was the Distinguished Visiting
Chair of Australian Studies at the University of Copenhagen, and is
currently co-editor of Australian Historical Studies.

Australians in Papua New Guinea 1960–1975

Edited by Ceridwen Spark, Seumas Spark and Christina Twomey

PACIFIC STUDIES SERIES

An imprint of UQP

First published 2014 by University of Queensland Press
PO Box 6042, St Lucia, Queensland 4067 Australia

www.uqepress.com.au
www.uqp.com.au
uqp@uqp.uq.edu.au

© Ceridwen Spark, Seumas Spark and Christina Twomey (compilation, introduction and interviews)
Essays © individual authors

This book is copyright. Except for private study, research, criticism or reviews, as permitted under the Copyright Act, no part of this book may be reproduced, stored in a retrieval system, or transmitted in any form or by any means without prior written permission. Enquiries should be made to the publisher.

Cover design by Kate Barry
Typeset in 11/15 pt Electra LH by Post Pre-press Group, Brisbane
Ebook produced by Read How You Want
Printed by Lightning Source

UQ ePress Pacific Studies Series Editorial Committee:
Professor Clive Moore (Chair)
Professor Brij Lal

Cataloguing-in-Publication Data available from
the National Library of Australia
http://catalogue.nla.gov.au/

UQ ePress pacific studies series
978-1-921902-43-7 (pbk)
978-1-921902-45-1 (pdf)
978-1-921902-44-4 (epub)

CONTENTS

SELECT ABBREVIATIONS

ADO	Assistant District Officer
CPC	Constitutional Planning Committee
CRA	Conzinc Riotinto
DC	District Commissioner
LMS	London Missionary Society
PHD	Public Health Department
PMC	Papuan Medical College
PNG	Papua New Guinea
UPNG	University of Papua New Guinea

TOK PISIN GLOSSARY

bilas	decoration
boi haus	accommodation for domestic help
dokta	doctor
haus boi/haus meri	male domestic help/female domestic help
kaikai (abbrev. kai)	food (noun), eat (verb)
kaukau	sweet potato
kiap	Administration/patrol officer
laplap	length of cloth worn around the waist
luluai	senior village leader
manki masta	male domestic help, valet (indigenous)
masta	white man or employer
meri	indigenous woman/wife
misis	white woman/wife
nambawan	first, best, most important
pikinini	child or junior
singsing	song, ceremonial dancing and singing, party
taim bipo	before, once, previously. Can refer to the pre-Independence period
wantok	relative or friend (usually someone speaking the same language)

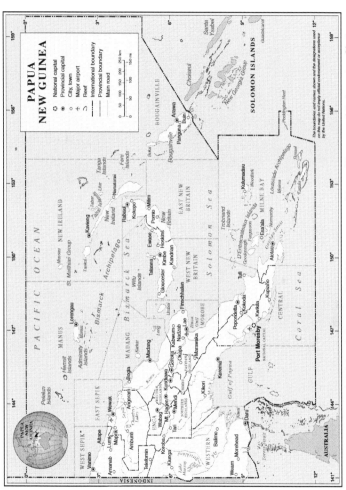

Papua New Guinea, Map No. 4104 Rev.1, January 2004 (www.un.org/Depts/Cartographic/map/profile/papua.pdf) Sourced and reproduced with permission from the United Nations.

Stories about Australians in Papua New Guinea from the 1960s to Independence in 1975 are not often told despite the wealth of people who were a part of that time. Australian public servants, teachers, missionaries, medical researchers, doctors, nurses, botanists, coffee plantation owners and commercial entrepreneurs were among the many who went to PNG. And because they were there, so too were their children.

When Ceridwen, Seumas and Christina approached me to write a foreword to their book, I jumped at the chance. Ceridwen, Seumas and I are the children of people who lived in PNG during this era, one which saw the birth of a young nation after decades of Australian 'colonisation'. In 1960, my father went to Bougainville as a *kiap*, a Government Patrol Officer. My mother, a teacher, joined him later. My parents left Goroka 36 years after my father had first arrived in PNG. My sister and I were both born in the country. Along with Ceridwen and Seumas, we grew up in Goroka in the Eastern Highlands, where I was fortunate to have been taught by their mother, Helen, at the International Primary School. At the school, children from over one hundred different nations were brought together as a result of their parents' shared interest in living in PNG.

There is nothing I enjoy more than listening to my parents' stories about their time in PNG. My mother, a young city slicker from Melbourne, had to learn to wash her clothes on a rock in a river. My father recalls the coronial inquiry he chaired which found that a ghost had caused the death of a drunken man who fell off a swing bridge one dark night. Another of his stories involves a young man who, having broken taboos by sleeping with a menstruating woman, was saved thanks to a couple of multi-vitamin pills.

While I do not remember the years before Independence (I was three in 1975), my parents discuss how foreigners approached living and working in another people's country. Some respected the cultural differences and were fascinated to learn of another society, while others wanted to be part of some colonial past, ringing bells for house boys or girls to meet their needs.

In order to progress, it is important to know your past. This book will enable many people in PNG to understand their recent history, trigger memories for those who lived it, and expose other Australians to the lives of our nearest neighbours. In her interview for the book Meg Taylor states: 'Papua New Guinea gets under the skin and it holds you to her'. This is true. My passion for PNG, and that of Ceridwen and Seumas and many others, lives on. Through this book, so too do the stories.

The Hon. Lara Giddings, MHA
Premier of Tasmania, 2011–14

Introduction
LIVING ON THE EDGE OF THE WORLD
Ceridwen Spark, Seumas Spark and Christina Twomey

A few years ago Seumas was reading about the Stolen
Generations. Among the Australians who raised awareness of
Aboriginal rights and issues from the 1950s to 70s were people
he associated with Papua New Guinea. Charles Rowley, for
example. An advocate for Aboriginal rights and author of
seminal works on indigenous Australia, Rowley had a close
association with PNG over several decades, including as
Professor of Political Studies at the University of Papua New
Guinea from 1968 to 1974. His book *The New Guinea Villager*
has long occupied a place on the Spark family bookshelves. Two
more familiar names were Ronald and Catherine Berndt. In
the 1950s these pioneering anthropologists conducted research
in the Eastern Highlands of New Guinea, where Seumas and
Ceridwen grew up.

Other prominent and successful Australians who had lived and worked in PNG soon came to mind: Fred Chaney, politician and university chancellor; Ross Garnaut, ambassador and government adviser; Alan Gilbert, historian and university vice-chancellor; Michael Jeffrey, soldier and governor general; Alan Morris, senior public servant and international consultant; Drusilla Modjeska, author and editor. What took these people to PNG? What did they hope to gain from living there? How did the experience influence their lives and careers? The idea for this book was born.

Subsequently, we decided to focus on the 15 years before PNG became independent in September 1975, in part because there is a lack of writing about the country during this period. Historian Hank Nelson believed that people have been deterred from writing about this crucial time in PNG history because of the country's post-Independence difficulties. We hope the reflections written for this book, and the interviews undertaken for it, contribute to filling this gap. With the timeframe settled, all that remained was to invite Papua New Guineans and Australians resident in PNG during this period to reflect on their experiences. How do they remember this time? What are their perspectives on the Australian influence from 1960–75? As for many Australians, these years proved fruitful in the lives and careers of many Papua New Guineans.

There had been a British or Australian presence in PNG since the late nineteenth century. Prior to the Second World War, there had been two distinct territories: Papua and New Guinea. Queenslanders, in particular, had watched nervously as Germany annexed the northeastern part of the island in 1884. In response, largely at Australian insistence, Britain annexed Papua, or the southeastern quarter of the island, territory contiguous to German New Guinea. In 1906 control of the Territory of Papua passed from Britain to the newly federated nation of Australia. One of Australia's first actions during the First World War was the successful capture of German New Guinea. Thereafter, Australia retained possession of the Territory of New Guinea, under a League of Nations mandate. According to the Covenant of the League of Nations, the mandates system was directed at 'peoples not yet able to stand by themselves under the strenuous conditions of the modern world' (Article 22, Covenant of the League of Nations). This effectively transferred former German and Ottoman colonies to Allied control. Australia, as a beneficiary of the mandates system, was charged with the 'well-being and development' of New Guinea as a 'sacred trust of civilization' (Article 22, Covenant of the League of Nations). The mandates system instituted a system of Australian colonial control in New Guinea.

While the Japanese invasion of both Papua and New Guinea during the Second World War temporarily inter-rupted Australian governance, the coming of peace restored it, albeit in altered form. The colonial overtones remained. Henceforth, Papua and New Guinea would form one admin-istrative unit, the Territory of Papua and New Guinea. From 1949 Australia was the administering power of Papua and New Guinea under an international trusteeship system created by the United Nations. Papua, that is, was no longer immune from international oversight. Trusteeship, a direct descendant of the mandates system, more clearly articulated a purpose for 'progressive development towards self-government or independence' (Charter of the United Nations). Other trust powers included New Zealand in Samoa, Britain and France in the Cameroons, and Belgium in Ruanda-Urundi. Many of these United Nations trust territories gained independent nation status in the 1960s. By the 1970s, PNG was one of the few remaining trusts. 'The whole world believes that … we run one of the world's last colonies', Australian Prime Minister Gough Whitlam told a gathering in Port Moresby in 1971 (Murray-Smith 1984, 281).

This book focuses on the final 15 years of Australia's period as the administering power in PNG. In doing so, it traces the end of a colonial regime, not through violent over-throw, revolution or coup, but via a voluntary relinquishment of power. Its contributors reflect on the challenges that the transition to independence posed for Papua New Guineans, and for the Australian officials and administrators charged with effecting the change. They also consider the legacy of the connection between Australia and PNG that has existed for over a century, and the relationship between power and responsibility.

In his interview for this collection, Ken Inglis discusses whether or not independence came 'too early'. Reminding us that it is necessary to consider the alternatives, he asks: 'Would there have been terrible violence if PNG independence had been delayed? … Did the country have enough skilled and highly educated people, public servants, and politicians … to run a country? … [W]as the alternative thinkable? Who knows?' Charles Lepani comments that while 'things probably didn't go as we had expected and hoped … a delay would have made things worse'. Despite the doubts that may have arisen since, most of the contributors recall the optimism and excitement of the times. Bill Gammage, for example, is certain that it was appropriate to pursue independence.

Another topic common to the essays is the relationships of Australians with Papua New Guineans. There are diverse perspectives. Some see their relationships with Papua New Guineans in terms of a 'shared humanity' (Michael Alpers). Others, Margaret Smith for example, remark that there were limited opportunities to interact with local people and that this was not 'discrimination but a recognition of difference'. Meg Taylor, one of our contributors, is the daughter of Jim Taylor, an Australian-born patrol officer and explorer, and Yerima Taylor, a New Guinean woman from the Wahgi Valley. Having grown up acutely aware of the distinct groups of people that lived in and near Goroka, Meg makes clear that while racism was for many a normal and accepted part of everyday life, some Australians had equal and mutually respectful relationships with Papua New Guineans. One thing seems clear; those who lived in villages and hamlets were in a better position to appreciate indigenous perspectives. Michael Alpers, Ian Maddocks and Carol Kidu are remarkable Australians (or former Australian in the case of Carol Kidu) who have benefited from their openness to this experience. As Isi Kevau notes, the intimacy created through sharing life in the same place made a difference to the everyday practice of medicine, not least because people trusted doctors not to use medical samples to perform sorcery.

The relationship between Australia and PNG is based on a unique shared history, yet many Australians see PNG only as the biggest recipient of Australian aid. Given this, and the experiences and insights of the contributors, it is helpful to read the opinions of several on the subject. Charles Lepani, who has reviewed Australian aid to PNG on several occasions, wonders whether Australia's provision of aid produces a dependency relationship that ultimately is detrimental to bilateral relations. Ken Clezy has a different view, arguing that we 'must hang on for the long haul', while Inglis wonders whether arguing to cut aid is mean-spiritedness disguised. Their perspectives are reminders of the value of looking back as we continue to negotiate the complexities in the Australia-PNG relationship.

As this collection is precisely about looking back, it is apt that the title of this introduction is taken from Ken Inglis's contribution. With characteristic poeticism, he reflects on his family's experience of being in PNG: 'The experience of living there gave us a temporary foothold in a world that wasn't our own – a glimpse into a world that was exciting, alien, and constantly challenging our understanding. And that continues even to this day. That sense of having lived on the edge of another world has stayed with all our kids, as with us.' We concur. PNG was home for Seumas and Ceridwen in the 1970s and 80s. Since our return to Australia, it has dwelt within us, providing a constant source of memory, inspiration and awareness of cultural difference for which we are grateful.

***

The book is divided into three sections, the first of which is 'Medicine and Science'. This field has a long and distinguished history in PNG, testament in part to the many Australian doctors and scientists who have been attracted to the country.

The memories of several are recorded here, as are those of Isi Kevau, for whom PNG is both home and a place to practise medicine. We trust that Robin Radford, historian, social worker and archivist, does not mind her contribution, co-authored with her doctor husband, appearing in this section. The second section, 'Policy, Governance and Justice', contains the reminiscences of public servants who played important roles in building the political, legal and administrative framework of independent PNG. In Charles Lepani's case, his public service to PNG continues 40 years on. His chapter is one of four in the book that is an edited transcription of an interview conducted with one of the editors. Also in the second section is the contribution of Bill Brown, of whom a special request was made. In the belief that the book should include a chapter on Bougainville – the island's troubles have been central to PNG history – we asked Bill, who was stationed on Bougainville for several years, to focus his writing accordingly. The third section is 'Education, Race and Social Change'. In the 1960s and 70s UPNG was served by a number of visionary scholars who, in the best traditions of education, sought not only to gain knowledge but also to share it. The memories of two of these scholars are followed by the thoughts of three women, each devoted to PNG, on colonial life, social change and the future of the country. In the conclusion Jonathan Ritchie of Deakin University places the contributions into context and discusses themes raised in the book.

References

Article 22, Covenant of the League of Nations. avalon.law.yale.edu/20th_century/leagcov.asp#art22.

Charter of the United Nations, Chapter XII: International Trusteeship System, Article 76 (b). www.un.org/en/documents/charter/chapter12.shtml.

Murray-Smith, Stephen (ed.), *Dictionary of Australian Quotations*, (Melbourne: Heinemann, 1984).

MEDICINE AND SCIENCE

1

MEDICAL RESEARCH IN THE HIGHLANDS: BEING PART OF THE COMMUNITY DOES MAKE A DIFFERENCE

Michael P. Alpers

I went to the Territory of Papua and New Guinea in October 1961 to study kuru, a fatal neurodegenerative disease found only in a remote corner of the Eastern Highlands (Alpers 2007; Collinge & Alpers 2008). I was a young medical doctor from the University of Adelaide and my original intention had been to come on a fellowship arranged through the University. Early work on kuru published in 1958 had suggested that the disease had a genetic basis, and the Administration decided to restrict the movement of the Fore people and other groups who suffered from kuru, in order to prevent the spread of the putative delete-rious gene. It was not long before the authorities realised that, whatever the ethics of it, this plan was not feasible and it was quietly scrapped. The only outcome was the proposal to place, in compensation, a full-time research medical officer in the

Okapa Sub-District (now District) of the Eastern Highlands District (now Province) to study the disease. The Administration approached Professor H. N. (Norrie) Robson, my Professor of Medicine, to see if by any remote chance he could find some-body to fill the position. Since I was there, poised to go, he was able to put my name forward before the authorities changed their mind. So I arrived as a medical officer on the government payroll and was assigned to the small Research Division of the Department of Public Health. My boss was Dr Frank Schofield, but I did not meet him until about five months later.

My airfare and those of my wife Wendy and eight-month-old daughter Kirsten were paid to Port Moresby, where I signed a few papers, and we were promptly sent on to Goroka. By serendipity a six-week linguistics course run by the Summer Institute of Linguistics was about to start in Goroka at exactly that time. By a stroke of genius on the part of someone in the Public Health Department I was assigned to attend this course. It was open to all members of the public service in the Territory and to patrol officers from Netherlands New Guinea (now the Papua Province of Indonesia). There were not many from our side of the border but the Dutch officers were keen students and good company. For me the course was a revelation. I had no knowledge of linguistics and no understanding of how to learn and analyse an unwritten language. What I learned about phonetics and phonemics and the structure of language was intellectually exciting; moreover, these new skills and insights proved to be very useful in the work I was about to undertake. We also learned a little Gahuku, the language of the Goroka people. I am not sure how often the course was held or whether the Department of Native Affairs ever showed more interest in it, but the fact that it was held at all showed that someone, somewhere in the Administration was thinking straight. On the Dutch side of the border the district staff were clearly much more engaged with the local people on their own terms than was the case on the Australian side. Nevertheless, on both sides there was the prevailing belief that the process of pacification and modernisation of the 'natives' had only just begun, and ideas of independence were completely premature and could be deferred for a generation or two. So I learned a lot during the course, from my teachers and my fellow students, about the Melanesian people among whom I would be working and the colonial world which I was entering. My political education, however, soon became outmoded when the prevailing belief was challenged, firstly by the recommendations made by the 1962 United Nations mission to the Territory, led by Sir Hugh Foot, and secondly by a Dutch program to prepare rapidly for local independence. This was thwarted by the Indonesian colonial takeover in 1962 (Langdon 1971, 42–59).

I also learned about pigbel. There are three diseases which are peculiar to PNG and have made the country famous in medical circles: kuru, pigbel and swollen belly syndrome. I had come to work on kuru. During my time in Goroka, before I had set foot in the kuru-affected area, Wendy, Kirsten and I stayed with Tim Murrell and his family. Tim was an old school friend and was working as a medical officer at the Goroka Hospital. He was just beginning his work on pigbel, a serious gangrenous disease of the small bowel in children which was associated with large pig feasts, and naturally he told me about his ideas (Murrell 1984, 3–10; Walker 2003). I occasionally went with Tim to the hospital and thus it happened that I saw a patient suffering from pigbel before I had seen one with kuru.

From my linguistics course I learned how complex and sophisticated the local languages were, which gave me a deep respect for their speakers. During the course we would go to the Goroka market, where large numbers of people, all in traditional dress, arrived on Saturday from surrounding villages. We had to make an effort to speak to them in Gahuku. This was my first real contact with Papua New Guineans, and I was struck by their friendliness, patience with my bumbling talk, and beauty – especially of the young women. Relations were easy within the market itself but the local people were not allowed in the town after dusk, and I did notice that once they had left the comfort of the crowded market place they slunk away quickly through the town streets to make their way home. One of the most striking changes in PNG after Independence was that when the local people came from their village to town, they came in modern dress and walked about proudly as if the place belonged to them.

Once my course was over it was time to go out to Okapa. We had a house assigned to us on Okapa station. We were in touch with the *kiap* in charge of the sub-district and we flew by charter to Tarabo, where there was a Lutheran Mission airstrip that served the Mission and the government station about 15 kilometres away. The plane buzzed the station to announce our arrival and then flew to Tarabo and landed. The Assistant District Officer, Mert Brightwell, was already there to meet us. On the road to Okapa he had the driver stop the car on several occasions so that he could get out and 'berate the natives', usually for not properly maintaining their section of the road. It was clear that this was done largely for my benefit. I was not impressed. I was struck by the beauty of the countryside we were driving through and excited by the new and challenging tasks ahead of me. I realised that I had a lot to learn and I was eager to get on with my work. My first lesson was clear: I should not throw my weight around or behave in an arrogant, superior manner. When we reached Okapa we were met by Dr Andrew Gray, who was the medical officer in charge of the hospital on the station, and taken to our house. I had met Andrew in Adelaide, where he had come for further obstetrics training, and he immediately made us feel welcome. Our house was made of bush materials and was situated on a knoll above the tennis court, along the road that ran between the station office and the new houses built for senior administrative staff.

Okapa station had been built on a grassy hill with magnificent views in all directions. It had been beautifully laid out and the trees were beginning to grow. Originally the patrol post was to have been located down by the pine forest, which was a well-known part of the sub-district since seed had been gathered there for the pine plantations in Bulolo. However, when the station was being established it was realised that this low-lying area was malarious and so the station was summarily moved to the high ridge by Moke village. Since the name 'Okapa' had already been gazetted it was not changed; the name of the village near the pine forest was changed to 'Okasa', and everyone was happy. However, the locals were not fooled: the Fore translation of 'I am going to Okapa station' was 'Mokenti wowe'. The view from our house was towards Mt Michael, which can also be seen in Goroka from another direction, and in the early morning it was magical, with mists rising from all the intervening valleys. Below us, over the road and down in the first valley, was the village of Pusarasa.

Andrew was very solicitous and took good care of us. He introduced me to the hospital and his staff. He had built a leprosy ward where patients could stay and get long-term treatment; he was passionate about his leprosy patients, one of whom I employed as gardener and caretaker around our house. At this time there was no tuberculosis in the Highlands and yaws had been effectively eliminated but leprosy was common. It had come up from the coast through the traditional trade routes; one such route followed the Purari Valley to Karimui, where there was a lot of leprosy, and passed through the Gimi, where leprosy was common, to the Fore, where leprosy occurred but less frequently. Most of Andrew's patients, therefore, came from the Gimi linguistic group. Andrew also helped me to explore the area and taught me how to go on patrol. 'The first thing you need is an umbrella', he said, and he bought me one. Sadly, I have a tendency to ignore good advice, and when the umbrella broke, as it soon did, I never acquired another. Most afternoons in this Highland world it rained so heavily that the simplest thing was to get thoroughly wet, and dry out when the rain stopped or you reached your destination. While we were settling into our house in Okapa and when I was not out with Andrew, I borrowed one of Andrew's hospital orderlies so that he could sit with me at home and teach me Fore.

I saw my first patient with suspected kuru with Andrew and we both agreed that he did not have kuru. He was in the Okapa prison serving a sentence for murder. He had been the self-confessed killer of an alleged kuru sorcerer and was a hero in his home community. While in prison he had come down with a strange disorder that resembled kuru; however, the clinical features fluctuated and were not progressive and, after we had examined him, Andrew and I diagnosed his 'kuru' as hysterical. Despite our opinion but probably for good reason, the ADO released him from prison and sent him home to his village. The story had an interesting denouement. Six months later, when I was well into my kuru field studies, I saw this man again in his village. He still showed the same hysterical features, though less florid than before. I filmed him with my large Bolex camera on its tripod. This excellent camera had been provided for me by the University of Adelaide and, though it was an encumbrance, I took it with me (carried by two of my team) on all my trips to see patients. Not all patients were willing to be filmed but we used the camera whenever we could. Some weeks later I got the message that our hysterical patient had fully recovered from his kuru. This was no surprise to me but was generally considered amazing. Then I started to get deputations of people from all over the kuru region, even far north in the North Fore, where I only occasionally visited, asking me to come and see their relatives suffering from kuru. I was doing my best at that time to see as many patients as possible and I was enheartened by this public surge of support for my work. It took me a while to tumble to the fact that the 'cure' of the man I had filmed had been attributed to the camera: that was what people wanted for their sick relatives and not my personal attention or careful clinical examinations.

When I was in Adelaide planning my fieldwork I thought that I would try to base myself in a village and follow patients in their home environment from the beginning of their course to the end, with as much clinical and cinema documentation as possible. Professor Robson had given full support to these ideas, which is why he had managed to get me equipped with the best camera available. However, it had also been agreed that my program was flexible and could be adapted to whatever circumstances I found when I reached Okapa. As I settled into the colonial life on Okapa station it became abundantly clear that basing my work in a village community was indeed the way for me to go. I set about finding the right community and visited several possibilities. I had for a long time studied the maps of the area and knew the names of the villages where kuru occurred. From Okapa there was a road system that connected to the airstrip at Tarabo and by another road north reached Kainantu and joined the road to Goroka. There was no Highlands Highway: it was nine hours by road from Okapa to Goroka, which is why we did not go very often. There was also a road south to Purosa. Halfway along this road was the village of Wanitabi, where two anthropologists, Robert and Shirley Glasse, were working (Shirley later became Shirley Lindenbaum). They were supported by a Rockefeller Fellowship from the University of Adelaide, similar to the one that I might have come on, and had a short-wheel-base Land Rover that they were asked by the University to share with me. They were very friendly and helped me a lot.

The village of Waisa was an hour's walk off the road on the opposite side from Wanitabi; it was a rival to Wanitabi and, although there was intermarriage between the two villages, they were on mutually unfriendly terms. This general area in the middle of the South Fore had the highest incidence of kuru and villages away from the road had had little direct contact with outsiders. Waisa therefore seemed like a good choice for several reasons and I visited to explain my intentions. I was warmly welcomed, and so the matter was quickly settled. I then moved into the village on my own, met the people from different hamlets and arranged for a small house to be built for my temporary personal use. In response to the community's desire for my more permanent presence, I was allocated land. I compensated its previous users and we engaged carpenters from the North Fore to build a house there of pit-sawn timber and other local materials for me and my family.

Meanwhile I set about my work. I employed assistants from the village, whom I taught to read and write in Tok Pisin, which I was still in the process of learning myself. Two of my assistants I taught how to dress sores, give penicillin injections and keep records, and we set up a clinic in the village. Andrew Gray kept us fully supplied with the necessary medications. Since everyone in the community at that time had tropical ulcers, and the young children and older people commonly suffered from pneumonia, we were kept very busy in the clinic, especially after word got around and people started coming to us from distant villages. Soon I was able to leave some of the team in charge of the clinic and go out with the others seeing kuru patients in surrounding villages, usually requiring half a day's walk or more to get there. Eventually the big house on my ground at Yagoenti was completed and Wendy and Kirsten joined me in Waisa. We still kept our house on the station, which became mostly a transit house for me, but when I went on patrol or was waiting in another village for a patient to die, the family would settle back in Okapa, and they spent relatively more time there after James was born in November 1962.

I had read what anthropological papers there were on the Fore people and neighbouring groups. I suspected that the people of Waisa would be difficult to understand, suspicious of me and culturally alien. They expected me, naturally enough, to be like other white men that they had had dealings with. They knew that I was a doctor so they probably decided I was a risk worth taking. I was aware that their contact with the modern world was very recent, and that everyone over the age of 15 years had grown up in a traditional society using stone tools, with little knowledge of the outside world. I could not expect too much of our relationship. When I came, some of the young men latched on to me, I met the *luluai* Yaiigi and *tultul* Againaga and we talked together and in larger groups about my plans. The *luluai* was the headman of the village appointed by the Administration; he was sometimes but by no means always the traditional leader of the community. The *tultul* was the deputy headman of the village appointed by the Administration; he was usually from a different clan from that of the *luluai*; unlike the 'medical *tultul*' of the German Administration he had no specific function related to health.

I walked all over, up and down, the village grounds and began to learn their names, of which there were many. I visited each hamlet and scanned the boundaries of the village from different vantage points. I ate with people in their gardens and in their houses and made an effort to learn everyone's name. Without even thinking about it, seamlessly, from the beginning, there was mutual acceptance. We recognised our common humanity and moved on from there. It was the easiest thing imaginable. There was still much for me to learn and much that I did not understand, but that did not affect the reality and sincerity of our mutual acceptance. I now know that this was a privileged experience to which I have an obligation to bear witness. It supports, moreover, my gradual realisation that the discipline of anthropology was flawed at its core since it was based on the concept of the Other, and there is no Other. There is but one human race – and that is the only proper use for the word 'race' in the context of the subspecies *Homo sapiens sapiens*. The concept of ethnicity provides an inclusive combination of genetics and culture to describe human groups but there are no exclusive 'races' into which humankind can be divided – though, regrettably, we still need a word for racism. The core of anthropology should be our common humanity, from which all the ethnic differences arise. Though most anthropologists may think this way today it is hard to separate the discipline from its original core, which continues to constrain the way that inherently fascinating ethnographic information is written up. Moreover, the traditional owners of this information do not normally take part in anthropological conferences, nor are they included as co-authors of anthropological books and papers, though there have been exceptions (Majnep & Bulmer 1977; Whitfield et al. 2008; Wiessner & Pupu 2012).

The ADO or *nambawan kiap* on the station was the local lord: Queen's representative, chief of police, magistrate, governor of the prison, coroner, commander of transport, principal road engineer, postmaster and so on. Mr Brightwell was helpful and friendly but he always had to make clear who was boss. Since I was a government medical officer he was obliged to take care of my official needs, but my needs were few so he had little to do in that regard. He always helped Wendy and made sure that her order went in when the station vehicle made its weekly run to Kainantu to pick up stores. I had use of the Adelaide University Land Rover but if I needed transport Mert would do his best to provide it. However, occasionally it went the other way, when the station vehicle broke down and Mert had to request help from me. He found it hard to swallow his pride to do that, and I got a secret pleasure in helping him out. The *kiaps* on the whole were benign rulers, hard-working, tough, fair and committed to their task of bringing the 'natives' into the modern world through education, economic development and a peaceful and just civil society. Many individuals in all walks of life committed themselves in dedicated service to the betterment of people's lives and to the training of Papua New Guineans (Clezy 2011). Clive Auricht (2011, 42), writing of his experiences in PNG, declares that he is 'very proud of the contribution made by my fellow Australians' during the era of '*Taim Bilong Masta*' (the time when the white masters were in charge). It is true that a large number made admirable and valuable contributions over many years, but one has also to acknowledge that the system was colonial and racist. The local people were the 'natives' and they were certainly Other, officially discriminated against in all kinds of ways. No matter how idealistic young patrol officers may have been when they entered the service and received training in many useful skills and disciplines, including anthropology, and no matter how strongly they maintained that idealism throughout their careers, the system was colonial and no-one could escape that – except by leaving the service.

When I lived in Goroka after Independence one of my treasured friends was James (Jim) L. Taylor, the great explorer who expanded government control through first contact with

Highland groups in the 1930s. Jim loved PNG and he loved its people, and did so from the beginning of his remarkable career. He had a relationship with a Highland woman and they had a daughter. This was common enough among *kiaps* and indeed many such liaisons could hardly be dignified by the term 'relationship'. Such behaviour may not have been officially sanctioned but was considered perfectly acceptable. However, if a *kiap* wished to marry a local woman he had to leave the service. With his next relationship Jim did just that: he left the service and, not long afterwards, married Yerima. He remained married to Yerima until he died. Jim and Yerima also had a daughter; later, Jim's first daughter was incorporated into his new family. They all played a special role in my life in PNG.

Some kind of colonial control of the island of New Guinea was inevitable. Outsiders were moving in to exploit its resources, its people were being taken away as labourers, and missionaries were establishing outposts in this challenging new mission field. The nations of Europe were carving up what was left of the world between them. One or more of them would feel obliged to take charge of New Guinea, be responsible for it, protect it, own it or express their sovereignty in some other way, and thereby exclude others from grabbing it. Nikolai Miklouho-Maclay was a remarkable scientist and pioneer ethnographer whose life and work (Webster 1984) is a model for us all. Russian children growing up with his stories and drawings of life in a Melanesian village had the benefit of his wisdom but elsewhere few people have heard of him. In 1871 he came and lived with the people of the Rai (Maclay) Coast near Madang. When he first arrived in the village he lay down on its central ground and went to sleep, indicating his peaceful intent to the anxious and puzzled inhabitants. Years later, he did everything he could to prevent their exploitation by 'the invasion of a white race in New Guinea, able easily or almost certainly to bring deplorable catastrophe in its wake' (Greenop 1944, 164). In the event, when the Germans came to Madang in 1884, they unscrupulously used his local prestige to ease their way in. In the same year the British proclaimed their right to Papua and in doing so promised to protect the rights of the local people (Souter 1964, 62; Langdon 1971, 42–59). Colonialism throughout the world may only rarely have reached the savage depths of the heart of darkness of the Belgian Congo, but it was always, at the very least, paternalistic. This was hard to live with, even in its benign form in the Territory of Papua and New Guinea. Unthinking racist comments were part of everyday conversation. Racism was deeply embedded in colonial society and could never be questioned or discussed. Travelling with members of my field team presented difficulties of accommodation since 'natives' needed to know their place', and even obtaining a soft drink and a meal required careful consideration, let alone getting a beer, which was illegal for 'natives' to drink until late 1962. The hospital in Goroka was a 'native hospital' with European wards on the side of the ridge above it. Of course if you lived entirely in a white colonial world you were not conscious of these slights and difficulties and had cordial relationships with many happy 'natives' because, by and large, the 'natives' did 'know their place' and caused no disturbance.

When I first arrived in Okapa I was told very firmly by Mert Brightwell that I could conduct no autopsies, since the local people had been very upset by autopsies carried out by medical research workers in the past and the authorities had given him strict instructions to forbid the practice. I made no comment but bided my time. I soon learned that the local people had indeed been upset by autopsies; however, it was not the autopsy itself that worried them but the fact that it was done in secret in a hospital away from the person's home ground, and in particular when it was done a long way away in Kainantu. It was an essential part of my work to obtain autopsies on patients whom I had followed throughout the course of their disease, especially after we had planned experimental transmission studies in the United States. I discussed the matter with community leaders and relatives of patients and then went to see Mert. I explained why I needed to undertake autopsies and the attitude of the local people, and that I would be doing a limited autopsy to obtain inoculation material with the help of family members in the house where the patient had died. He agreed that this was acceptable. We made an arrangement that I would seek permission for the autopsy from the family and if I obtained it I would inform him of the details. He would issue a coroner's certificate authorising the autopsy, and I would report to him when it was done. Of course it was only possible to make this arrangement in the case of an inevitably fatal disease with a protracted clinical course. This procedure worked well and was followed for every autopsy that I carried out.

It was not only the authorities that got excited about autopsies and kuru. They seemed to fascinate everybody, even doctors. In 1957 research into kuru was initiated by Carleton Gajdusek, an American paediatrician and polymath, Vincent Zigas, the government doctor based in Kainantu, and Jack Baker, who was then the *kiap* in charge of Okapa. There were widely circulated stories about guests dining with Jack Baker while Carleton and

Vin 'shared the same table as they went about their business of carving up brains and other body parts for dispatch to overseas laboratories', as Alan Ross (2012, 57–8), who visited Okapa in 1957, testifies. Anthony Radford in his book of experiences in PNG has a section on kuru that includes an extraordinary discussion of autopsies (Radford 2012, 244). He has a direct quotation from me about the increasing 'cost' of obtaining an autopsy: 'I don't know how many blankets (and tomahawks) I gave out'. I never said this. If I had mentioned blankets, which is quite possible, it would have had nothing to do with autopsies and everything to do with patients, to whom I have given out hundreds of blankets over the years, because this was, sadly, one of the few helpful things we could do for them. Such quotations ensure that historians will continue to be confused about autopsies. Radford makes reference to Warwick Anderson (2008), whose wonderful book about kuru moves into fantasy when it comes to the discussion of autopsies and the collection of lost souls. Recent work has clarified our understanding of transumption and the souls of the Fore (Whitfield et al. 2008), though most of these findings are as yet unpublished. The Fore have a pragmatic view of such matters and did not become overexcited about autopsies, provided, as I have said, that they themselves were involved and proper respect was paid to the dead. Their perspectives are recorded in a film documentary on kuru (Bygott et al. 2010). The autopsies that I carried out were difficult emotionally but matter-of-fact affairs technically that achieved their purpose without high drama. Their scientific purpose was also achieved when the experimental transmissibility of kuru with extraordinarily long incubation periods was demonstrated (Gajdusek et al. 1966).

I left the Territory at the end of 1963 to undertake these experimental studies, but I continued to work on kuru for the next 50 years. Much of this time was spent as Director of the Papua New Guinea Institute of Medical Research (PNGIMR) after Independence. When I came the Institute was housed in the old European wards of the Goroka Hospital after the rest of the hospital had been demolished. The world of PNG had changed greatly by then. Most government positions had been localised – Jack Baker was in charge of localisation until he localised himself and left. What should have been attempted was a partnership for development, something Miklouho-Maclay would have supported one hundred years before. If it had been tried, how many would have accepted such a relationship is something we will never know. The irony was that after Independence there were still lots of expatriates buzzing around, but they were all 'experts' and 'consultants' on high salaries and allowances who spent their aid money and their brief time and made little contribution to the development of PNG. We still have to learn that aiding development requires a long-term partnership along the lines of the PNGIMR model, where many expatriates over many years worked within a Papua New Guinean institution and left their mark, not only in helping to improve the health of Papua New Guineans but also in training PNG scientists and in strengthening a PNG institution where these scientists could continue to work happily. The Institute also created its own international support network. My brief essays (Alpers 1997; Alpers 2003) and unpublished lectures on this subject were composed with medical research in mind but could equally be applied to other contexts.

References

Alpers, M. P., 'A History of Kuru', *Papua New Guinea Medical Journal*, 50 (2007), 10–19.

Alpers, M. P., 'Research and Development', *Papua New Guinea Medical Journal*, 40 (1997), 115–18.

Alpers, M. P., 'The Buttressing Coalition of the PNGIMR: An Example of International Collaborative Research', *Trends in Parasitology*, 19 (2003), 278–80.

Anderson, W. H., *The Collectors of Lost Souls: Turning Kuru Scientists into Whitemen*, (Baltimore: Johns Hopkins University Press, 2008).

Auricht, C., *Medicine Beyond Kokoda*, (McLaren Vale: Clive Auricht, 2011).

Bygott, R. (director), B. Alpers (director), F. Hope (producer) and P. DuCane (producer), 'Kuru: the Science and the Sorcery'. Film documentary, (Melbourne: SBS Television, 2010).

Clezy, K., *Now in Remission: A Surgical Life*, (Adelaide: Wakefield Press, 2011).

Collinge, J. and M. P. Alpers (eds), 'The End of Kuru: 50 Years of Research into an Extraordinary Disease', *Philosophical Transactions of the Royal Society (B, Biological Sciences)*, 363 (2008), 3605–763.

Gajdusek, D. C., C. J. Gibbs Jr. and M. P. Alpers, 'Experimental Transmission of a Kuru-like Syndrome to Chimpanzees', *Nature*, 209 (1966), 794–6.

Greenop, F. S., *Who Travels Alone*, (Sydney: K. G. Murray Publishing, 1944).

Langdon, R., 'A Short History: Sixteenth-century Explorers and Twentieth-century Ballot Boxes' in P. Hastings (ed.), *Papua New Guinea: Prospero's Other Island*, (Sydney: Angus and Robertson, 1971).

Majnep, I. S. and R. Bulmer, *Birds of My Kalam Country*, (Auckland: Auckland University Press, 1977).

Murrell, T. G. C., 'The First Six Years of Pigbel – A Historical Analysis' in M. W. Davis (ed.), *Pigbel: Necrotising Enteritis in Papua New Guinea*, PNGIMR Monograph No. 6, (Goroka: PNGIMR, 1984).

Radford, A. J., *Singsings, Sutures & Sorcery: A 50 Year Experience in Papua New Guinea. A Dokta at Large in the Land of the Unexpected*, (Melbourne: Mosaic Press, 2012).

Ross, A., 'The Okapa Pine Forest', *Una Voce*, 4 (December 2012).

Souter, G., *New Guinea: The Last Unknown*, (London: Angus and Robertson, 1964).

Walker, P. D., 'Obituary: Timothy George Calvert Murrell', *Papua New Guinea Medical Journal*, 46 (2003), 87–9.

Webster, E. M., *The Moon Man: A Biography of Nikolai Miklouho-Maclay*, (Melbourne: Melbourne University Press, 1984).

Whitfield, J. T., W. H. Pako, J. Collinge and M. P. Alpers, 'Mortuary Rites of the South Fore and Kuru', *Philosophical Transactions of the Royal Society (B, Biological Sciences)*, 363 (2008), 3721–4.

Wiessner, P. and N. Pupu, 'Toward Peace: Foreign Arms and Indigenous Institutions in a Papua New Guinea Society', *Science*, 337 (2012), 1651–4.

2

HOOKED FROM DAY ONE

Ken Clezy

The brutal mid-afternoon blast from the shimmering, sunstruck tarmac of Jackson Strip as I disembarked from the Qantas Empire Airways DC-3 late in November 1952 was an unforgettable introduction to New Guinea. I was in the first tranche of senior medical students that Dr Gunther invited to the Territory of Papua and New Guinea for six weeks paid employment each summer in the hope that some would eventually join the PHD. Despite the heat and humidity I was hooked from day one and spent the next eight years training, with employment by the PHD at the forefront of my mind.

The Reverend Ben Butcher, a notable London Missionary Society pioneer in Papua, and the first LMS member to venture onto Goaribari Island after his colleagues James Chalmers and 11 others were killed and eaten in 1901, had already aroused my interest in the country. In 1947 Butcher spoke at a large interdenominational youth meeting in Adelaide and told us we weren't meant to muddle our way through life or do our own thing, but should aim to discover what God had planned for us and do that. If we were willing to follow, God would show us the way. Although I was a believer from a Christian family this was new and seminal advice, but it shouldn't have been: a text (Proverbs 3:6) on my parents' dining room wall said, 'In all thy ways acknowledge Him and He will direct thy paths.' It was obvious to me now that I'd never fully comprehended it. The missionary experiences of friends influenced me too, and I entered medical school aiming to work overseas, perhaps in New Guinea. My parents were happy about this and more importantly, so was Gwen, my wife-to-be, who had a similar background and shared my beliefs. Gwen's relatives had worked in Borneo and Bolivia for many years she wasn't fazed by the prospect of us spending an indefinite period abroad. The only questions were, where and in what capacity?

My six-week stint with the PHD, mostly on Bougainville, where the Sohano doctor and other Administration personnel were encouraging and supportive, was enough to attract me to a career in the country, despite the opprobrium frequently heaped on Christians, missionaries in particular. ('He came to do good and stayed to do well', was a common barb, and a contemptuous 'mercenaries, misfits and missionaries', in descending order of merit, was another.) But I was horrified by the range of competencies required of an outstation general duties medical officer. Surgeons seemed to be in short supply so I chose to narrow my sights in that direction, intending to join the many others who saw employment in the public service as the practical outworking of their Christian faith. After my specialist training in Adelaide and the UK a surgical position became available at Nonga Base Hospital, Rabaul, at exactly the right time and I applied in high hopes, so was dismayed when I failed the medical. Elsewhere I detail the reason for this hiccup, and how it was overcome (Clezy 2011, 79). I began in Rabaul in January 1961 and left the service for good in November 1988.

I realise now that, like several other doctors in or out of the public service, I was something of a loner, which made working in surgical isolation less of a problem than it might have been. Nonga's limited range of investigative facilities didn't worry me either – this was long before the days of ultrasounds and CT scans, of course. I'd been taught and believed in the overriding importance of clinical history taking and physical examination, repeated if need be, an approach to the diagnostic process that I've always tried to inculcate in my students.

The huge variety of surgical fare, with new conditions appearing with great regularity, meant that the hospital work was exhilarating. I'd seen one case of mouth cancer before going to New Guinea; now they were my bread and butter. (This cancer is especially common in those who chew betel nut.) Excision wasn't a problem but reconstruction of the resulting defect demanded new skills, which I learnt from Frank Smith in Port Moresby.

Bone and joint tuberculosis was common too, but the only case I'd ever seen had been thrown at me in my final FRCS examination in London. I took a particular interest in spinal TB (Pott's disease) and soon was performing the radical surgery for it recently invented in Hong Kong. In the mid-sixties I decided that this was a marvellous operation looking for an indication, and abandoned it for simpler procedures except in certain special circumstances.

I had never seen the cancer that results from years of recurrent or unhealed tropical ulcer, and eventually realised that this cancer begins not in the ulcer itself but in the totally depigmented scar surrounding it. Therefore such cancers resemble those in burn scars, and are caused by exposure to the ultraviolet light, rather than by some mysterious quality of unhealed ulcers. This explains why ulcers on the soles of leprosy patients' feet very rarely become malignant; in the nature of things the sole has little exposure to the sun.

A regular problem all over the country was the ruptured spleen, most commonly resulting from personal violence. Every surgeon in the world removed them to prevent death from bleeding, and the sooner the better. Some of our patients died suddenly, months or years later, and when we heard that children in the West without spleens often died of late overwhelming sepsis we suspected (correctly) that our adult patients were doing the same, perhaps from pneumococcal infection or from *falciparum* malaria, both major problems in otherwise healthy New Guineans. Patients often came in days after injury, clearly not bleeding to death, so perhaps the rush to remove spleens was unnecessary and dangerous. Several of us found that we could safely transfuse most patients, with splenic removal to prevent exsanguination rarely necessary. Although paediatric surgeons had managed ruptured spleens non-operatively in children for years, this became standard policy in adults in PNG ahead of the rest of the world.

Good textbooks were available and the occasional visiting surgeon was helpful, but experience was the great teacher, often in areas remote from those seen in most general surgical practices in metropolitan Australia, as in those mentioned above. I learnt that unless patients were *in extremis*, it was usually best to observe rather than meddle with doubtful or mysterious cases, in the expectation that either the passage of time would clarify the situation or the patient would recover. If I know when not to operate, I learnt that in New Guinea.

Nonga had a good nursing school and I was invited to take part in the teaching program, which I enjoyed. I saw that more than talk and chalk was required, and carefully prepared duplicated lecture notes that became, years later, the basis of a surgical text for Health Extension Officer trainees (Clezy 1967).

In the seventies I was at the Port Moresby General Hospital, where I was briefly Dean of Medicine and Professor of Surgery at the University of Papua New Guinea. I became Dean because the Sudanese incumbent was moving to Australia, and was elected by faculty not by default but because other worthy putative candidates were believed to have their own barrows to push.

When Professor Ian Maddocks left the country for Adelaide we expected his replacement to be another physician, but for reasons best known to him he advised the vice-chancellor, Professor Ken Inglis, to appoint me to the single chair in the Department of Clinical Sciences. A series of unsatisfactory appointments in other departments had made Ken suspicious of glowing references and impressive CVs; better to have a known quantity even with little research experience. I was appointed Professor of Surgery without so much as an interview.

I didn't enjoy my time with the university. I was at far too many professorial board meetings discussing matters that were presumably of importance to people on the main campus at

Waigani but which seemed irrelevant to us in the medical school at Taurama. Meanwhile my hospital patients suffered in my absence. And the university seemed to be absurdly democratic, with professors not necessarily being heads of department. I now realise this was to allow Papua New Guinean junior academics to learn leadership by leading rather than by observing, which was an appropriate policy.

Senior hospital doctors accepted under- and post-graduate teaching as part of their brief, and for most of the time PHD and university staff worked together well, but even in our small faculty we had fair copies of the irresistible force and the immovable object, and for years we unwittingly harboured a fraudulent PhD, who nevertheless was well worth his salary.

Early attempts to identify future national specialists, surgeons in particular, weren't spectacularly successful, but we all knew that sooner or later the right people would appear. If any foreigner perceived that they would inevitably take over before we were ready to retire, it wasn't mentioned.

Always being flat out in the hospital helped insulate me from the developmental processes going on in society around us, matters in which I had little interest anyway. I was a surgical worker bee with few other competing interests and without political antennae, but nevertheless I spent a morning hearing Sir Hugh Foot, the leader of the 1962 UN Trusteeship Council delegation, inform a mostly Tolai audience that the sooner they and their fellow countrymen changed up to self-governing mode the better. There was a soft appreciative buzz from the locals but his unexpected and egregious advice drew uninhibited belly laughter from the handful of foreign planters at the back of the hall. While Administration personnel heard him out respectfully, if any agreed with him they didn't say so. I was as square as a chessboard, so sided with the many other conservatives who reckoned he was talking nonsense. Now it is difficult to see how events could have unfolded in any other way, with or without Gough Whitlam.

Elections were memorable, even for foreigners who didn't vote. Before one poll a hopeful national government heavy-weight from Simbu laid on beer in mega-monstrous amounts; thousands lined up to drink it and then voted for someone else. And one night in Goroka we admitted a truckload of Simbus after a tribal fight because, according to one side, the wrong politician had been elected, undeservedly and perhaps crookedly. My junior staff managed their injuries, none very serious, and the one case I remember from next morning's ward round was an old man lying in bed, still in his arse-grass (the bunch of leaves Highland men wear in the natal cleft), complaining bitterly but with little to account for it. A nurse came in to say his son was on the phone, and when I asked her to tell him his father should be ready for home in a day or two she said I should speak to him myself because he was calling from New York. I did so and found he was with the PNG delegation to the UN. This incident encapsulates the enormity of change PNG saw in one generation.

Apart from being active in church life our community involvement was limited. I tried to coach the Nonga baseball team but unfortunately I lacked the hallmark of successful coaches – charismatic authority. Like most specialists I qualified, along with my wife, for more invitations to the District Commissioner's residence or to other soirees, in Rabaul and elsewhere, than our standing would have warranted at home.

When visiting other districts as a regional consultant I dutifully called first on the DC and was amazed – still am – at the deference these princelings often showed to doctors junior to them in every way.

In colonial government circles doctors were usually second in the pecking order, and the more senior the better. DCs rarely had tertiary qualifications, and rose to the top by virtue of years of successful dealings, many of the first-contact type, with wild and sometimes dangerous tribes. This field experience gave status to Department of Native Affairs personnel that unquestionably put the best of them in a league of their own – their swagger suggested that some were well aware of it, too – but apparently this was rarely enough to dispel the mystique attached to a medical degree, especially a specialist qualification.

We went to Rabaul in 1961 with three little girls, had another that year, and finally a son in Madang in 1965. Because we always lived in provincial centres our children had good primary schooling, but the older three had to leave home for their secondary education. It was Gwen who saw them off – I was always too busy – so she bore the brunt of tearful airport departures. Our second daughter was more severely affected by this dislocation than we realised, and her death after years of devastating illness was ultimately due, at least in part, to its effects. It was small comfort to know that ours was far from being the only expatriate family affected in such a way.

Although she gladly hosted missionaries stuck in town for medical or other reasons, sometimes for weeks on end, usually Gwen found looking after the family quite enough, even with a servant. But in itself this can scarcely explain why we rarely entertained Papua New Guineans in our home until we were in Goroka in the late eighties, when our children had long since departed. In Rabaul our *haus boi* came from Nonga village but I don't remember visiting him there, and if I ever knew his second name I've forgotten it. It was the same story elsewhere.

Others, notably Anthony and Robin Radford, became widely and deeply involved in the community wherever they went, as his book attests (Radford 2012). The Radfords lived mostly in rural areas whereas we were base hospital types, but this only partly explains the contrast between their lives and ours. They were inquisitive in the best sense of the word but we weren't. When one considers the superlative richness of PNG cultures and the exotic magnificence of so much of our surroundings, it seems shameful now that we paid such scant attention to the country's people or to the natural wonders that tourists still fork out big money to see. Gwen took the kids swimming and to the Port Moresby Show, but that was about it.

In some expatriates this degree of disengagement would have indicated disdain for the country and its people; this wasn't so in our case, perhaps best illustrated by my willingness to have our eldest daughter Meredith enter the fledgling UPNG medical course. Here, as I'd expected, the 5+2 training program (5 years at university and 2 years compulsory internship) turned out a far more rounded young doctor than did the 6+1 combination offered in Australia. We would have been happy to see her make a career in PNG, but four years after graduation she married a man from Brisbane working temporarily in Port Moresby, and he took her south. Her PNG training prepared her well for practice in Australia, where she scaled the notorious hurdle for foreign medical graduates with ease.

From the beginning I was eager to learn from other surgeons working in the tropics, so I travelled regularly in this regard, most notably in 1964, on a WHO fellowship and *en famille* for once, to Vellore where I had the immense privilege of spending nine months in Paul Brand's last class in India. Paul was one of the twentieth century's most original surgical thinkers, and almost single-handedly revolutionised our understanding of every aspect of deformity in leprosy. The missionary son of missionary parents, he was a convincing template of mature spiritual equipoise, a Christian leader in a class of his own, a brilliant communicator and justifiably world famous for his innovative work. Despite his eminence, to the end of his life he remained the personification of grace and humility, as has been acknowledged repeatedly by the writer Philip Yancey, who came to revere him as a father figure (Yancey 2004, 14). I rate my time with Paul Brand as by far the richest experience of my professional life. Not only did he teach me virtually everything I know about leprosy and the management of its deformities, but also he was a uniquely inspirational exemplar of the balanced Christian life.

For five years after our return from India I spent one week in Madang and the next visiting leprosaria all over the country performing operations to correct leprosy's deformities, and did a little general surgery when necessary. Later I was to treat leprosy patients in Indonesia, the Solomon Islands, the New Hebrides (as it then was) and Samoa. I was able to perform complicated operations in these places only because each had, or temporarily imported, a physiotherapist with the essential specialised skill to manage cases post-operatively.

Observing visitors and their hospitalised friends, in New Guinea and elsewhere in the Third World, taught me the inherent merit of quietude. In the West we seem to think that when words run out it's time to get up and go. Not so. Sick Papuan New Guineans and their visitors were content to enjoy each other's company without the constant yacking that we so often regard as essential if socialising is to be meaningful. The presence of the friend or loved one is what really matters, chatter or no chatter.

And long before the idea of informed consent surfaced and became standard practice in the West, when 'doctor knows best' was almost invariably the watchword, Papua New Guineans taught us that the unquestioned acceptance of medical advice didn't have to be a foregone conclusion. Some of us were slow to learn this truth, which we found particularly distressing when parents refused what we insisted would be their child's life- or limb-saving treatment. Occasionally we twisted their arms in one way or another, but thought twice next time after being humiliated, as we sometimes were, by seeing subsequent events prove the parents' judgment correct, if for the wrong reasons. Heroic surgery often failed when patients came in late, as in a child I saw deeply unconscious from a brain abscess. I persuaded his unwilling parents to allow me to operate, and had him die on the table. They didn't say, 'told you so', but I have the feeling they thought it.

Many doctors and others worked in the Territory temporarily and hopefully on their way to what they saw as bigger and better things at home or elsewhere, and the subsequent careers of many were, I suspect, even more successful than they could have hoped for. Many became distinguished professors; one of these, Ian Maddocks, was a most worthy Senior Australian of the Year in 2013. Another, Dr Michael Alpers, was elected a Fellow of the Royal Society. Short of a Nobel Prize there is no more illustrious scientific award than the FRS.

I was among those who went to New Guinea expecting to spend a working lifetime there. Around the time of Independence most foreigners departed but others signed new contracts that highlighted our training role, in essence telling us we were to work ourselves out of our jobs. Although I enjoyed teaching and was pleased to see our Papua New Guinean trainees developing surgical competence, I failed to appreciate, if only because the demand for surgical services would increase faster than we produced specialists, that this could result in the truncation of my own PNG career. I suddenly and painfully learnt this lesson when my contract came up for renewal and I was offered a one-year extension – a polite indication that my time was up. What now?

At the end I was ready to go anyway, because I was facing some of the standard post-colonial frustrations – fractious and, in my view at least, irresponsible junior staff making team-work difficult, and the availability of essential equipment and disposables (even oxygen and blood) becoming increasingly unpredictable. At this distance I am prepared to admit that, under pressure, I may have displayed irritating traces of the anachronistic colonial master, but if that was the case nobody has ever told me so.

Once again, we saw the hand of God at work when an excellent position opened at exactly the right time. We went to Tasmania and I spent ten good years in Burnie, after overcoming the palpable hesitation some showed in trusting this chap from the wilds of New Guinea. The breadth of experience I'd gained there was good preparation for rural practice in Australia. As always, I insisted that my trainees use their eyes, ears and hands properly before, or instead of, ordering expensive investigations, a *modus operandi* that I gather didn't survive for long after my 1999 departure for Jibla in the Yemen highlands.

PNG had prepared me even better for the rather different surgical and security challenges at the Jibla Baptist Hospital, where I volunteered to mind the shop for one year while the new American career surgeon studied Arabic. We found the hospital in urgent need of a more permanent surgeon with wider experience than that of the string of retired, narrowly-specialised Americans who had done their best to keep the place going for years, each serving for three months. There was too much work for one surgeon anyway, and because we clicked with Jibla we didn't finally leave until 2005. That Gwen and I enjoyed Yemen more than PNG may seem strange; I ascribe it to our being part of an overtly Christian missionary effort deep in the Muslim world that we found especially satisfying.

Wherever I was stationed I did my best to teach good surgical practice to all who would listen, and was told recently that my influence in this respect is still acknowledged in PNG (as it is in Yemen) but I have to admit, as others have done, that I believe I got more out of my PNG time than I put in. In particular, I was forced to develop an unusually broad surgical competence, with particular interests in hand surgery, neurosurgery and several other specialised areas that stood me in good stead elsewhere. The various awards that have come my way would have been highly unlikely if I had spent my life in an Australian practice. I was delighted to see our children grow up with a wide view of the world, mercifully devoid of brash nationalistic sentiment; they are better Australian citizens for that.

Whatever the downside may have been for the rest of us, living as we did far from Australian cultural attractions and other luxuries of metropolitan life, it was my wife who really paid the price, as so often happens, and not only because mealtimes were so unpredictable. This isn't the place for details, but Gwen had enough bad PNG memories for me to wonder if it would ever again be feasible for us to work in the developing world. In 1997 I took her to visit medical missionary friends in Ethiopia, hopefully as a sort of opener for our next phase, which proved to be at Jibla, where she was much loved.

I've been back to PNG twice, about 20 years ago to teach a surgical course for Health Extension Officers in Madang, and again for the 2010 jubilee of the founding of the Papuan Medical College, where we saw old students doing well professionally, a source of great pride for their older teachers. I was impressed by how articulate many current students are, but like the rest of our party I was appalled at the evident deterioration of health services in the city, and by others' descriptions of the far worse state of affairs further afield.

About 50 years ago Sir John Gunther returned from a trip to the Dark Continent averring that Africa had nothing to teach us, but how wrong he was. Whatever we thought at the time, Africa has been teaching us that there is a fairly standard and inexorably seamy developmental process for newly independent countries, with hordes of politicians, bureaucrats and business people having their hands deep in the till until they are sidelined by the next crowd desperate for their turn. With greed so rampant, naked and unashamed in modern Australia and in the world generally – 'in Greed we trust' – and remembering for a moment our own grubby national histories, what right have we as outsiders to point our fingers at avaricious Papua New Guinean leaders, some of whom hadn't even seen a wheel when we were still in three-cornered pants? Sometimes their methods may be less sophisticated than ours, but they aren't categorically different.

The foreign aid line item in the Australian budget looks like being under increasing pressure for many years, and the time may come when some in government wish to seriously limit the largesse we bestow on PNG, but any honest assessment of our legacy there – and I don't mean only Ok Tedi, Bougainville and suchlike – must demand that we hang on for the long haul. This may necessitate much more than providing hard cash; for example, it isn't entirely fanciful that sooner or later the Indonesian Papua/PNG border will need defending. With most Australians assessing our military engagement in Afghanistan and Iraq as at best nugatory, or at worst flagrant all-the-way-with-LBJ type buccaneering, we may have little stomach for more conflict, even this close to home. As always, the pragmatists must be expected to prevail.

In our retirement Gwen and I live in Adelaide, the domicile of a surprisingly large number of old New Guinea hands, many of them medical, and our declining years are enlivened by regular opportunities to join them in chewing over the past. If the nostalgia is sometimes rendered less saccharine by nagging fears that we may have had rather less positive and less permanent influence on PNG's development than many of us like to imagine, no matter. There is little point in wondering. Be they ever lambent or be they dulled by time, the memories we treasure of what were our glory days in a unique land, the New Guinea that most of us insist we saw at its best, must be enough.

References

Clezy, K., *Now in Remission: A Surgical Life*, (Adelaide: Wakefield Press, 2011).

Clezy, J. K. A., *Surgery for Health Extension Officers*, (Port Moresby: PHD, 1967).

Radford, A. J., *Singsings, Sutures & Sorcery: A 50 Year Experience in Papua New Guinea. A Dokta at Large in the Land of the Unexpected*, (Melbourne: Mosaic Press, 2012).

Yancey, P., *In the Likeness of God*, (Grand Rapids: Zondervan, 2004).

3

THE CHALLENGES OF CHILDBIRTH IN A PRIMITIVE SOCIETY

Margaret Smith

My husband Frank Smith and I worked in PNG from 1964 to 1971. Frank wanted to work in a place that would test his skills as a surgeon. I had no desire to go there and went under sufferance. We had completed our postgraduate degrees in Britain and I had been given a university teaching post in our home city, Adelaide. Already we had been away from home for five years, with only airmail to connect us with family and friends, and the thought of living in a developing country was somewhat daunting, especially when I heard I would be the first resident obstetrician/gynaecologist in the Highlands. Previously gynaecologists had made only occasional short-term visits. I was well-trained, but aware I would probably have to face obstetric problems I had not encountered before. I would just have to cope.

In mid-1964 we arrived in Port Moresby. Despite the fact that we had been told to come urgently, things were not ready for us in Goroka, where we had been posted. In the meantime, Frank was sent to Rabaul which, in those days, was considered the most beautiful town in PNG. Port Moresby was not beautiful. The heat was stifling and not at all pleasant for a redhead like me, used to the cold weather of the United Kingdom. I knew no-one and wondered how I had been talked into coming to such a place. I was the temporary replacement for Dr Stan Reid, an Australian GP and obstetrician who was to go to London to sit postgraduate obstetric exams. Australian GPs in Port Moresby looked after the expatriate women while Dr Reid cared for the indigenous women.

I lived in a small *donga* (house) in the grounds of Boroko hospital. There was no airconditioning. I had large cockroaches in my one-room living quarters, and at night, on the path that led to the labour ward, there were many slimy toads on which I slipped. The work was alarming. I had to deal with women who were anaemic because of malaria and thus it was very important to prevent any excess bleeding. Many of the women came in to the hospital having been in labour for many days. I had to deal with dead or nearly dead babies in abnormal positions, which meant a destructive operation (crushing the head) to deliver them vaginally. Caesarean section was not an option since such women would probably not return to a hospital for their next delivery, putting them at risk of rupturing a uterine scar. I had had no training in this destructive method of delivery and was appalled by the instruments I was given to use. The arrival of a thoracic surgery team from Melbourne – who visited each year to do chest surgery all around PNG – gave me some much needed company. While Frank enjoyed Rabaul enormously and met every surgical challenge, which was galling to hear, I felt I barely coped. It was a relief to go to Goroka after six weeks.

Goroka Hospital, which looked like a village, was on a large, sloping grassed area that led down to a river. It was comprised of a mixture of buildings, some left from the Second World War and others made of bush material. All had concrete floors. The laundry was an open shed. The washing was hung out to dry on long lines among the buildings, although there was also an ancient and rusted Hills Hoist – probably the only one in the whole of the Highlands. There were no showers but there was a river in which the ambulant patients could bathe. There were always little groups of people in the hospital grounds and an occasional dog or pig. Most patients were accompanied by their friends or relatives. There was no kitchen. The staple diet was *kaukau*, which was boiled up in a big drum. We doctors went home for lunch.

My ward for New Guinean women had 15 wooden-slat beds, old blankets and only one sink – in the labour room. There was an old hospital bed for delivery of babies but most women preferred to squat during labour. It was all very primitive. The labour ward had a pungent smell to which I had to become accustomed. It was a mixture of blood and unwashed bodies with a touch of decay since many women were brought in *in extremis* – dead or dying. During the day most 'native' women patients preferred to be outside the ward. For the very sick ones there was an old hospital bed to which we could attach an intravenous drip; even then the patients still preferred to be outside the ward rather than in it.

The laboratory in the hospital was very basic. A few Bunsen burners, an ancient microscope, many test tubes and some reagents comprised its meagre resources. The operating theatre, an old army hut with a concrete floor, was similarly primitive. There was no running water, so we scrubbed up in metal basins in a small ante-room. From this room steps led down to the wood-fired boiler, attached to which was an ancient steriliser. It all worked surprisingly well. Windows on one side of the theatre allowed patients' relatives to stand in the coffee plantation and view proceedings. We had six theatre 'boys'. They were local men who had been trained by Mogish, a Papuan, who was literate and had basic theatre skills. He could give an anaesthetic and also acted as a theatre sister.

In the early days the hospital was run by a handful of specialists. Frank was the surgeon and Dr Frank Rhodes the physician. I was the obstetrician. Since there had been no full-time obstetrician before me in Goroka, it took a year for me to establish a service. Rae and Ian Riley, two younger doctors, had anaesthetic, public health and general medicine training. When Rae arrived in Goroka as an anaesthetist we were able to get a Boyle's machine to give relaxant anaesthesia instead of using open ether through a gauze facemask – a method which leads to post-operative vomiting and makes for a messy and unpleasant experience for all concerned. Sister Margaret Giddings came to Goroka as our theatre sister in 1965. We seconded her from Port Moresby, where she had worked with the visiting thoracic surgery team. This experience led to a decision, perhaps made with a little persuasion from me, to work permanently in PNG. On her arrival in Goroka, Margaret reorganised the theatre and was able to upgrade our instruments and other equipment. Mogish was glad to have her and she was able to teach him many things. We hosted visiting doctors from Australia who were doing specialist training in their home hospitals. Medicine in PNG was an eye-opener for all of them. One of these visitors was John Pearn, who became professor of paediatrics in Brisbane and remained in contact with PNG.

There were many difficulties in providing medical care for New Guinean women. Birth dates were unknown, unless our patients had been born in a mission hospital that kept records. Taking a history of the presenting complaint, as doctors always do, was made difficult by language barriers. Although we foreigners mastered pidgin English, most of our patients spoke only their local tongue, so we relied heavily on *wantoks* from the same village who spoke pidgin. On one memorable occasion I was operating in theatre when one of the 'native' nurses opened the door and said, 'Doctor missus come quick! Meri bilong bed 3 emi die!' ('The woman in bed 3 has died!') I downed tools and raced over to the ward. As I walked in, the woman in bed 3 sat up. I chastised the nurse: 'You said this woman had died!' She replied, 'Oh emi no die pinis, emi die liklik tasol.' ('She did not die fully, she just fainted.')

Because of their lifestyle New Guinean women were prematurely aged. They did all the heavy work and gardening, and carrying of loads. They breastfed each baby for at least two years. The nubile breasts of young teenagers became drooping sacs and I was often surprised to see babies suckle from these apparently inactive organs. The prolonged suckling helped to regulate the spacing of babies, and in some villages nursing mothers were forbidden to have sexual contact.

Despite the absence of a clinical history, by the time patients reached the hospital there were usually gross physical signs to provide a diagnosis. The first indigenous patients I had were in poor condition and some had dead babies stuck in the pelvis. Often they were brought in from outlying villages by missionaries who had found them cast out of the village and crawling along bush tracks. If a woman could not give birth to her baby she was considered to be cursed and likely to bring bad luck to others.

I rarely performed routine gynaecological surgery in Goroka; mostly it was severe infection requiring drainage or fistulae needing repair, an occasional ruptured ectopic pregnancy, and a few Caesarean sections. Some women came in draining faeces and urine through the vagina because of fistulae caused by obstructed labour. In Ethiopia, Dr Reg Hamlin and his wife Dr Catherine Hamlin had devised surgery to cure this condition using a muscle graft to plug the holes. (Frank and I knew the Hamlins. They had taught us when we were trainee doctors in Adelaide.) Frank visited them in Ethiopia during one of our breaks away from Goroka and learnt this technique, which we were able to use. (We recorded our experiences in an article: 'The problem of Vesico-vaginal fistula in The New Guinea Highlands', *Papua and New Guinea Medical Journal*, 11, 1 (1968), 19–21.)

The other notable problem I had not encountered before was severe intra-abdominal infection (peritonitis) after delivery of the baby. It was usually associated with anaemia due to blood loss. In European women post-partum infection usually is confined to the pelvis and is treated with antibiotics to prevent spread. Any excessive blood loss at delivery is prevented, or at least treated adequately. These 'native' women were very ill indeed, so conservative management was necessary. We drained the pus abdominally through a small hole and left the drain in until the flow stopped many days later. We gave intravenous antibiotics and waited weeks before operating to remove the damaged tissue. (I wrote about this in the *Papua and New Guinea Medical Journal*, 10, 4 (1967), 131–4.)

The pain threshold of indigenous women was extraordinarily high. They did not scream or moan during labour and even when they presented with a bellyful of pus they merely grimaced. On one notable occasion I made a mercy flight to pick up a woman who had been in labour for four days. This was not her first child so there was obviously something very wrong. We had only a small plane so she could not lie down. When we got her back to the hospital I laid her on a table and found that her blood pressure was very low and her whole abdomen was rock-hard. She was in severe shock. She was grimacing but did not utter a sound. In theatre I resuscitated her and at operation found that she had ruptured her uterus. She survived and appeared grateful. I will never forget her smile as she held my hand in thanks when she was able to go home. At such a time words are unnecessary.

Treatment of indigenous women was best carried out in the base hospital, where there were facilities and equipment. However, it was not always possible for patients to come in. Many could not get to hospital because of the mountainous terrain and scarcity of transport. Often I went out by small plane to assist doctors in my region with difficult births or to transport gravely ill women back to the hospital. On one emergency call-out to a small hospital near Kainantu I performed a difficult forceps operation to deliver a stuck baby. Circumstances meant I stayed the night. Next morning I was picked up by a small plane to go back to Goroka. The pilot tried to persuade me to go on with him to Madang 'just for the ride', but I had work to do in Goroka. He flew off and never came back, having been trapped by cloud in a high valley. Small planes with no oxygen could not fly over 12,000 foot mountains and had instead to find gaps between them. There were several such losses during my time in Goroka.

I was welcomed as an obstetrician by white women throughout the Highlands, who previously had gone to Port Moresby or Australia to have their babies. These women received antenatal care from their local medical officers or me and then came to Goroka for the last few weeks of their pregnancy. This gave me the reassurance that normal obstetrics was still possible. We had an eight-bed 'European' hospital with a labour ward in the hospital grounds. A British midwife who came to work at the hospital cared for its patients and delivered babies if all was normal. The separation of expatriates from indigenous women was not discriminatory but necessary because of very different standards of hygiene. The expatriate part of the hospital was up a steep, gravelled dirt track, along which patients were carried on stretchers. The orderly boys groaned loudly when they had to carry any large European patient back from theatre.

Although I was an obstetrician/gynaecologist, I was also the anaesthetist when necessary. And as there was no GP in town, the expatriate doctors, Frank and I included, also attended to the general health of the expatriate population. Expatriates were not, however, encouraged to come for routine surgery.

Frank had strong feelings about this. He said he had come to New Guinea to look after New Guineans, not expatriates. I, on the other hand, felt privileged to look after expatriate women: my care for them meant they did not have to travel elsewhere.

Frank performed surgical operations every day, mostly on patients from outlying areas. His surgical ward and the two medical wards were of bush material and had about 20 or 30 beds. There were no firm paths between the buildings so patients were carried on stretchers by our theatre boys. On one occasion, Frank was waiting in theatre for his next patient. The boys carried the man in and put him on the operating table. Frank was very surprised to find that this man, who had looked so ill the day before, now appeared well. The man had a nasogastric tube running into his stomach and a drip in his arm. Frank asked if the boys had the right man. The boys went back to the ward and found the real patient lying under the bed looking very ill indeed. His brother had taken over the bed and had not complained when he was prepared for theatre.

Frank was well-trained in general surgery and resourceful. This proved important, for he met problems not encountered in developed countries. Pigbel, *enteritis necroticans,* was one such challenge. After a feast of pig some of the meat was left in insanitary conditions. Women were rarely allowed to eat the meat but men and some children ate tainted meat, which then caused ulceration and perforation of the small bowel. These people were very ill indeed and needed surgery. I gave the anaesthetics for many of these operations. Dr Tim Murrell, a fellow Adelaide graduate, defined the aetiology and epidemiology of pigbel. Between 1960 and 1964 he was District Medical Officer for Goroka, Wabag and Kundiawa. He moved on just as we arrived.

The other common problems requiring surgery were gastric ulcer and gastric cancer. In modern society it used to be thought these were caused by stress. Why would primitive men get ulcers? What stress were they under? It is a pity we did not draw the analogy between this condition and pigbel, i.e. that an ingested organism was the cause. This puzzle was solved in Perth (where I now live and work) a decade or so ago when two brilliant researchers, Professor Barry Marshall and Dr Robin Warren, showed that ulcers were caused by bacteria – *Helicobacter* and *Camphylobacter*. For this they were awarded a Nobel Prize. Treatment is with special antibiotics. But drawing the analogy may not have helped us because by the time men with ulcers came to us the disease was far advanced and surgery was necessary; even then it was often too late.

One such case, which I will remember forever, happened on a long weekend when Frank, against his will, had been sent to Lae as cover for the resident surgeon who was away. (There were only four Health Department surgeons in PNG at this time, one each in Lae, Rabaul, Port Moresby and Goroka. In addition, there were mission hospitals, such as that at Yagaum near Madang, where the legendary Dr Braun provided all branches of medical practice.) Lae was a busy, more populous town than Goroka and it was thought there may be more surgical emergencies there. As night fell our physician, Frank Rhodes, called me to see a patient in his ward who had severe bleeding from his stomach. We had no further blood of his type available so the only option was to operate on him to stop the bleeding. I had not trained in general surgery. As a gynaecologist I operated usually in the area below the umbilicus. But we could not get our surgeon back as planes could not fly into Goroka after dark. Compounding our problems, at that time we did not have a dedicated anaesthetist on staff. Frank said he could manage to give the anaesthetic under my direction, so I had to be the surgeon. I looked up my husband's surgical textbook to familiarise myself with the anatomy. When I opened the patient's abdomen I found the ulcer had invaded all the surrounding tissues, including the head of the pancreas. Gastrectomy (removal of the stomach) was impossible so I identified and tied off the main bleeders and closed up.

That weekend was very busy. I removed a spear from the chest of one young man and put in a chest drain. I removed an arrow from a cat's abdomen. I also delivered several babies and set a broken arm. When Frank came back from Lae he was ropable. He had had almost nothing to do for the whole weekend. Later he operated on the man with the ulcer, who subsequently died. As Frank told the story, 'My wife operated on a young man and saved his life. I operated on him and killed him.' Not true, of course, for the condition was inoperable. Frank was dedicated and devoted to his work.

Our laboratory technician, Ted Shelton, was a gem. He was a 'before', meaning he had started work in PNG before the Second World War. He was trained as a medical assistant and had served at many remote outposts in the Highlands. I think he just picked up the laboratory work without having specific training. In those days pregnancy tests were done by injecting the patient's urine sample into a toad. I sent in a sample of urine for an urgent test. Ted's report was brief and unhelpful: 'Pregnancy test. Result unknown. Toad absconded.' Ted had inadvertently left the window open and the toad had taken off into the coffee plantation after being injected.

Some of the 'befores' were eccentric characters indeed. One such was our local magistrate. He was responsible, among other things, for signing death certificates. A mystery illness sometimes claimed the life of young men. The New Guinea doctor boys were sure this was some kind of sorcery, but our magistrate had his own theory. He said the death was due to 'ground vacuum'. He was convinced that anyone, anywhere, could walk into a space containing no air and drop dead. Since post-mortems conducted on the young men did not prove otherwise, the magistrate stuck to his theory, making it official by signing their death certificates. How I wish I had kept a copy of one of these documents. I never heard of any authorities questioning the magistrate's theory.

Another eccentric I met was Dr Carleton Gajdusek. He won a Nobel Prize for his scientific proof that kuru (so-called laughing disease), which affected the South Fore tribe in the Okapa region of the Eastern Highlands, was caused by a slow virus. He stayed at our house a few times in between field trips. Usually he slept on the floor under our dining room table as he was accustomed to sleeping on the ground. He did not often shower. He talked incessantly. His brain cells, Frank commented, seemed to be directly connected to his vocal cords. Gajdusek seemed to me to inhabit a different world from the rest of us – an authentic genius.

We were privileged to work in Goroka. The weather was beautiful – Goroka lies 5,200 feet above sea level – and the town is surrounded by spectacular mountains, including Mt Michael at 12,000 feet. When we first arrived in Goroka there was one general store selling only frozen and tinned food – no fresh bread, milk or meat. There was a hotel and a bank, but no restaurant. When, a couple of years later, the Collins and Leahy company began to supply fresh milk and meat, and the local people brought fresh vegetables to sell at market, paradise was complete. We lived simply and had very little contact with the outside world. This ensured we looked forward to the mail with almost childish excitement. Apart from news from home, we received books from the Mary Martin bookstore and records from the World Record club: music and books helped to prevent the feeling of isolation I had experienced in my first few months in PNG. Eventually, the isolation became part of the charm of living in Goroka.

The only phones in town were for local connection to the hospital and its staff. On one occasion I had an expatriate woman bleeding internally from a ruptured ectopic pregnancy. We needed blood for transfusion urgently, which meant a phone call to the blood bank nurse. There was no response from the local switchboard in the main street. I jumped in the car and drove there to find the New Guinean switchboard operator fast asleep. The door was locked. I went next door and woke up the on-duty policeman who shouted loudly enough to wake the operator. We called our Australian blood bank nurse. She checked the patient's blood group and found she was Rh negative. All our stored blood had come from New Guineans, who are always Rh positive. Our resourceful nurse had a list of expatriates with Rh negative blood, including two young bank tellers. It was a Friday night and the bank boys were partying. The nurse extracted the required two units of blood and we transfused our patient as I operated to stop the bleeding. On wakening the woman was very grateful and said she felt very well indeed. I suspect that as a non-drinker of alcohol she was on an artificial high.

Social life in Goroka was somewhat limited. There were about 600 expatriates in town when we arrived, most of whom worked for the Australian government. Others were on mission stations and some had plantations, mainly coffee. The Sports Club was the main drinking hole. Twice a year a ball was held there. While there was no movie house in Goroka, ancient films sometimes came our way, whereupon all adjourned to the Asian storehouse with fold-up chairs and a supply of grog. The film invariably broke down and a couple of fellows who fancied themselves as stand-up comedians would entertain us. There was a nine-hole golf course bordering the hospital and airstrip. If I were needed while out playing, one of the orderlies, message held aloft on a stick, would come to find me. A beautiful 18-hole golf course, away from the town, was opened two years before we left Goroka. We did not socialise with the local people – the only New Guineans we met were either hospital workers or patients. There were never indigenous trainee doctors in Goroka as the medical school in Port Moresby was in its infancy. Our only junior doctors were those seconded from Australian hospitals.

Our new hospital in Goroka opened in 1969. Frank and I had been allowed to comment on the design and suggest possible improvements. We were warned by the local people that the new hospital was to be built on a site that they called 'ground nothing'. They alleged the land had seen many clashes between warring tribes and was cursed, but building went ahead nonetheless. Local people stayed away at first, but as the main referral hospital for the Highlands it still had plenty of customers. It was large and spacious – a big concrete monolith – with custom-built operating theatres, proper beds in the wards, and a modern laundry. There were patient trolleys and no hills to climb. Indeed, there were none of the charming difficulties to which we had become accustomed in the old hospital by the river.

In 1972 we went to Perth for Frank to undertake special training in thoracic surgery. The idea was to learn the service provided in PNG by visiting surgical teams. We doctors were on contract and had no thought our jobs would be permanent, but nonetheless Frank and I were surprised when we were not asked to return. Later, PNG independence came as a surprise. We had not thought about it or heard it discussed during our time in Goroka. In any case, I felt relieved when our move to Perth became permanent. I settled down into teaching and private practice in obstetrics and gynaecological endocrinology, with some good medical stories to tell my students. I welcomed the return to all the advantages of medicine in a modern society.

My time in Goroka was of immense benefit to me. I learnt to cope with some of the most difficult problems in obstetrics and to appreciate simple living and solitude. I had great respect for the village women of the Highlands, their quiet dignity and tolerance of pain. On market days, as they squatted on the ground beside their wares, they would pinch my legs, fascinated by my stockings which they thought were some kind of abnormality. One commented, 'skin bilong yu lus tumas' ('your skin is too loose'). I felt privileged to care for these women. At the same time, I was aware of a huge medical need which we could not fill. There were overwhelming communication problems – in language and in transport.

I have only revisited Goroka once. In 1980 Frank and I hired a Land Rover and drove up the Highlands Highway to all the places we had heard about but were unable to visit when we lived there. In particular, we went to see birds of paradise and orchids in wild and remote areas of the Eastern Highlands. We visited the hospital only very briefly. Frank knew the surgeon and had worked there a couple of times after we left PNG. It no longer felt familiar to me.

When we lived in Goroka we did not have to lock house doors or car doors. Women were safe to walk the streets and go shopping alone. But Port Moresby was not safe even then and I understand that nowadays expatriates live in fortresses. From media reports it is clear that PNG, which had to make the sudden leap from tribal culture to civilisation, has been beset by corruption. It is my belief that Independence was granted too soon to people who were not sufficiently well-trained to take over. Our lifestyles were so disparate and we had little in common. This echoes my comment that we did not have social contact with indigenous people in Goroka. This was not snobbery; just recognition of difference.

I keep in touch with PNG only indirectly via Jim Sinclair, who now lives in Queensland and still visits PNG frequently, nearly every year. I know little of modern PNG and have no desire to work there. However, I understand only too well the difficulties of supplying adequate health services to remote areas given the nature of the terrain, the lack of appropriate transport, and the budget constraints. I gather that not much has changed for people in remote villages and that their general health remains poor. About this I am immensely saddened.

4

AUSTRALIANS IN PAPUA NEW GUINEA, 1960–75: A PERSONAL PERSPECTIVE

Ian Maddocks

My personal appreciation of the contribution Australians made in PNG in the years leading to Independence in 1975 is based primarily on residence in Port Moresby between 1961 and 1974, but expanded by reflection on vacation experiences in 1953 and 1954 and regular visits between 2000 and 2012.

Student encounter: 1953–4

As a Melbourne medical student, I was employed during two successive long vacations as a 'temporary medical assistant' attached to Malahang Native Hospital near the town of Lae. A Department of Territories bursary offered a promising introduction to my professed aim of becoming a medical missionary, possibly in the New Hebrides. For its part, Territories hoped that bursaries would encourage students to work in PNG after graduation, which it did for more than a few. Such vacation opportunities were succeeded in the late 1950s by the offer of medical cadetships, providing undergraduate support for students who committed to later service in PNG.

It was a heady experience. The country's towns were still recovering from the destructions of the 1939–45 war, and many of Lae's surviving structures – the Malahang Hospital, the airstrips, the jeeps which were major means of personal transport – had been left behind when Allied troops departed. I was a fourth-year student, previously little exposed to patients but now accorded immediate clinical responsibility – making diagnoses, administering injections and open ether anaesthetics, assisting at operations, instructing 'native' orderlies, and all under only casual supervision by available doctors or European medical assistants. 'On patrol' in the hill villages of Momalili I lined up populations for rapid physical examinations.

I appreciated being a *masta*, bringing to my relationships with local New Guineans a mix of arrogance, good intentions and ignorance, along with a fascination for the exotic cultural environment, on display at the great New Year *singsing* where males in elaborate headdresses topped with bird of paradise plumes stomped interminably to monotonous chants alongside bare-breasted maidens. I slept in a single man's *donga*, and ate at the government officers' mess where stout Australian females supervised and incessantly berated the *bois* who waited at table. I learnt to speak pidgin and gave instructions to my *haus boi*. I frequented the RSL Club and learnt to drink alcohol. The main entertainment of the town's whites appeared to be drinking and all and sundry were honorary members of the RSL Club. Those who gathered there were mainly single males, many of whom,

I suspected, were escaping from difficulties back in Australia.

I saw PNG as a country of scattered individual villages, each a collection of houses constructed of rude timber and thatch clustered around a small central square or street, with perhaps a larger church-cum-school of the same construction. In some there was an aid post where an aid post orderly kept a small supply of dressings and medications. The villagers I encountered were wary, responsive, subservient, waiting for instructions. I met missionaries and traders, but spent most time with government officers who commonly were accepting a range of responsibilities far greater than they could ever have assumed in Australia. They exercised their authority in unashamed racial tones, barking their orders in pidgin in a tone redolent of speaking to children. The final rising 'eh' at the end of a sentence conveyed 'Did you understand that, you ignoramus?' I found myself doing the same.

I was aware that the culture was different in the Highlands, but my only acquaintance with that region was on a 'milk-run', travelling in a DC-3 and calling at airstrips through to Wabag to deliver mail and supplies. My permission to go was facilitated as a favour by District Commissioner Horrie Niall, whose word, it appeared, was law. I suspected he had ordered a refrigerator to be off-loaded to fit me aboard. It took all day, sitting sideways against the windows of the plane, with patrol boxes, string bags, mail and stores stacked down the centre. Goroka, Hagen, Wabag and where else? By the end of the day I was vomiting from the constant uneven motion. Some stops were just a strip with a house for the *kiap* and hordes of naked men congregating around. I remember particularly the wig men at Wabag. At one stop a young New Guinean arrived with a drink of cold water from the local Lutheran missionary. When I thanked him, he replied in clear American, 'You're welcome, sir.' At another, two missionaries sheltering under the shade of the wing were discussing a colleague's letter: 'He didn't mention the name of the Lord Jesus once.' They were two small incidents that made me think again of the plan of being a missionary, and bringing my culture and religion to PNG.

After graduation from medical school and resident training, I undertook a blood pressure research project in Fiji and the Gilbert Islands. Each of those colonies had the advantage of one common language, so different from PNG, and they were administered within the global British colonial structure by officials who brought confidence and experience from other colonies. In Fiji and the Gilbert Islands, the health establishment included local medical graduates. PNG clearly had a long way to go before it could match either.

Physician and academic in Port Moresby: 1961–74

By the end of 1960 I was qualified as a Member of the College of Physicians, but there was no opportunity available to work as a medical missionary. I had the church's blessing to go instead to Port Moresby and work in government service at the newly opened medical school. I arrived in February 1961 with wife Diana and our one-year-old son.

The Department of Territories cadetship scheme was already bringing results. More than 30 individuals had accepted a cadetship and though some paid it off or defaulted, at least 20 were readying for placement in PNG. They were mainly married males, many from strong Christian backgrounds, and they brought with them idealism and commitment.

The suburb of Boroko housed most of the newcomer government officials; older hands had more favoured accommodation with beautiful gardens on the slopes of Paga or Tuaguba Hills in town, or along from the steep Lawes road that formed a short cut to Konedobu for those who sought audience with the heads of departments. Boroko was expanding in the open valley behind the first line of hills, filling with standard government houses, new churches, a high school and two primary schools – one for Europeans, one for 'natives'. Housing was at a premium as increasing numbers of Australians arrived to staff government departments, banks and businesses. We were allocated the house of the Director of Medical Research, who had departed on leave for a year leaving his personal furniture and valuables locked in one of the three bedrooms. We set up house without our own effects – a large pantechnicon filled with furniture and books and our Volkswagen sedan – which arrived by sea several weeks later. We were intending to stay. Dr Stan Wigley, who had interviewed me in Melbourne, had noted: 'There is a career for you in New Guinea, Dr Maddocks, but not one for your son'. That was prescient for the time; many in Canberra and Port Moresby could not see independence coming to New Guinea until at least the year 2000.

A childless couple came with the house as domestic servants, occupying a standard single room dwelling which was at the rear of the block and attached to the laundry. There was a shower/toilet for their use. We had no experience with managing servants and were embarrassed by the opportunity. We were required to keep them in employment so that the family on leave would have them waiting upon return, otherwise we might have tried to manage on our own. They were able to instruct us gently, going about the activities they were accustomed to undertake, and negotiating in pidgin with Diana about any variations. Like most new arrivals we were keen to present a colourful and neat garden, watering lawns and plants through the dry times. There were no fences. It seemed unnecessary to lock doors.

I was appointed Lecturer in Medicine at the fledgling Papuan Medical College, located midway between the Walter Strong Wing ('native' hospital) and the MacGregor Wing (European hospital). The College was based in buildings designed in Australia as an animal house for the new Taurama Hospital. Cages were removed to form a lecture room. Increased Australian resources were expected, and in the meantime we felt encouraged to make do. The Principal, Dr Eric Wright, had worked as a medical assistant in Papua before the war, then completed medical training and returned to private practice in Rabaul before being appointed to oversee courses for nurse and medical training. Dr Ian Reid, who had been a missionary doctor, a couple of Australian medical assistants and a school teacher comprised the initial faculty. Two Papuans, former medical assistants, provided support as storeman and laboratory assistant.

The pioneer medical student group was commencing the second year of a five-year course. I was to teach physiology and biochemistry until the students were ready to begin clinical studies. My physiology class consisted of 12 students, all from coastal areas of PNG. Highland communities were just getting their schools, often introduced by missionary organisations. My students were highly selected, in many ways the pick of the country, pioneers in its first truly tertiary education institution.

Sogeri High School and teacher training were in operation, but teachers were graduating at lower than the Queensland Junior Certificate standard which the Medical College had set as an entry qualification. In addition to my teaching duties, I was the town's second physician specialist, supervising one half of the 80-bed medical ward in the 'native' hospital. The other half was under Dr Charles Campbell, already a highly respected physician in the town. We each had a 'resident', two of the first PNG graduates from the Central Medical School in Fiji.

It was universally anticipated that graduates would staff rural hospitals. This meant me taking the physiology class (minus females) for a 'rural experience'. In 1961 we went to villages on either side of the Kumusi river in the Northern District, and in 1962 we travelled by double canoe to coastal villages near Marshall Lagoon. We conducted a census in each place, drew maps, and analysed the data we were collecting: height, weight, skin fold, peak flow rate, haemoglobin. We stayed in government 'rest houses', shared the cooking, and under the pressure lamp in the evening exchanged jokes and stories. At the end of 1962 I recruited Luke Rovin, a medical student from Bougainville, to accompany me to the Eastern Highlands to conduct further studies on blood pressure similar to those I had completed for my MD. We found Eastern Highland populations to have blood pressures that were lower in older age groups, the reverse of findings in European populations. Luke was cheerful and good company, as close a 'friend' as seemed possible across the distances of race, affluence and education.

Port Moresby's churches were important places for the Europeans of the town to meet, and long-lasting family friendships were forged. A motivation to see the Australian colonial enterprise develop well, with a sense of mission and optimism, was common among the Australians we knew best. We attended the United Church, which was for those with Protestant connections. Its minister had initiated the Contact Club to encourage Australians to gather with Papuans and New Guineans. It met monthly, and self-consciously attracted the few locals with backgrounds that allowed them the fluency in English and confidence required to accept this opportunity. There were individuals in government service with strong mission backgrounds, like Albert Maori Kiki and his wife Elizabeth. There were some from Kwato, where the Abel family had fostered a community schooled in English language and custom. Kwato expertise included technical trade skills and cricket.

Otherwise Australians commonly met indigenous men or women only in places of employment or as their domestic servants. The 1961 Port Moresby phone book held only expatriate names: there were no Papuans or New Guineans listed. At the hospital, there were some senior Papuan staff whose names became familiar. There was no suggestion that they might be friends, however, or might dine with us. We tried to bring the medical students into our lives: occasionally they came for a meal, and some from the Methodist areas of Milne Bay, New Britain or New Ireland attended the Boroko church.

Family social life involved church, dinner parties with fellow Australians, cinema outings, Ela Beach, or weekend drives to Sogeri, where the cooler air and the rubber plantations of Koitaki and Itikinumu were an attraction. In 1960 the Port Moresby community comprised approximately 6,000 in villages and urban settlements and approximately 6,000 expatriates, most of whom were Australian. Eighty per cent of the indigenous population of the town had been born in the Port Moresby region. In the local villages almost 3,000 were Motuans. They were not often chosen as domestic servants. More usually pidgin speakers from the New Guinea side were favoured for these jobs. We began to distinguish particular groups. Young Mekeo males were dandies with big hair and effeminate ways; from Marshall Lagoon came fully framed men known for their skill as house painters; Sepik people had elaborate decorative scars; those from the Gulf/Daru areas darker skins and hooked noses; and Goilalas were smaller and reputed to be untrustworthy.

In 1962 the law changed to allow 'natives' to drink alcohol, which we felt gave us permission to forgo the teetotal approach we had adopted since arrival. A student approached me: 'Doctor, I want to drink beer'. Apparently he faced the opportunity with apprehension about how it might affect him, so I bought a bottle and we shared it.

Port Moresby resembled in size and structure a small North Queensland town – we could recognise private cars from a distance there were so few – but one with delusions of grandeur, for it was also a national capital with all the various institutions appropriate to that status. Within our first few years I became involved with the Medical Society, the medical journal and the Medical Board. We talked of the strength of the *wantok* system in PNG, whereby individuals were bonded with anyone who spoke their language and they could rely implicitly on that relationship. The Australians in government service had their own *wantok* system. Individuals holding positions of influence were often known by name, met with socially, and accessible by phone. We soon learnt how to get things done, and achieved a confidence in management that stayed with us when we returned to the more complex bureaucracies of Australia. To receive my MD degree in person I applied for support to go to Melbourne. The request was referred to the Assistant Administrator, and Dr Gunther demanded to see me. He made it an occasion to look me over before stamping his approval.

The Australian *wantok* system also operated outside of Port Moresby. I visited mission and government health centres in the Western District and travelled between them by air, my arrangements being confirmed on the daily wireless 'sked' which linked the various centres. Locals could gain access to this manner of communication or air travel only through the good offices of their resident missionary or government officer. Without that access they moved by dug-out canoe or 'talked' with drum beat messages.

I enjoyed the particular challenges of PNG medicine, with diseases not much studied in a Melbourne medical course – malaria, leprosy, dysentery, life-threatening lobar pneumonia. There were major limitations on investigations and treatment, but we worked around them, building clinical skills. The Port Moresby hospital pathologist, Dr A. V. G. Price, had vast experience of PNG diseases, having worked on the New Guinea side prior to the war. He was legally blind, but continued to manage his service unchallenged. He and his wife were devoted to PNG. He was fluent in Motu and had recorded valuable conversations with Hanuabada elders about traditional customs. His wife was a powerful advocate for Girl Guides and social action.

There were regular opportunities for health workers to take up overseas travel or further study, and many who started in PNG with basic medical qualifications were able to expand into more specialised areas. In 1963 a WHO scholarship allowed me to spend six months in Uganda at the Department of Paediatrics, Mulago Hospital, Kampala, and subsequently I was supported to take the Diploma of Tropical Medicine in Liverpool. I presented PNG blood pressure findings at an international conference in Edinburgh, suggesting that the low salt intake of Highland communities was important in their absence of hypertension. Through that travel I recognised that research in PNG held messages for world medicine, and came to appreciate that Australian efforts in PNG were not inferior to colonial activity in other parts of the developing world.

By 1964, the College had a full complement of staff, basically one teacher in each major academic discipline. Each teacher enjoyed a sense of control in the role, and there was a heartening development of teamwork. Staff-student sporting contests and 'Island Nights', in which both staff and students presented skits and performances, added to morale. The first three graduates of the Medical College completed their course in 1964 and entered resident training.

1964 also saw the Currie Commission into Higher Education, which led quickly to the establishment of the University of Papua New Guinea. By 1966 the University was taking students, many being primed for leadership roles in the years ahead. The Commission report had assumed that the Medical College would move into the University, and that was the clear hope and expectation of the staff and students of the College. We were visited by newly appointed UPNG professors. One expressed some surprise: 'You have no gremlins here', meaning no sign of the competitiveness and backstabbing he had known in Australian academic institutions. Canberra, however, expressed concern. Medical schools were notoriously expensive, and it was surely better to keep the graduates at a level that would require them to remain under government control, and not qualify for practice overseas.

I was by then Dean of the College, and I encouraged, as far as I was able, an escalation of protest over the next three years, demanding that the College become the medical faculty of UPNG. I foretold a loss of staff, decline in standards and difficulty in recruitment of students unless earlier expectations of full university degrees were fulfilled. As public servants, we felt prohibited from making overt public protest. Instead, we worked through the Medical Society. Its chairman, ophthalmologist Father Frank Flynn, was quite free to voice our concerns in press and letter. In addition, we recruited Australian consultants, who visited the College to teach or examine our students, to raise their voices on our behalf. Canberra remained intransigent, however.

A major development in 1967 was the formation of the Pangu Pati, the first serious attempt at creating an indigenous forum for expression of the aspirations of Papuans and New Guineans and of preparing for eventual independence. It quickly spawned other political groupings. Student Ebia Olewale, whom we met at church and who later became a leading political figure, brought us the small Pangu membership card. We paid the fee and, at least in name, were early members.

Throughout 1965 and 1966 I visited Pari village, five kilometres out of town, to conduct measurements relevant to blood pressure, similar to those made earlier in Fiji and the Highlands. In the course of house-to-house visitation, I met a youngster who was one of a small group of Papuans and New Guineans studying at the largely expatriate Port Moresby High School.

Immediately it was clear that he had difficulties in completing study and homework in his crowded single room house, lit only by a single lamp, no privacy, and with limited family understanding of what was required of him. I suggested that he might benefit by staying at our house, close to his school, Monday to Friday. We were moving to more equal relationships between staff and pioneer students, and the offer was less unusual than it might have seemed a few years earlier. Isi Kevau and his fellow Pari student, Nou Oru, spent the school week with us for the remainder of 1965, and we were pleased that both did well enough in their difficult New South Wales examinations to proceed to further study – Isi to medical school, Nou to theological college to train for the ministry.

The initial plan to study Papuans' apparent freedom from hypertension and ischaemic heart disease led to a second interest in Pari. From hospital practice it was clear that local Motuans, in particular, had understandings of illness, its causes and appropriate management that were quite different from accepted Western practice. When a disease did not respond quickly to hospital treatment, family members commonly took their sick one away. We wondered if a better picture of what underlay this distrust might emerge if we became more familiar with village life; if we went to live in Pari. The idea progressed in conversations with Isi's father, who offered a site close to his own house over the sea. The house posts were erected with much village cooperation one weekend, and later two Pari carpenters completed a small dwelling for us.

We moved to Pari in 1968 and stayed for six years. They were busy and happy times. My volunteer wife and I provided a basic medical service for the village at the small village clinic and at our house. At the same time, UPNG, which still aimed to incorporate the Medical College, appointed me acting Dean of the proposed medical faculty. I was charged with developing plans for the faculty, including physical structure and funding. The opportunity afforded me to design a new medical school was not untypical of the challenges that PNG offered to Australians at that time. Planning went ahead even as the lobbying with Canberra was still proceeding. There was an increasing restlessness among experienced PNG government officials at the distant control continuing to be exercised from Canberra.

In Pari we amassed records of 22,200 sickness episodes that the 1,000 or so residents brought to our attention. More important than the medical statistics was the opportunity afforded us to develop friendships and participate in daily village life and special events. We began to gain insights into the history and traditional life as it was in old Pari, hearing the stories and songs of the old folk, and recording genealogies back 14 generations. Closer contact between indigenous and expatriate was becoming more common and easier. Over the next few years young graduates began to emerge from UPNG, nurtured and known by their teachers. They were being prepared for major roles in an independent PNG. Independence was becoming more a matter of timing than conjecture as global decolonisation policies strengthened. Canberra eventually approved the transfer of the Medical College to UPNG, leading to my appointment as Professor of Clinical Sciences and Dean in February 1970.

Life in Pari had separated us from our former social life as Port Moresby suburbanites. I now attended Pari church on Sundays, and spent evenings seeing Pari patients, and weekends collecting stories and taking photographs in the village. Suburban

Moresby was changing rapidly. Fences were being built around houses and dogs were kept as defence against casual theft. Pari seemed a much safer environment than Boroko. Highlanders with their different backgrounds and more aggressive ways were migrating to the coast in increasing numbers, and especially to Port Moresby. After an incident at a major rugby match, Papua versus New Guinea, a riot broke out. Pari village panicked as rumours spread that New Guineans were coming to attack. The village chief, rarely evident as a figure of authority, appeared on the beach and ordered women and children to be ready to take to the water, and some families loaded their canoes.

Pari, with its early access to education opportunities, was well-placed to participate in the urgent changes now being promoted towards localisation, with new positions of status becoming available for locals with talent. Isi Kevau became the first PNG graduate in the UPNG MBBS program, and was later Professor of Medicine and Dean; Nou Oru, an early theological graduate, was later a bishop; Buri Kidu went on from schooling and a law degree in Australia to become the first indigenous chief justice; Oala Oala was already Port Moresby's first mayor.

We left PNG at the end of 1974 with mixed feelings, sad to leave Pari village, but keen not to stay on and pretend old authority or exercise unwelcome influence in the new juris-diction. Those whom we had come to 'help', an attitude with which we were increasingly uncomfortable, were taking over. Local medical graduates, once my students, were now achieving status in the Health Department or securing junior teaching roles at UPNG. It was time to get out of the way, I thought. Also, our son was ready for the upper forms of high school, and would probably benefit from exposure to a wider environment. Yet we were apprehensive about moving back to Australia. Much had changed there too.

We planned to return to Australia in company with another medical family which had shared much of our life experience – Melbourne University, Student Christian Movement, teaching at the Medical College, housing among PNG families (in their case at Hohola). Our aim was to live as a community in Australia, in part further to explore some of the lessons about community we had appreciated in PNG. An Adelaide friend located a large house able to fit us all in. Our plans were greatly facilitated by the generous compensation arrangements made for those PNG public servants who were being encouraged to retire as Independence approached – a substantial lump sum and tax-free annual payments for five years.

Our community experiment continued for three and a half years, by which time we were taking up individual professional employment. During our time in PNG, Australian medical specialties had moved on with new technologies and instrumentation, inhibiting an easy clinical transition for us. Nevertheless, my reputation from PNG gave me acceptance as a visiting specialist at the newly opened Flinders Medical Centre with university associate professor status. Many colleagues from PNG found similar opportunities as new initiatives in academic or administrative aspects of community medicine were launched under Whitlam. Neither financially nor professionally was experience in PNG counted as a disadvantage.

A Time of disappointment: 2000–12

For two decades following our departure in 1974 I had only limited contact with PNG. In the 1990s, Dr John Waiko, pioneer UPNG student and academic, visiting Adelaide in his capacity as PNG Minister for Education, came to breakfast. We discussed issues in education and John noted, 'I could put you on the Council of the University', which he eventually did. I stayed a member for over a decade, participating carefully when an Australian academic observation seemed appropriate. I was impressed by the calibre of the students and the vigour of debate as councillors sought to squeeze – from inadequate and usually delayed government grants and frugal student fees – sufficient resources to meet growing student numbers and expectations. I quickly became aware of, and distressed by, UPNG's inadequate infrastructure. A tour of student accommodation showed that any item that could be moved had been stolen – there were no lounge chairs, no toilet seats, no mirrors, no shower heads.

PNG had not become the country envisaged by the Australian colonial administration that handed over sovereignty in 1975. With hindsight, the expectations held by the departing Australian civil servants, who believed they were leaving behind a new nation on the path to good governance and self-sufficiency, seem naïve. While not oblivious to the fact that in other former colonies acquiring independence there was commonly a failure to establish a workable democracy, a public service free from corruption, a sustainable infrastructure and sound economic growth, Australians hoped that PNG would somehow be an exception – that the structures and processes of government that Australian officers had designed in consultation with the emerging PNG leadership group in the early 1970s would be maintained and strengthened, and that benevolent oversight and support from Australia would continue to guide the young nation.

It could be justly claimed that the constitution prepared for PNG was 'home-grown'. It was hoped this might have been enough to ensure peaceful and effective development. We wanted to believe that PNG held a kind of primitive innocence, unspoiled by the examples of Western history and urban life, and sustained by the widespread acceptance of Christianity, which would protect the new nation from the dangers rising in other newly independent states. However, when the 2008 Waigani Seminar, *Living History and Evolving Democracy*, held at UPNG, reviewed the goals and principles enunciated by the Constitutional Planning Committee, Bernard Narokobi, a member of that committee, and author, scholar and statesman, could only lament, 'Nearly 40 years on, we celebrate our miserable failure'.

In retrospect, there can be little doubt that we Australians might have been more guarded in our expectations or more sceptical. But not *all* has failed. The constitution has not been suspended or superseded, and a semblance of democracy remains in place, albeit overlaid with blatant corruption. A major difficulty remains the nation's regional divisions and the more than eight hundred distinct language groups that inevitably constrain ideals of nationhood, cooperation and service for the common good. And while the decision to establish multiple provincial governments was a valid attempt to lessen the domination of Port Moresby, it added another layer of bureaucracy and additional opportunities to skim money from budgets for personal gain.

In visits over the last decade, I have become aware how corruption gradually has infiltrated all levels of society. Some, whose position or employment allows them to profit – whether through demanding bribes from commercial interests seeking advantage, or siphoning off percentages from overseas grants, or stealing saleable items from government stores – make a good life, building new houses protected by dogs and three-metre fences. A far greater number, low wage-earners or unemployed, live with poverty and hunger far more intense than was usual in traditional life. At all levels of governance, inaction and delay characterise official responses, allocated monies disappear, contracts are not fulfilled. Even in church affairs it seems people find it difficult to avoid participation in corrupt practices.

Prior to Independence, much had been expected of the cohorts of medical, legal and teaching graduates beginning to emerge from UPNG, but a high proportion moved out of government service. They rejected employment in regional areas and established urban private practices, helping them afford private schooling for their children or houses in Queensland.

By 2012, when I resigned my position on the UPNG Council, Port Moresby had become a city with a population of nearly half a million, a hugely different place from the small town of the early 1960s. Its infrastructure had not kept pace with this growth, and roads, water, power and telephones were quite inadequate. Maintenance of all kinds, public and private, continued to be neglected, and much public housing had fallen into such disrepair as to be uninhabitable. Car theft and burglary were commonplace, as was the use of firearms. Port Moresby was no longer a place of the Motu, or even of coastal Papuans; it thronged with 'outsiders', particularly from the New Guinea Highlands, who formed aggressive gangs ready for arbitrary violence. The sheer numbers of those who arrived from the New Guinea side meant far greater competition for employment; university graduates were no longer assured of a job.

Could it have been otherwise? Where did we go wrong?

During a century of paternalistic oversight, coastal Papuans and coastal New Guineans had been prevented from engaging in warfare, encouraged to live in peace and accept Christian principles. They were rendered dependent on the instructions of government officials, while being denied any real participation in the management of issues beyond the purview of a family. Now they face large Highland groups, with only brief exposure to the control of law, who have maintained their inter-group hostilities and continue to engage in conflict with both traditional and modern weapons, bringing those ways to the daily life of the coastal cities.

The Motuan groups with whom Diana and I were most familiar have seemed powerless to withstand this upsurge in urban violence. Their reefs are dynamited, their gardens despoiled. Some observers have blamed the protectionist policies implemented by Sir Hubert Murray during his long pre-war governorship; some suggest that independence came too quickly; others hold responsible the fragmented demography of the nation and the primacy of relationships within the one language group, whereby all others are rivals, foreigners or enemies fit only for exploitation. Whatever the reason, the result is a Port Moresby described by some observers as one of the world's least comfortable and safe locations, and the views shared among those of us who survive from the years leading up to Independence are uniformly ones of sadness and disappointment.

5

AUSTRALIANS LIVING IN PAPUA NEW GUINEA, 1960–75: FROM MEMORY

Sir Isi Henao Kevau

An honour

I feel honoured to have been invited to write about life in my beloved PNG in the period from 1960 to 1975, the latter year being when we gained independence from Australia. The editors of this book have asked me to write about my memories of the role played by Australians during that time, what they brought to the Territory and what they may have gained through being here. As I reflect, I feel it is important to share with readers just how different life in the 1960s was for us 'natives', as we were referred to then.

Second World War

I come from the Motu tribe and my village, Pari, is only eight to ten kilometres from the centre of Port Moresby. Because of its closeness to that city, the villagers had to be evacuated when

AUSTRALIANS IN PAPUA NEW GUINEA 1960–1975

Japanese warplanes bombed Port Moresby. The people of other Motu villages, including Hanuabada and Vabukori, also were forced to move. Between 1942 and 1945, my people were placed at a location 40 to 50 kilometres east of Pari and Port Moresby. At the end of the war, they were given clearance to return home to rebuild their broken village.

Tau Bada and *Sina Bada*

In the Motu language, the word for 'man' is *Tau* and that for 'woman', *Hahine* or *Sina*. The latter word, *Sina* has a specific meaning and that is mother. There is another Motu word, *Kurokuro*, which refers to the colour white. *Bada* is the Motu word for big. Men of Australian and European descent were referred to as *Tau Bada* (big man) or *Tau Kurokuro* (white man). *Tau Bada* was used to address a white man at work or at any meeting place while *Tau Kurokuro* was a descriptive term used commonly by village folks in their story-telling. So Mr Smith was *Tau Bada* Smith and Mrs Smith was *Sina Bada* Smith.

The Motuans referred to the *Tau Badas* and the *Sina Badas* as beings from the mysterious *Tauru*. If you ask a Motuan where *Tauru* is, the response would be a finger pointing south, indicating the direction of the ocean. The uncertainty of the origin of the *Tauru* invaders with their foreign language and unusual characteristics and possessions caused fear, and perhaps awe and respect, in the minds of Motuans.

Tau Badas in the Workplace

The 'natives' had very little or no formal education and had not had the chance to learn English under the church's education system. Basic numeracy and literacy skills were taught, but the language of expression was Motu, our mother tongue. My father learnt numeracy in a church building (of the London Missionary Society), using a fountain pen. He was good with pounds, shillings and pence calculations. I still keep his diary, in which he wrote all sorts of things and recorded information such as the dates when a *Lakatoi* [Motu trading vessel] left Pari for Kerema and when it returned.

From the 1950s to the early 1970s my father was a carpenter with Port Moresby Freezers (PMF), a construction and joinery company in Port Moresby which was under the management of some Australian men. There were a dozen men from Pari working at the same place. Every morning, from Monday to Friday, the workmen were picked up from the village in a lorry. They were dropped off in the afternoon after work. This truck became the major mode of transport for the working men from the village, including those who worked for other smaller companies in town. It was also very useful for school children, including me, as we had to walk three to four kilometres to school.

From 1963 to 1966, while attending Port Moresby High School, I had the opportunity to witness the relationships between my father, his fellow village folks and their white masters. In the afternoons I would go to my father's work place, the 'PMF Workshop' as it was warmly known, and wait around until 4.30pm, 'knock-off' time. I was allowed to walk into the workshop only when my father was there. Generally the white bosses at PMF were friendly, although it seemed to me that they could also be quite strict with the 'natives'. One or two of the bosses were rough, including the paymaster, a gentleman who shall be known only as Mr K. We thought he had a superiority complex and his rough language irritated and embarrassed my father and his village folks. They felt that their pride as fishermen, gardeners and responsible village and family men was being trampled upon. In return, they would say things in their language to Mr K; knowing that he did not comprehend provided a sense of satisfaction.

The workers, all Motuans, were quite content with what they received from their white bosses. I cannot recall exactly what they were paid but I can say that at no stage did I hear talk of low pay or a strike. There was, as far as I can recall, no confrontation between the masters and the workers over working conditions.

Fridays were very special

Every Friday, the workers had something to take home to their families. One Friday it was the pay package and the next Friday it was 'rations'. Rations, which came in a bag, included rice, flour, tea-leaves, salt, sugar and tinned goods, especially tinned fish. I remember the contents as I was the first to open the bag, with or without my mother's permission. It was something to look forward to.

'You beauty'

I want to mention this phrase because it exemplifies the wonderful working relationship between the Motu men and their white bosses at PMF: most of the bosses respected their Motu workers. It was Thursday afternoon, the last working day before the Easter celebrations. I cannot remember the exact year but I think it was 1962. There must have been a company party and the men had been given some special food. There was certainly no alcohol because 'natives' at that time were not allowed to drink. When the PMF truck arrived in the middle of the village, the phrase 'You beauty' came from every worker's mouth. Soon their sons and daughters were saying it also. During the entire Easter weekend, 'You beauty' was uttered constantly, sung as a song almost. Motu families had adopted the language of the white men.

Mr Smith's store at Badili

A certain Australian businessman known to Pari people as Mr Smith is worth remembering. He owned a retail shop at Badili which sold rice, sugar, flour, tinned fish and tinned meat – the usual goods – to the 'natives' at very reasonable prices. A most memorable feature of this shop was the trust and respect Mr Smith and his management gave to the PMF-employed 'natives', who were allowed to obtain goods through a credit scheme. My father and his co-workers were able to obtain food, such as rice and sugar, on credit as long as payments were made on the due date. I remember this because a sizeable part of my father's debit was due to my regular requests for meat pies. I loved meat pies.

One could argue that Mr Smith's credit scheme was no big deal. But it must be remembered that this was the 1960s when 'natives' faced many restrictions, so to allow them to take goods home for their families without cash payment was of great significance. I remember vividly how every second Friday afternoon the men would jump off the lorry, walk into the shop with their yellow pay package, clear their balance, buy more goods, get back on the truck and go home with great satisfaction and pride.

A special Australian doctor and his family

Professor Ian Maddocks, AM, Foundation Professor of Clinical Sciences and the first Dean of the Faculty of Medicine, University of Papua New Guinea, deserves special mention. Ian, his wife, Diana, and their three children Simon, Sarah and Susan, earned themselves a special place in the hearts of the people of Pari village.

The starting point of the Maddocks story was the chance meeting between Ian, the physician, and me, the village lad, on Pari beach in 1966. Playing rugby league on the beach was a regular Saturday afternoon event and I was the captain of one of the teams. On that particular afternoon I was nursing an acutely swollen left leg caused by a nasty stonefish sting suffered when fishing a few days earlier. What I was doing with my life became a point of interest to the white doctor, and when it was revealed that I was attending the Port Moresby High School, the school which all white kids in Port Moresby attended, Ian's interest seemed to take a deeper form. From our conversation, it became apparent I had lots of incomplete homework – including special projects like a book review on a famous Australian – and that deadlines had come and gone. It must have been obvious to Ian that I was not too worried about these unfinished school assignments and that rugby league and fishing were more important to me.

At the end of the afternoon, two things happened: my team lost and I made an appointment to visit the Maddocks' home on Monday. A few weeks later I took up residence there. Soon I was joined by another village boy, Nou Oru. Both of us stayed in the Maddocks' home and did our studies, homework and our book reviews, mine on William Dobell and Nou's on Albert Namatjira. We prepared well for the forthcoming School Certificate examinations under the New South Wales Wyndham Scheme. The following year, 1967, I went to the newly established UPNG and commenced studies to become a doctor, while Nou went on to pursue a career in the Church. Later he became Bishop (Urban Region) of the United Church in PNG.

The Maddocks' impact in Pari village

In 1968 the Maddocks family moved into my village. They moved into a house that was built, at their expense, by village men using manual skills. Initially, their decision to move to Pari to be part of the Kevau family and the Kahanamona clan was not taken seriously. When I mentioned this idea to my father and uncle at a family gathering, they thought it was a joke. They could not think of a similar occurrence in any other Motu villages, nor in any village in wider Papua. Their knowledge of life in the other parts of Papua was based on what they saw and experienced in the Gulf district through the Hiri times, and they could not recall seeing or hearing about a white family living in a Gulf village.

For what they did then, and even now, we, the people of Pari village, have an enormous amount of respect for the entire Maddocks family, Ian and Diana in particular. Both are household names in Pari. The fact that they chose to live in a local village during that time (1968–74) was quite something. White people were regarded as gods, thought to be perhaps a reincarnated group of people from another world. In the beginning there was uncertainty and some confusion, but gradually the village people accepted the Maddocks family.

There was no electricity in the village and water had just been made available from the town water supply. The water piping system ended at taps in selected locations. Those sites were not selected randomly but according to *iduhus* or extended family units. The Maddocks family used the tap for my family clan. When all the taps in the village were turned on, our tap was either trickling or completely dry by the time the big doctor was in need of water. Many times, Ian had to wait until the early hours of the morning before he could get any water. Sometimes, he had to go and turn off the taps designated for other clans. There were some risks in doing this. The first was being chased and bitten by street dogs. The second was being accused by the village people of being a *vada tauna*, the Motu term for a sorcerer, because the dogs had barked at him.

As Pari people remember, Ian and Diana had a very positive effect on the village clinic. There was already a clinic when they arrived, but it changed for the better thereafter. Mrs Maddocks, a trained nurse from Melbourne, brought better organisation and quality service to the clinic. And village people remember her as the force behind the Maddocks home being converted to an evening clinic where patients could be seen and evaluated by Dr Maddocks. As Ian and Diana advanced the clinic, their popularity soared and they gained the hearts of the patients. They would drop everything to attend to the village patients, and even offered a cup of tea to many, providing a level of care not seen in any public hospital or health centre. Clearly, this was very special. Ian and Diana truly were loyal to the people of Pari. Nowadays when visitors from Pari and other Motuan villages come to my family's Korobosea home in the evenings, on weekends and in the early hours of the morning for consultation and treatment, my children often refer to the evening clinic run by the Maddocks team.

Tuberculosis (TB) was, and still is, PNG's number one medical problem. The failure to control TB in this country is worth a chapter on its own. My short essay is not going to dwell on the subject, except to say that Ian and Diana made a huge contribution to how village people who contracted this disease were assisted. They diagnosed the disease, registered the patients, treated them, made sure the patients actually swallowed the medication, followed up with them and visited those who defaulted. The Maddocks approach pre-dated the DOTS (Directly Observed Treatment, Short-Course) strategy initiated by the World Health Organization several years ago.

In the Pari model, confidence and trust of the patients in the health workers, in this case Dr and Mrs Maddocks, were vital to success. People knew that the sputum collected was going to be stained and examined under the microscope by Dr Maddocks to diagnose TB and that the blood collected was going to be stained and put under the same microscope by the same doctor to diagnose malaria. People had no fears that these specimens could be used to perform sorcery. It was also very important that the Maddocks team visited in their homes those villagers who had defaulted on their TB treatment. This not only ensured continuation of treatment, but also reduced quite significantly the stigma attached to TB.

Physicians and surgeons

I had the opportunity to work with some very prominent Australian clinical specialists after completing my medical training at the end of 1972. Along with Professor Ian Maddocks, the physicians included Dr Michael Price and Dr Keith Powell, while in paediatrics I worked with Professor John Biddulph. As a Resident Medical Officer, I worked with Australian surgeons including Dr Ken Clezy and Dr Frank Smith. And it would be discourteous of me if Dr Frank Rhodes, a South African physician, and Dr David Hamilton, a New Zealand surgeon, were not mentioned here.

All these specialists had an impact on the patients they looked after in the wards and on the students they trained. As a junior Resident Medical Officer, my ward rounds were very intense. They involved me, Dr William Bye, the Medical Registrar, and Dr Powell and Dr Rhodes. I had to be alert at all times, making sure that all results were obtained from the laboratory and pasted on the back of the in-patient record. Each case was presented to the bosses, either by Dr Bye or me, with all the supporting investigation results. The bosses would then check the patients for the physical signs we had mentioned during the presentations. I found this process very scary. These men were serious, learned and experienced clinical specialists who had obtained overseas (British, Australian, South African) fellowships such as Fellow of the Royal College of Physicians (FRCP) and Fellow of the Royal Australasian College of Physicians (FRACP). I remember making a presentation on a patient with right-upper-quadrant abdominal pain and a very tender liver. After auscultation I found a noise over the liver, a 'bruit', and diagnosed a liver cancer. I remember Dr Rhodes putting on his stethoscope to double-check. I cannot forget the relief I felt when the big specialist smiled at me. It was most encouraging.

While all the physicians knew their general medicine, my registrar and I knew Dr Powell was especially knowledgeable on two disciplines within general medicine, namely nephrology and gastroenterology. Dr Rhodes, on the other hand, was the expert on tropical medicine. A healthy clinical and academic rivalry developed between the two heavies, which made our ward rounds very interesting. These specialists had worked hard and read widely, and the ensuing clinical discussions were great learning opportunities for us young doctors.

Dr Powell was interested in the question of whether a kidney inflammation called glomerulonephritis causing nephrotic syndrome was caused by the malaria parasite *Plasmodium malariae*. Nephrotic syndrome comprises generalised oedema (legs and the face, especially around the eyes), lowered protein (namely albumin) in the blood (hypoalbuminaemia), and loss of protein in the urine (proteinuria). To answer this question, Dr Powell was engaged in a research project that entailed performing renal (kidney) biopsies. He sent the tissues obtained to Dr Vince McGovern, senior histopathologist at Royal Prince Alfred Hospital (RPA), Camperdown, Sydney.

The classification of the different types of glomerulonephritis causing nephrotic syndrome was very complicated. It was like learning a new language and Dr Powell knew it. Dr Rhodes often expressed critical comments, making for very entertaining discussions. On one ward round, we had exhausted ourselves with a feast on nephrology and malabsorption syndrome, particularly tropical sprue, when a patient was wheeled in with a protruding abdomen. Dr Rhodes made the spot diagnosis of liver abscess; Dr Powell was not so sure. These were pre-ultrasound scanning days when one relied on clinical acumen based on years of experience in the tropics. Prior to coming to Port Moresby, Dr Rhodes had worked at Goroka

Base Hospital in the Eastern Highlands Province. The ward round was diverted to the procedure room where Dr Rhodes, confident in his diagnosis, performed a liver aspiration. This revealed pus consistent with an amoebic liver abscess.

Royal Prince Alfred Hospital registrars

In the 1960s a special arrangement was forged between PNG and the RPA Hospital in Sydney. Under this arrangement young Australian doctors working as registrars or clinical specialist trainees in areas such as internal medicine, surgery and pathology were sent to hospitals in Port Moresby, Rabaul, Lae, Goroka and other parts of PNG to work and gain clinical experience, particularly in tropical medicine. Many bright young Sydney doctors came to the Territory, including William Zylstra, Geoffrey Duggin, Ian Bailey, Bob Chia, Diane Howard, Peter Fletcher, Alex Bune, William Bye, Peter Bye, Ron Trent and Bruce Hall, among others. The Port Moresby General Hospital attachment was four to six months in duration and two doctors came up in each rotation.

My experience as a medical student and as a young resident doctor was affected positively by this PNG-RPA arrangement. In teaching and in clinical work, the RPA registrars were role models for the medical students and young doctors in the Territory. The registrars took their clinical duties seriously. These young professionals brought with them an enormous amount of theoretical knowledge. In PNG they were to consolidate this knowledge into clinical gains. Even though they did not always have the clinical experience and specific knowhow to begin with, the registrars seemed confident in every new situation. They consulted with the senior consultants like Drs

Maddocks, Price, Powell and Rhodes, and they took to the medical library regularly to gain more knowledge from the literature.

One thing the registrars were good at was systematic examinations and evaluations of the symptoms and signs in patients and then making a provisional diagnosis. In weekly clinical meetings or on medical rounds, these registrars were key players. Dr Duggin once ran off to Koki Market in search of a leprosy patient he wanted to present at the medical round. His detective work was successful and within half an hour he was back at the lecture theatre with the patient.

Benefits for Australia and PNG

In relation to what these medical registrars gave to PNG, especially its young doctors, what they learnt from the experience, and what they took back to their hospitals in Australia, there is so much to write about. But I have space only to offer two main reflections.

The first is based on a comment from Dr William Bye or Bill as he was more commonly known. Bill told me that before he came to the Territory, he assumed that clubbing of fingers and toes was caused by congenital heart disease. He thought this every time he saw cases of clubbing in young patients in Sydney. Bill was perplexed and often frightened by the complexities of this form of heart disease. From his PNG experience, he learnt that bronchiectasis was the most common cause of clubbing. As he told me later, this knowledge helped him enormously when, after returning to Australia, he sat his clinical examination for Membership of the Royal Australasian College of Physicians (MRACP) and was given a case of clubbing to examine and comment on. He performed and responded confidently, eventually succeeding in that particular examination because of knowledge he had gained in PNG.

The second reflection concerns the impact the RPA scheme had on PNG physicians. In addition to allowing Sydney doctors to spend time in PNG, it allowed PNG doctors to spend a year to several years at RPA. This had an enormous impact on the professional lives of many PNG physicians and warrants huge acclamation. Dr Adolf Saweri was the first PNG doctor accepted by RPA to work there as a Resident Medical Officer. He was even given the opportunity to work with Professor Blackburn in the RPA Professorial Unit, a placement that I gather was only for the top University of Sydney medical graduates. After a year's experience at RPA, Adolf went to the Liverpool School of Tropical Medicine in England and, following that, came back to PNG. He became the first PNG doctor to become an academic at the Faculty of Medicine, UPNG, and the first PNG physician with a special interest in respiratory medicine.

Following Dr Saweri, a number of PNG doctors went to RPA. While the length of stay varied, the average was four years. I was one of those given this opportunity, as were Drs Puka Temu, Goa Tau, Banare Zzefirio, Paul Mondia, Paisen Dakulala, Mark Paul, Jerry Minei, Barnabas Mavo, Kindin Ongugo and Kilage Vanuga. All of us were trained as physicians under the highly regarded Royal Australasian College of Physicians (RACP) training program. All but three returned home and have been engaged in public hospitals as specialist physicians or in the UPNG medical school as academics. Two went into private practice and one into politics. For me, the clinical experience gained at RPA during my preparation for the FRACP examination (1977–80, formerly the MRACP examination) and later when I undertook a PhD (1988–91) placed me in good stead for my work in PNG.

Chapter 6
ONE FAMILY'S EXPERIENCE IN PAPUA NEW GUINEA, 1959–2012
Anthony and Robin Radford

This is the short story of a couple who went to PNG before Independence. We developed two quite separate careers – Anthony as a doctor, teacher and academic, Robin as a homemaker, historian, amateur anthropologist, development apologist, journalist and researcher – and together grew a family. Why PNG, and why has the experience never let go of us?

Early morning sun lighting blue sea, an irregular coastline with occasional villages built out over the water, green hills, winding rivers, Jackson's Airstrip and, at last, Port Moresby. A wave of hot, humid air with the scent of tropical dampness and the tang of eucalyptus welcomed us in March 1963. Ever since, arrival by plane in PNG has held a sense of excitement and anticipation. Much has changed – the strip is now an airport surrounded by urban sprawl and bitumen roads. Conglomerates of buildings, planes and equipment have replaced the barely functional, hot tin shed which served as a terminal. 'European' passengers are now a small minority amongst Papuans and New Guineans. And yet, 50 years later, to our delight and surprise, at the airport we could meet the grand-daughter of an Oro friend selling brewed coffee or a grey-haired medico or nurse, once students of ours.

For Robin, who on return in 2010 after 40 years absence was prepared for much change, a kind of culture shock set in, one we had not experienced in our excitement on first arrival in the 1960s. Roads crowded with people, cars, umbrellas, billboards, traffic lights and roundabouts. No 'traditional' dress but colourful clothes. Multistorey buildings and roadside stalls, even a tunnel and a mosque. There were no familiar landmarks, but flowering poincianas, frangipani and shady 'rain trees' gave a feeling of hope. This hope dimmed as we passed heavily secured houses, graffiti, signs of wanton destruction, and verges covered with smoking rubbish. While she had anticipated change, Robin hadn't really faced the sense of being helpless, stripped of independence of movement and aware of potential violence.

***

Anthony's first connection with New Guinea was during the Pacific war when a medical uncle sent him a pressed, brilliant blue Ulysses butterfly from the Australian base at Hombrom Bluff, outside Port Moresby. A desire to study medicine was cemented when Paul White, the author of the Jungle Doctor books, spoke at a school assembly. We had both grown up with a sense of social justice and an awareness of the need for priority care for the disadvantaged, and we determined to spend some years working in situations where this need was greater than in Adelaide. Thus, when in 1956 Anthony was offered a cadetship and a salary to work in the Territory of Papua and New Guinea, he accepted gladly and signed up for a three-year cadetship in exchange for four years of service after graduation. We stayed ten.

The premise of Robin's social work and community develop-ment training was to help people help themselves – to facilitate and encourage people to take control of their own situations. At university we had many international student friends and in the summer of 1958–9 were both part of an Australian university delegation to India, giving us our first cross-cultural experience and insight into the enormity of mass poverty and disadvantage. Together we planned a future in the Territory. We devoured books such as Colin Simpson's *Adam in Plumes* and *Adam with Arrows* and Grimble's *Pattern of Islands*. We joined the Anthropological Society of South Australia to gain a greater understanding of cross-cultural issues. We hoped to immerse ourselves in PNG, the land and its cultures, and expected to both give and receive. Perhaps we were different from most of our colleagues, neither better nor worse, just making different choices.

***

Our experiences spanned three phases. The first was for two months when, as a final year medical student in late 1959, Anthony was dropped into a small enclave of 'casual racism' (Hank Nelson's phrase) – a community of Europeans at

Kundiawa. (Only in New Guinea did we hear Australians classifying themselves as 'European'.) Kundiawa was in the Chimbu District, surrounded by the towering mountains of the central Highlands. Students who held cadetships were expected to spend their long vacations 'in the Territory' to become professionally sensitised and geographically, climatically and socially acclimatised. During his time as a student – a *pikinini dokta* – Anthony soaked up as much as he could of the land in all its dimensions, taking every opportunity to visit villages, plantations, other stations and mission centres.

At this time Port Moresby was a sleepy tropical town of about 10,000 people. One was immediately conscious of a colour bar. No drinking was allowed for the 'natives', although they served drinks to the *wait mastas* and *missus*. A notice at Ela Beach reminded all that it was for 'EUROPEANS ONLY', in front of which someone had scratched 'NON' in charcoal. The winds of impending change were beginning to blow. In church the 'Europeans' sat on one side and the 'natives' on the other. When a white child came in with its parents and went to sit on the 'wrong' side the child was jerked back to the 'right' side. The Europeans took communion, and left, first. A few years later, indigenous parishioners sat at the back, and by the turn of the century the congregation was entirely mixed – male and female, black, brown and white.

* * *

The second phase of our PNG experience was from 1963–72 when, as a family, we lived for a year in Boroko, Port Moresby – close to the Papuan Medical College and Taurama Hospital where Anthony took up his initial appointment – then at Kainantu in the Eastern Highlands, followed by two years at Saiho Hospital in the Northern District, now Oro Province. Later we returned to Kainantu before spending a final two years in Port Moresby. We took one child with us to PNG, had a second a year later, and a third was born in Scotland while we were on study leave. Government officers were given three months leave after 21 months of service, with medical officers having the option of an extra six months if they undertook relevant postgraduate study. We had two study periods overseas, which gave us opportunity to reflect on our experiences.

PMC opened in 1960 to train local medical personnel. (In 1970 it morphed into the medical faculty of the University of Papua New Guinea.) Our first home was separated from the small Boroko shopping centre by a kunai grass swamp. Unfortunately there was no short cut to the shops and we had to push the stroller around the dusty streets to get to BP's store, the post office, the chemist and the newsagent. When the truck spraying for mosquitoes travelled through the unsealed streets it churned up as much dust as it dispensed clouds of DDT.

Government houses were known by their design description and the number of bedrooms, for example AR2 and M3. Our first was of an older design and included a big open space, where a passage and an extra room would have been much more useful. The laundry was about 20 metres behind the house, semi-enclosed with cement floor, double cement troughs and a cold water tap. Outside were the wood-fired copper (for 'boiling' clothes) and a clothes line of the two posts with wire between. The *boi haus* was adjacent to the laundry. Basic furniture and appliances were supplied by the government: stove and refrigerator, a table and four dining chairs, four aluminium 'lounge' chairs with plastic plaiting, one double bed and a single bed. We had to borrow essential items for living from the hospital until our boxes arrived many weeks later – a situation to be repeated with each move. Sheets served as bedroom curtains until we could buy material and make our own. We accumulated minimal belongings as we had to crate and store everything each time we went on leave and then transport these crates to the place of our new posting – only once did we return to the same place.

Making do was an everyday challenge and working out innovative solutions became second nature. The first major cross-cultural situation we encountered was finding domestic help – a *haus boi* – then learning how to manage this situation in both practical and culturally appropriate ways. Word travels quickly and there was no shortage of uninvited applicants for the vacant position, which came with the bonus of a *boi haus*. In later years, these essential buildings were no longer provided as better electricity supply, washing machines and other labour-saving devices became available. In the early days house help was invaluable, for facilities were primitive, water had to be carted, and white women wilted in the tropical climate, especially when the missus was pregnant again.

The medical assistant, nursing and medical students often came to our home, with the nurses, separated from their extended families, delighted to act as babysitters. As we were barely three to five years older than many of them, we were more like older siblings than teachers and often acted *in loco parentis*. We did not see or feel ourselves as being patronising, and the interaction was mutually enjoyable. We hosted weddings and, in 1963, helped in negotiations on behalf of West (New Guinea)

Papua students when the Indonesians demanded their immediate repatriation to Irian Jaya. We joined a Bahasa class which
one of them taught. This special relationship with the West
Papuans has continued until today. Another student started
classes in Police Motu which we also attended.

Anthony became player-coach for the Taurama rugby team
and rugby reporter for the *South Pacific Post*. Later he coached
university rugby teams, whose members included numerous
'wannabe' politicians and public servants. He played district
rugby league and cricket for Kainantu and regional rugby
union for the Highlands, until he dislocated a hip in the South
Pacific Games trials. We led full lives, centred around family,
our workplaces, the Anglican and Lutheran churches, and our
friends, expatriate and national.

Our national friends included administration officers as well
as villagers in the rural areas to which we were appointed. In our
early years we enjoyed friendships with many of the growing
PNG elite through the Contact Club, which met regularly to
discuss issues of the day. There was no consciousness of black
and white, as we recall 50 years later. Many of the 'nationals'
who participated in the Contact Club went on to senior administrative, professional and political posts. In later years such
interactions kept us abreast of the groundswell for change.

We made some special friendships. One was with paramount *luluai* Anarai'i Wake of Punano No. 1 village at
Kainantu. (He was the first *luluai* and then the first paramount
luluai appointed by the Administration in the Highlands.)
Anarai'i was a major informant for Robin when she was
collecting oral histories about first contact. He gave our children Agarabi names, taught them the names of the various

types of arrows – 'the young', he bewailed, 'are no longer interested, let alone know how to make them' – and gave our elder
son archery lessons. He also visited us in town, once so we
could help him dress to meet the Duke of Kent.

The people of the small village of Soroputa on the other
side of the river from Saiho Hospital embraced our family
and included us in their celebrations and daily lives. We have
remained lifelong friends. They dressed us in tapa (beaten bark)
cloth and other *bilas* to dance with them at Christmas and
Easter, and gave our children Orokaiva names, even allocating
land to our eldest. When we left in 1967 they composed and
sang a special farewell song. In 2011 they celebrated the return
of Anthony and the boys with a traditional welcome of dance
and feast as we laughed, cried and danced the years away. Over
the years some of their young have visited us in Australia while
undertaking higher education. These relationships, forged
pre-Independence, are very special. They are reciprocal and
'relational' and we have been greatly enriched by them. While
outwardly the cultural differences are enormous, we enjoy and
share the common human threads of life and family. The boys
have pledged to continue these relationships into the future
with their own children.

Anthony's work included visiting village health workers and
projects, taking students to live in a village for a time, and going
on patrol, as well as running a large hospital and its peripheral
services. While Robin couldn't be directly involved in this, she
became his research assistant and he hers. At Kainantu, as part
of her interest in the history of first contact between foreigners
and Highlanders in this area, she began an oral history project
which took us into a number of villages. (Robin was awarded

an MA from UPNG for her thesis on this research, which was later published as *Highlanders and Foreigners in the Upper Ramu: The Kainantu Area 1919–1942*, (Melbourne: Melbourne University Press, 1987)). Our children played happily with the local children, and our presence as a family helped to create a trusting and relaxed atmosphere. Everyone enjoyed these occasions, men and women, young and old, as we heard their stories of first contact: sometimes they re-enacted events, complete with fighting regalia and weapons. Their recollections and perspectives of the 1930s complemented and clarified the information recorded in the written Administration and missionary reports, and provided a significant new perspective. Many of these first-hand reminiscences came from people who were dead within a decade.

We loved living on outstations. At Kainantu, and especially at Saiho, we were part of the local rhythm of the station and its neighbourhood. Something was always happening; we had little need to plan anything; life was vibrant and fascinating. Market days, plane arrivals and departures, villagers walking past, occasional local fights, and village celebrations, to which we were often invited, were part of outstation life. There were countless visitors, expected and unexpected, to be fed and often accommodated. One year over 235 signed our guestbook.

In 1965 Robin wrote: 'There is something about Territory life. People are interdependent, the constant moving about though hard and frustrating at the time – means a wealth of friends and contacts in so many places and a welcome wherever.' Still, Robin sometimes felt lonely and isolated, especially at the small jungle compound of Saiho Hospital, where she had no access to transport, no telephone, no one close by for coffee and a chat, nor even a track smooth enough to take the children for a walk. There were no neighbours or family nearby to discuss the development and problems of our young children, and the only adult European conversation was with visitors and was predominantly medical. There was a strong community spirit among station women in some of the towns, but Saiho was too small for such a community.

Robin's most frightening experience occurred in Kainantu. Anthony was away on patrol and one of our houseboy's beloved twin daughters became seriously ill and died. Peter went berserk, furious that Anthony was away. For the first and only time Robin feared that Peter might pick up a bush knife (machete) and attack her and the children. She had a wakeful night, though there was nothing she could have done. Fortunately, morning brought calmer emotions.

One of the special delights of living in rural areas was the opportunity to get a different perspective of the country by doing 'other things'. These included climbing the highest peak, Mt Wilhelm, and volcanic Mt Lamington, as well as walking the Kokoda track/trail/road, before it became a public thoroughfare. We followed our anthropology and archaeology interests, tracing ancient trade routes and collecting artefacts for the National Museum in Port Moresby. For a time Robin worked as a research assistant in the Prehistory Department at UPNG. We explored the geography of the land, experienced its ancient and recent history, and delighted in our natural surroundings. We watched the world's biggest butterfly in our Saiho garden, listened for and tried to catch sight of birds of paradise in the jungle, and collected arboreal orchids.

We did not think of ourselves as colonialists, nor in the late fifties and early sixties did most of those we knew. Indeed, the term was hardly ever used until the young socialist-leaning academics came up to the Territory in the late sixties. As we saw it, from the ivory tower of the new university at Waigani they condemned much of what had gone before, assessing the activities of earlier years in the light of the political correctness of the late sixties and early seventies. In 1963 Dr John Gunther, Assistant Administrator of the Territory and later foundation vice-chancellor of UPNG, thought independence to be in the distant future, as did several Territory luminaries such as long-time missionary Percy Chatterton. Many planters and other 'B4s' had an even longer, 'if ever', timetable. (A 'B4' was someone who came to the Territories of Papua and New Guinea before the Pacific war. Later the term was loosely applied to those who arrived in the years soon after the war.) This was probably wishful thinking. Independence was mooted by the Minister for Territories, Andrew Peacock, then precipitated by Prime Minister Whitlam, and the colonial tag for past admin-istrations increased. These were pressure cooker times and the independence debate was all over a short 12 years later in 1975.

We noticed the expatriate terms for the indigenous people varied and changed rapidly in this period. *Kanaka* was a deroga-tory term used by many Australians and indeed by many Papuans, on the south side of the island, about New Guineans. The connotation was that New Guineans were 'bushies'. However, many New Guineans called themselves *kanakas*, meaning they came from villages. Other derogatory terms such as 'coon' and 'bung' were becoming less common. Increasingly the generic word for describing origin became 'local' and then 'national'.

Many expatriates outside the main centres had never met an educated Papuan or New Guinean, and introducing tertiary-educated students and staff into an outstation like Kainantu was bound to produce tension. It was a huge learning curve for all. We took the medical students to the Kainantu Club to watch movies, which was tolerated, but when Robin played mixed doubles tennis with a Papuan student there was a barely controlled outburst from some of the expatriate males. One afternoon Anthony arrived at a plantation with a medical assistant and, as usual, was invited in for a 'cuppa'. When Anthony indicated his colleague, the hostess replied, 'Oh I don't know about that. I don't know what my husband would say if he found him in the house. Especially if he came home with a few in him. We've never had one in the house'. Domestic houseboys didn't count, of course. One issue was that expatriates often behaved like whales in fishbowls, whereas at home they would have been minnows in an ocean. Many were not used to having and using authority. For example, Anthony, three years out of medical school, was the sole doctor for 50,000 people. He was in charge of a 100-bed hospital, a staff of 20 at the hospital and another 20 in the field, and was responsible for liaising with four mission health centres.

***

Towards the end of 1971 it was clear that the time for us to move on was nearing as Anthony wished to extend his teaching experience into the Australian academic medical scene. Forgoing the 'golden handshake', at the end of 1972 we moved to Liverpool, England, then in 1975 to Australia's newest medical school at Flinders University in South Australia. (The 'golden handshake' was a monetary provision given to public servants who had served in the PNG administration prior to self-government and Independence. The amount awarded varied according to length of service.) But it was not farewell to PNG. Between 1978 and 2011 Anthony made numerous trips back to PNG as a consultant to various national and international agencies, including WHO, UNICEF, AusAID and World Vision. This was the third phase of our PNG lives. In 2010 Robin made her first visit back to PNG since 'going finish' in 1972, while our two sons made the same trip in 2011.

In the years after 1978 there have been times of both joy and sadness. The joys include reunions with village friends and students who are now colleagues. In 2010 we returned to celebrate the fiftieth anniversary of the creation of the PMC. It was a memorable occasion as former staff and students relived old memories, re-walking and re-working the experiences of yesteryear. The medical and health sciences faculty had grown from 40 to over 500 students, and eighty per cent of staff members were national. Over the years five former students have filled the role of Dean, a particular pleasure for a former teacher.

At the same time it has been difficult watching the uneasy evolution of independence as PNG has sought an identity as a separate nation. Not only did health services and their infrastructure, especially in rural areas, retract as Anthony had predicted in 1971 (Radford 1972, 250–79), but the administration struggled to provide anything like equity of services for the different health units. The resources that do exist are now concentrated in the bigger centres. In the early years of the new millennium it was estimated that more than half of the village health posts which were operational in 1970 were no longer functional. After initial deterioration during the first decade after Independence, there has been some improvement recently in child death rates, but this has only brought the situation back to where it was 40 years ago.

These days Christian missions, now national churches with mostly national leaders, provide much of the medical care for those in rural areas and with unsociable diseases such as tuberculosis, leprosy and, more recently, HIV, which is rushing across the country like a bushfire. The missions have long played a major role in the provision of health services, education and training, making a significant contribution to the development of nationhood. Many old Territorians asserted that missionaries came to the Territory 'to make good and they did', referring to the huge tracts of land they appropriated for plantations. The relationship between church and state was variable and often minimal. But this should not blind us to the contribution made by missionaries.

The unique undergraduate rural training program that Anthony initiated in the 1960s was almost completely eroded by 1990, although by 2010 another expatriate South Australian doctor, working with the Baptist Church, had established a six-year postgraduate course for training doctors intent on a career in remote and rural medicine. He has also been appointed to a half-time position at UPNG to re-establish formal rural training within the undergraduate medical course. Many of the current health workers are heavy smokers, chew betel nut and are markedly overweight. This is despite their education and training. Affluence has brought changes to the lives of some senior citizens, and they are now dying prematurely from stroke, heart attacks and diabetes – the 'lifestyle diseases'. Obesity was rare in the 1960s.

Numerous buildings – those of the NDOH (the PHD was rebadged as the National Department of Health), church health services and many schools – are in a terrible state of disrepair. Many staff show little interest in their roles or in providing leadership. Desks in national and provincial offices are often deserted or occupied by staff reading the daily papers or, more recently, using their mobile phones. Other public servants with much to contribute are unable to do so. One, an old friend of ours, was a reporter with the ABC in 1963, manager of its Goroka office when he enlisted Robin as the reporter for Kainantu, and captain of the Highlands rugby union team of which Anthony was a member. He went on to become manager of the PNG South Pacific Games team and head of the national radio network until he was forced from office.

From 1963 to 1972 we had lived virtually free from random attack and constant fear. We could leave houses unlocked and shop, walk and travel freely, although by 1970 in Port Moresby we had to take more care. Our gentle dog was sufficient for us, but neighbours began to acquire security screens for windows and doors and to fence their premises. In the earlier days our children, barefoot and adventurous, lived outdoors when not at school, eating or sleeping. We knew that the Europeans, the station staff and the local villagers knew who they were and would care for them. On one station our children and those of Papara, our domestic help (we struggled with the term *haus boi*, in part because he was the same age as us), were happy playmates. The boys were kept from wandering too far off the beaten track – the jungle was all around us – by Papara's stern warning that if they did, the bad spirits (*embahe*) of the jungle would get them.

Stories of instability and violence on the roads and in the towns are now commonplace. Once we were held up on the Highlands Highway and held to ransom before the 'excavated' road was refilled to enable us to pass. One senior nurse, after walking 300 metres, complained the next day of extreme pain in her feet. 'I haven't walked so far in ten years,' she exclaimed, 'it just isn't safe.' One evening in 2011 Robin was showered with myriad pieces of glass when a *raskol* threw a rock, not a stone, at our car. The word *raskol* has taken on a new meaning; no longer just a nuisance, but a robber, prepared to use violence, even murder. Every week there are reports of attacks in the cities and, increasingly, in small rural towns. Stories abound of corruption at every level of government and society – corruption appeared minimal in our time – while dishonesty is exacerbated by pressure from *wantoks* on those who have access to resources. The Law Society reported recently that eighty per cent of women in cities and seventy per cent in villages suffer domestic violence.

For those of us who have spent so much time in PNG it continues to wound the soul to read of the ongoing violence, widespread corruption and the land being stripped of its forests. A recent assessment rated Port Moresby, now a city of over 500,000 people, as the third worst place on the planet in which to live, and this in a country of only 7,000,000 people with one of the highest per capita levels of natural resources.

***

We went to PNG committed to contributing where and how we could. We hoped to live and work outside the main centres, where we could cross cultures and perhaps provide support to bridge the gap between the modern world and self-sufficient traditional life. We looked forward to enjoying the natural environment, whether on the islands, coast, or in the mountains. There was an undefined expectation of discovery and adventure; on reflection we were not disappointed. And while colleagues in Australia had predicted that going to PNG meant getting off the professional ladder, reality proved the contrary. Australian doctors from PNG took up many of the senior posts in academic public health and general practice when they returned to Australia (Radford 2011).

How did life in PNG change Anthony's view of his profession? In PNG most are born, get sick and die in villages. One of the most difficult things for young doctors and nurses was adjusting to the frequency of death and the responses of communities. Children especially were often brought to hospital *in extremis* with easily preventable conditions. We came to appreciate that the provision of care to the most peripheral and needy meant that a significant slice of the health cake had to be carved away from centralised hospitals, where the demands of investigatory medicine and clinical care overwhelmed preventive and promotive health needs. Another realisation was that decision-making on health care and its priorities is not the exclusive call of doctors. These realisations confirmed Anthony's belief that much of medical education should be conducted outside large hospitals, with their 'centrifuged deposit of the total world of illness' (W. Osler, circa 1911, in Robinson 1949, 232). Most illness derives from, and is managed in, community settings.

We decided to leave PNG for several reasons. First, Anthony was offered a challenging new opportunity, which enabled return trips to PNG. Second, our children were approaching secondary school age and after a very erratic and mobile primary experience we wanted something more stable for them. Third, local people were reluctant to take on roles of responsibility and leadership while their mentors were still involved. With Independence coming sooner rather than later, we thought it was time to step out.

Our children, and now their children, have grown up and live as 'Third Culture' children and citizens. Their world view is international. They have lived in places where their nationality, colour and language made them a minority, and they have learnt to relate easily to people of different cultures and countries. Our experience in PNG permeated our lives and still influences our outlook on the world.

References

Radford, A. J., 'Northward Ho! Experience in Papua New Guinea and the Development of Academic Public Health and General Practice in Australia', *Health and History*, 13: 1 (2011), 65–89.

Radford, A. J., 'The Future of Rural Health Services in Melanesia: With Particular Reference to Niugini' in M. Ward (ed.), *Change and Development in Melanesia*, (Canberra: ANU Press, 1972).

Robinson, J., *Tom Cullen of Baltimore*, (London: Oxford University Press, 1949).

POLICY, GOVERNANCE AND JUSTICE

7

A POWERFUL, FORMATIVE EXPERIENCE: 1963–76

John Langmore

Why work in PNG?

Living and working in PNG was a far more personally formative experience than I could possibly have imagined when thinking in 1962 about what to do after graduating in economics and social work. Ten years in PNG established my own independence; and work, postgraduate study and the rich diversity of life there turned out to be a strong foundation for later activities. Those years greatly increased my knowledge and sophistication and this concretely influenced the policies I was able to propose as a political advisor and MP in Australia, as Director of the Division for Social Policy and Development in the United Nations Secretariat in New York, and as a Professorial Fellow at the University of Melbourne. Working in PNG turned out to be a fine foundation for a career in public policy.

However, the expectation of such valuable experiences had little to do with my decision to apply for employment with the Australian Administration in PNG. PNG had the attractions of idealism, independence and adventure intertwined. Growing up in a Christian family, missionary work as a possibility had circulated but this never appealed to me: I am not an evangelist or a salesman by nature, and anyway the concept seemed permeated with cultural superiority. It could well be argued that attempting to engage in economic and social development has something of the same imperial attitude. Although aware of this, there still seemed to be some potential value in participating in, articulating and implementing a cooperative and equitable approach to living in the modern world. Rapid change in PNG was inevitable, but that could happen in many different ways. Surely there was some scope for attempting to influence the characteristics of that evolution? Australia was the colonial government so perhaps it was reasonable for Australians with even embryonic opinions about the style and strategies of independent government to attempt to have some influence on the processes of change?

In my final undergraduate year at the University of Melbourne I had become fascinated by the subject of economic development and was attracted to working in that area. Family life and experiences also influenced my decision. My parents had friends who were medical and educational missionaries in PNG, Africa and Asia and we had students from PNG who were studying in Victorian schools to stay during the holidays. I also remembered my uncle, a plastic surgeon, and his wife, a nurse, and thin, traumatised and yellowed soldiers (from their anti-malarials) returning after the campaigns in PNG, one carrying a beautiful, flattened *Raggiana* bird of paradise. With hindsight, it seems clear that I wanted to establish independence from my mother. In any case she and my father were both supportive of my going to PNG.

I was recruited to the Administration as a base-grade clerk and after a two-week orientation course in Sydney in February 1963 was appointed to the Health Department's Malaria Service in Port Moresby. After a few months of wrapping parcels and entering figures it was plain that the Service Director had no serious work for me and I went progressively higher up the Administration hierarchy to ask for something more substantial to do, eventually reaching the Assistant Administrator, Dr John Gunther. Shortly thereafter I was appointed as a research officer in the Department of Labour. Life also improved after I married in January 1964 and Di joined me in Port Moresby. Owing to the shortage of housing we had no permanent accommodation for two and a half years. Like many others, we moved from one leave house to another.

There were several major tasks in the Labour Department. One was research on indigenous entrepreneurs in Port Moresby (Langmore 1967). Then in 1966 I was appointed Executive Officer of the Committee of Inquiry into Rural Wages. This involved organising meetings in each of the major regions of the country for the Chairman, Bill Conroy, the Secretary of the Agriculture Department, and six members – three European planters and three leading Papua New Guinean cash croppers – so that they could take evidence. They were fascinating trips. Bill wrote the report, and after a year of investigation the committee decided to increase the standard rural wage by 50 cents a month! The Inquiry had been a charade.

Colonial control

The Inquiry into Rural Wages illustrated the principal characteristic of PNG in the 1960s: Australian dominance. I wrote the following summary of the situation for a thesis submitted to Cambridge University in 1972:

Papua New Guinea combines the characteristics of a region of Australia and a distinct economic unit. For strategic, humanitarian and economic motives the Australian government used paternalistic policies from 1945 to the early 1960s to improve the welfare of New Guinea people, as defined by Australians. Social aims predominate, particular emphasis being given to extending administrative control, health services, education and communications. The main instruments of economic policy were steadily increasing grant aid, used partly to pay the salaries of expatriate public servants, and the stimulation of agricultural exports from private expatriate-owned plantations and indigenous smallholdings. During the mid-sixties Australia's aims shifted towards establishing a self-supporting economy by further encouraging expatriate private enterprises, improving the quality of the work force by greatly increased educational expenditure, and extending the infrastructure. Limited institutional changes were made to facilitate the process.

The result has been an economy controlled by expatriates, with wide income distribution inequalities, leaving New Guinean producers an important share of output only in agriculture. Australia has constructed a superstructure of foreign institutions and enterprises, but has not succeeded in effectively integrating these with New Guinean society. Policy makers assumed that relying on overseas aid and personnel would maximise the short-term rate of growth of

GDP and that this would automatically lead to growing PNG involvement in the economy. However the spill over has been slight and
the growing power of the foreign presence is making proportional
increases in the share of income and influence more difficult for New
Guineans. (Langmore 1972, 45)

Of course there were also progressive expatriates within the
Administration, the churches and the New Guinea Research
Unit. These wonderful people were consciously seeking
humane and equitable social relations. Some were cooperative
colleagues and they, and others, became close friends. I undertook voluntary activities, including performing the roles of the
Contact Club (a multiracial organisation which held monthly
meetings on public issues) and of the Port Moresby Council
of Social Service (which aimed to coordinate non-government
welfare groups and to advocate more equitable policies). Both
were worth doing, though of only limited effectiveness. After
experiencing the strength of control by the Department of
Territories, the dominance and complacency of many of the
foreign elite, and my own powerlessness, I became increasingly
disillusioned. Yet I continued to work with the Administration
partly because it had a policy of encouraging officers to
improve their qualifications. With an award of six months on
full pay which could be spread over a longer period, I was able
to study for two years at Monash University for a masters degree
in economics. This greatly strengthened my knowledge of
economics and led to a thesis on wages policy in PNG under
the supervision of Professor Joe Isaac, the most outstanding
scholar of industrial relations in Australia.

Accelerating political and social change

Shortly after I returned from Monash in 1969 Professor Anthony Clunies-Ross offered me a lectureship in economics at the University of Papua New Guinea, initially teaching macroeconomics and labour economics. The University had been established in 1966 with the appointment of the effective Deputy Administrator, John Gunther, as vice-chancellor. He oversaw the planning of fine, durable, well-designed concrete-block buildings and the recruitment of a number of outstanding professors and other staff. By 1969 the University was a flourishing academic community, focused on teaching subjects specifically designed for Papua New Guinean conditions and to prepare students for the likelihood of self-government. The Papuan Medical College, which had been established in 1961 by Professor Ian Maddocks, Dr Ray Mylius and others, had led the way with tertiary education of doctors (and was where I had acted as a live-in dean of students for six months in 1965 while still depending on temporary accommodation), and this had been incorporated into the University as the Faculty of Medicine.

The University decisively broke through the ethnic and therefore class distinctions in Port Moresby, energised an intellectual and cultural renaissance about movement towards nationhood, stimulated fine writing on Papua New Guinean history and prospects, such as Hank Nelson's *Papua New Guinea: Black Unity or Black Chaos?*, and, with the encouragement of Ulli and Georgina Beier and others, generated much creative art, drama and autobiography. When we moved to live on the campus, we became part of vital intellectual, social and cultural forums. Both Di and I benefited enormously because we were given the opportunity not only to teach but also to write and publish, and to establish some of our strongest friendships. She wrote her first biography there, *Tamate: A King* (1973) and I published a series of articles on aspects of economic policy and labour relations (which are listed amongst the references) and jointly edited *Alternative Strategies for Papua New Guinea* with Anthony Clunies-Ross. A notable University initiative was the establishment of annual Waigani Seminars where scholars, researchers, public policy makers, business people and civil society leaders debated many aspects of political, social and economic development. International ideological and intellectual innovators such as Ivan Illich, Lloyd Best and René Dumont were invited as keynote speakers. The excitement of that time has been insightfully narrated in Donald Denoon's history *A Trial Separation* and vividly in Drusilla Modjeska's novel *The Mountain*.

Lecturing was a great challenge because it involved preparing syllabuses which reflected PNG and its future needs, and this led to the delight of attempting to spread ideas and increase the students' analytical capacity and imagination. As well, I was commissioned to prepare estimates – to be used by consultants preparing a plan for the national capital – of the indigenous and non-indigenous population and work force of Port Moresby in 1980 and 1990 and to stratify the estimates by income. This intrinsically difficult task was made even more so by the inadequacy of contemporary data, though a census taken in 1966 which measured the population at 41,000 was a vital foundation (Langmore 1970, 'Forecasts'). I forecast the population 24 years later to be 270,000. In fact it turned out to be 193,000 in 1990 (Columbia Encyclopedia 2005), so my estimate was excessive, but this did at least have the benefit of challenging the planners to prepare for very rapid growth.

I used the consultancy payment to finance a five-week visit to four central and east African countries to study their economic and localisation strategies. They were a decade or two further advanced than PNG and so they offered innumerable lessons. The challenge was to discern positive and negative precedents and then to articulate them to students and the wider public (Langmore 1970, 'Localisation'). Continuing to feel the need for stronger intellectual preparation, in 1971 I applied to Cambridge University to take a postgraduate course in economic development and, astonishingly, was admitted. UPNG enabled me to take the course, and it was indeed highly stimulating and relevant. My thesis on a critical assessment of Australian economic policy for PNG since 1945 is quoted above. My results qualified me for admission as a PhD candidate but on returning to Port Moresby the opportunities for participating in national planning were so enticing that I withdrew.

After the House of Assembly elections in February-March 1972, Michael Somare successfully negotiated a new coalition led by his Pangu Pati and he became Chief Minister. The coalition included Julius Chan's People's Progress Party and he was appointed Minister for Internal Finance. The coalition won the first divisions in the House on 20 April. The Australian Minister for Territories, Andrew Peacock, sponsored amending the Australian PNG Act to set 1 December 1973 for self-government (Denoon 2005, Ch. 7), creating a firm framework for generating and adopting policies suitable for an independent PNG.

Social policy: incomes

During the 1960s wages policy was the most sensitive political issue in PNG. Wages not only determine the standard of living but also have immense symbolic importance as an indicator of social status. No other Administration action evoked such public discontent as decisions over wages and other incomes. Government control of incomes was much greater than in Australia because the Administration (and other Commonwealth agencies) employed such a high proportion of wage earners and because of its direct and indirect influence over statutory and negotiated private sector wage rates.

Until 1964 public service pay was related to Australian levels with additional allowances for expatriates to compensate for isolation and discomfort. The few Papua New Guineans appointed to the permanent service received the same salary as their expatriate colleagues though not the allowances. When the Commonwealth started to recognise the necessity of preparing for eventual self-government they rather clumsily reconstructed public service personnel policy by setting up a dual structure, with pay for local officers related to the government's estimate of the country's capacity to pay. The day the new Ordinance became operative, 10 September 1964, marked the start of a bitter political debate (Langmore 1973, 192). Local officers were to be paid between thirty and fifty per cent of the salaries of their expatriate colleagues, excluding the additional expatriate allowances, severely undercutting Papua New Guinean expectations. Educational qualifications for many positions were lowered, enabling improved promotion prospects, but this was secondary to the establishment of the dual wage structure.

Living in a society with a dual wage structure is constantly anguishing. Those on low pay are often resentful and those on high pay are often guilty about their affluence. The system felt unjust. Public protests about the new pay scales grew quickly in both PNG and Australia. In Port Moresby there were large protest marches and demonstrations. The Public Service Association made a claim which was heard by the Public Service Arbitrator. Bob Hawke, then Advocate for the Australian Council of Trade Unions, appeared as its advocate in the Local Officers' Salary Case. The president of the Port Moresby Council of Social Service, Rachel, Lady Cleland, wife of the Administrator, and I made a submission to the hearings on behalf of the Council. The Arbitrator decided on some concessions including a significant increase for a large group of local professional officers, substantial salary increases for Papua New Guineans in senior positions and pro rata increases for those in mid-level positions ('so that they could associate with counterparts in other countries as well as their own'), but there was only a minor increase in the minimum weekly wage to $8.50. The Administration introduced an inadequate family needs allowance for those on the minimum rate. I remember being outraged at an instruction from Canberra telling us how much rice and sweet potato we could allow for inclusion in the regimen for calculating the weekly family needs allowance – and that was just one of many examples of the autocratic pedantry of the Canberra bureaucrats.

Belatedly a single-line pay structure for both local and overseas officers was introduced which paid the same rate for the same occupation, but with large overseas allowances for expatriates. Further general increases were awarded in 1970 and 1972, but the differential leave and housing arrangements continued to be resented by many local officers as much as the pay differences (Langmore 1973). The permanent appointment of expatriate officers ceased in 1964 and those who remained after 1973 were offered partial 'golden handshakes' if they resigned after self-government or full compensation if they resigned after Independence.

In December 1972 Cabinet appointed an interdepartmental committee chaired by Campbell Fleay, Secretary of Labour, with Mekere Morauta, a former student of mine at UPNG and soon to be Secretary for Finance, and Dr Vern Harvey, assistant secretary of the Department of Finance, as members. The Committee was required to propose policies consistent with eight national aims (see below) that would be appropriate for PNG, which would reduce inequality, and to suggest measures for their implementation. Evidence was taken from employer groups, unions and others and, under the direction of the Committee, Bill Rees drafted substantial parts of the report. Immediately after returning from Cambridge in July 1973 I worked nearly full-time for the Committee completing preparation of the comprehensive *Incomes, Wages and Prices Policy* report which was submitted to the self-governing Cabinet in November 1973. The report covered: subsistence, cash crop and informal sector incomes; the national, urban and Public Service minimum wages; productivity; hours of work; pay of expatriates; rents; business and professional incomes; prices and marketing; personal, export, company and indirect taxes and tax administration; and machinery for implementation. In his foreword the Chief Minister, Michael Somare, wrote that he was encouraged to believe that the report was sound because Professor Isaac had written that: 'The analysis and proposals contained in the Report are fully consistent with the national economic aims and the consequential policy objectives' (*Incomes, Wages and Prices Policy*, 1974).

After the Somare Government adopted this report I appeared as a government representative in an Urban Wage Inquiry. Bill Kelty, who was by then ACTU advocate, represented the unions and he was a tough critic of the Incomes Policy. Later I was appointed to arbitrate in a dispute at the Kokopo desiccated coconut factory owned by Carpenters. The employees were working in a manufacturing enterprise located outside the urban area of Rabaul. They were paid the rural wage (which set minimum pay for plantation workers) but were claiming the urban wage. After taking evidence I decided in favour of their claim. A couple of days later Carpenters announced that they would shut the plant!

Economic development

Another of the initiatives linked to preparations for Independence was a commission I received from the Chief Minister's Office to prepare a proposal for establishment of a national economic planning office. Sir John Crawford had written ten years earlier that: 'We can perhaps afford, I think unwisely, to do without forward economic planning in Australia: I am sure we cannot afford the same luxury in Papua New Guinea' (Bettison et al. 1962, 74) and went on to describe what he meant and what could be achieved. Michael Somare and his staff may not have known of Crawford's insightful comments but they had the wisdom to recognise the necessity of setting goals, preparing plans for movement towards them and policies for their implementation. My paper was prepared in consultation with Anthony Clunies-Ross and others, and shortly led to the establishment of a Central Planning Office. The Office had four branches: General Planning and Projects, Resources and Industry, Social Planning and Area Planning. I applied to work there and was appointed one of the assistant directors under the Canadian David Beatty who had worked in Tanzania as well as New York. Beatty was certainly a 'do-it guy' (Denoon 2005, 129) and became most notable for his leadership in the renegotiation of the Bougainville Copper Agreement. Two major tasks for which I was responsible were leading the team that prepared *Strategies for Nationhood: Policies and Issues*, the first national medium-term economic and social strategy; and introduction of a new approach to national budgeting which ensured that national economic and social priorities were identified and embodied in the budget.

Economic strategy was one of the major subjects in the ferment about policies leading up to self-government. The desire to move responsibility for economic and social decision making from Canberra to Port Moresby was as strong amongst the expatriates committed to self-government as it was amongst Papua New Guineans. An early product of the Somare Government which was adopted by the House of Assembly was the articulation of eight national aims which focused on 'increasing the proportion of the economy under the control of Papua New Guinean(s) … ', on equity including equality for women, on decentralisation, small scale business, national self-reliance, and on active use of public sector activity to achieve the goals. The eight aims were the basis for *Strategies for Nationhood: Policies and Issues*. The purpose of that 164-page volume was described in Michael Somare's foreword, which was based on the draft I prepared for him:

> In this document our policies to ensure socially, economically and environmentally sound development for all our people are summarized. It has been the custom in most countries to focus policies on the attainment of economic goals … The hope implicit in this approach was that somehow the benefits from such growth would trickle down to the people. In fact in those nations pursuing those kinds of policies there has been little improvement in the quality of life of the people. Instead the lions share [sic] of any new wealth generated in these countries is captured by the elite. This will not happen in Papua New Guinea. Instead we are concentrating our effort directly on rural development, equality and self-reliance. The organisation of this volume shows our priorities. (Somare 1974, iii)

Using the eight aims we also proposed five questions to the Cabinet Budget Committee. These were discussed and then each of the members gave a numerical ranking to the categories of public expenditure; these were averaged and the outcome used in deciding which outlays to increase most and which should have a low priority. Unsurprisingly, education, health and agricultural extension headed the list and defence was last. These rankings were the basis for budget decisions and for another planning document, *Programmes and Performance* (National Planning Committee 1975). At the time, Beatty questioned whether these planning documents were sufficiently useful to have justified the amount of time expended in the consultation, drafting and checking which they involved. But even to write that description of their preparation indicates one of their major effects: they were a potent way of drawing scores of politicians, public servants and academics into the process of rethinking both national strategy and more detailed sectoral and departmental policies in the context of a commitment to genuinely Papuan New Guinean development.

One of my reasons for applying to work on Gough Whitlam's staff in Canberra and deciding to return to Australia in early 1976 was the contradiction involved in being an expatriate and still engaged in highly sensitive political issues like planning and incomes policy. It was obvious after Independence that such issues had to be not only decided by Papua New Guinean politicians but that they also had to be advised by Papua New Guineans rather than expatriates, no matter how sympathetic to the national goals one attempted to be. This was happening so it was necessary for expatriates to withdraw. Another factor was that Sarah, the eldest of our three daughters, Sarah, Naomi and Katie, was growing close to high school age.

Lessons learnt for Australia

A potent lesson I learnt in PNG was the importance of national politics. It was only when the movement to self-government began that it was possible to start to move away from autocratic rule by Canberra. It was only when Papua New Guineans began to utilise the power of their majority in the House of Assembly that the focus of public policy shifted from maximising national income to improving the wellbeing of Papua New Guineans. It was only when the eight aims were adopted that planning of provincial and local government structures began. It was only when a Port Moresby City Council was elected that construction began of footpaths along the major roads in the city, something for which the Council for Social Service had campaigned for many years. But of course, democratic elections are a necessary but not a sufficient condition for effective representative government.

A comprehensive incomes policy can be an influential tool for simultaneously reducing inflation and increasing employment. That was amongst the goals of the Papua New Guinean Incomes Policy. Experience with that Policy was one of the factors which led me to propose, with Ralph Willis's encouragement, to the Labor Parliamentary Executive in Canberra, what became the Accord. Few people know that the innovative experience with an incomes policy in PNG was one of the examples which added strength to the proposal for the Australian Accord. One of the specific qualities of the PNG incomes policy which was a precedent for Australia was its comprehensiveness, including not only wages but other incomes, prices and taxation.

The value of foresight in development of economic policy was another useful precedent for Australia. The experience with the PNG Central Planning Office was one of the factors which suggested the value of establishing the Australian Economic Planning Advisory Council. Bob Hawke was receptive to this idea so it was included in the Labor Party Economic Platform in the early 1980s and the Council was established soon after the National Economic Summit in April 1983.

Experience in PNG also increased my scepticism of trickle-down economics and greatly strengthened my recognition of the importance of what can broadly be described as social democratic strategy, concerned with wellbeing, the common good and environmental responsibility. This was a lesson which was harder for Australian governments to accept.

Consequences and hopes for PNG

In March 1991 I visited PNG with nine other Australian parliamentarians. We were given a warm and polished welcome. We visited nine towns spread through most regions and the message was the same everywhere, 'Give us tied aid', which meant aid for particular national and provincial projects. The implication was that confidence had been lost in the effectiveness of the national government's priority setting and financial administration.

Law and order was the most commonly discussed subject informally. We were all distressed by the stories of crime and violence. Rapid social change had led to a breakdown of community constraints, and this was exacerbated by frustrated expectations, unemployment, alcohol and so on. Local courts were being established too slowly. The police were severely understaffed and most officers were inadequately trained. The astounding Australian decision in 1975 to close the Police Training College to accommodate cuts in aid – in the year of Independence – had caused enormous, enduring damage. Police housing was antiquated and inadequate; the police had too few radios and couldn't even get enough notebooks. The identification of this profound problem offered hope that it could be addressed, but after 20 further years there has still not been sufficient action. Australian governments bear some of the responsibility for the situation because, later, Foreign Affairs Minister Alexander Downer had required that Australian police advisors offered for work in PNG not be subject to Papua New

Guinean law! How could police responsible for administrating the law not be required to comply with that law? This was arrogant neo-colonialism, to which the Papua New Guinean Government naturally reacted by declining the 'assistance'.

Members of the parliamentary delegation were impressed with the competence, good sense and openness of many of the politicians and public servants with whom we spoke. It was clear that despite severe financial and organisational constraints many senior Papua New Guineans were working with dedication and professionalism. Sixteen years of independence had increased the authority and self-confidence of many leaders. It was clear that there was a desperate need to expand the number of high schools, and to improve funding for expansion and especially maintenance of roads, housing, health centres, schools and universities. It was also clear that the churches were major and essential sources of the provision of all services.

The delegation concluded that PNG had established its independence and that the time had come for more general recognition of the natural interdependence of Australia and PNG. More restrained supportive action by Australia would be warranted including: increasing funding for the police support project; increasing funding for higher secondary, technical, agricultural and tertiary education; upgrading of agricultural research on existing and new tropical crops; establishment of a Papua New Guinean mediation service; strengthening the embryonic science policy; resumption of medium-term economic policy making; and expansion in the number of national parks.

In 2013 it is clear that there is Australian government recognition of the importance of relations with PNG, for both

Prime Ministers made official visits during the first half of the year. But there is not nearly sufficient recognition within the whole Australian community that the wellbeing of the people of PNG is vital to Australia's wellbeing, not least because it is now and always will be our closest neighbouring country. All the recommendations in the previous paragraph are still insufficiently realised and continue to be essential. My hope is that many Australian individuals and groups will establish and sustain friendships with individuals and groups in PNG, and that these will flourish in scores of mutually beneficial ways. A more mature, equitable and attentive relationship between Australia and PNG is essential to the wellbeing and common good of both countries.

References

Bettison, D. G., E. K. Fisk, F. J. West and J. G. Crawford, *The Independence of Papua – New Guinea: What are the Pre-requisites?*, (Sydney: Angus & Robertson, 1962).

Clunies-Ross, Anthony and John Langmore (eds), 1973, *Alternative Strategies for Papua New Guinea*, (Melbourne: Oxford University Press, 1973).

Columbia Encyclopedia 2005, www.encyclopedia.com, accessed 30 July 2013.

Denoon, Donald, *A Trial Separation: Australia and the Decolonisation of Papua New Guinea*, (Canberra: Pandanus Books, 2005).

Incomes, Wages and Prices Policy: Report of Interdepartmental Committee, (February 1974). (Mimeographed.)

Langmore, John, A *Critical Assessment of Australian Economic Policy for Papua New Guinea between 1945 and 1970*, (Port Moresby: University of Papua New Guinea, 1972). (Cambridge University thesis.)

Langmore, John, 'A Role for Foreign Investment?', *Meanjin*, 34, 3 (1975), 260–71.

Langmore, John, 'Agricultural Wages', *New Guinea*, 6, 1 (1971).

Langmore, John, 'Any Lessons for Australia?: Planning in PNG', *Newsletter of the RIPA ACT Group*, 5, 1 (1978).

Langmore, John, 'Contractors in Port Moresby', *New Guinea Research Bulletin No. 16*, (Canberra/Boroko: Australian National University, 1967), 41–58.

Langmore, John, 'Economic and Demographic Forecasts', *New Guinea Research Bulletin No. 37*, (Canberra/Boroko: Australian National University, 1970), 3–41.

Langmore, John, 'Labour Relations in Papua New Guinea, 1970–1972', *The Journal of Industrial Relations*, 15, 2 (1973), 158–74.

Langmore, John, 'Localisation in Eastern Africa' in Marion Ward (ed.), *The Politics of Melanesia*, (Canberra/Port Moresby:

Australian National University/University of Papua New Guinea, 1970).

Langmore, John, 'Opening Address: Papua New Guinea – Australia Colloquium', *Proceedings and Recommendations*, (James Cook University of North Queensland, August 1988).

Langmore, John, 'Recent Developments in Industrial Relations in Papua New Guinea', *The Journal of Industrial Relations*, 12, 3 (1970), 387–96.

Langmore, John, 'Rural Wage Policy in PNG' in Marian Ward (ed.), *Change and Development in Rural Melanesia*, (Canberra/ Port Moresby: Australian National University/University of Papua New Guinea, 1972).

Langmore, John, 'The Bougainville Crisis: Opening Address' in Matthew Spriggs and Donald Denoon (eds), *The Bougainville Crisis: 1991 Update*, (Bathurst: Crawford House Press, 1992).

Langmore, John, 'Wage Determination in Papua New Guinea', *The Industrial Review*, 8, 1 (1970).

Langmore, John and Roger Berry, 'Wages Policy in Papua New Guinea', *The Journal of Industrial Relations*, 20, 3 (1978).

Modjeska, Drusilla, *The Mountain*, (Sydney: Vintage Press, 2012).

National Planning Committee, *Programmes and Performance 1975–76*, (Port Moresby: Central Planning Office, 1975).

National Planning Committee, *Strategies for Nationhood: Programmes and Performance*, (Port Moresby, Central Planning Office, 1974).

Nelson, Hank, *Papua New Guinea: Black Unity or Black Chaos?*, (Melbourne: Penguin, 1974).

Somare, Michael, 'Foreword' in *Strategies for Nationhood: Policies and Issues*, (Port Moresby: Central Planning Office, 1974).

8

FROM COLONIAL BACKWATER TO VIBRANT INDEPENDENT STATE – IN A DECADE

John Ley

My motivation for working in PNG

In 1962, as a young solicitor who had never been out of the country, I was looking for some adventure and stimulating legal experience outside the Australian mainstream. I had read Peter Ryan's book *Fear Drive my Feet*, about the Australian coast-watchers in Papua and New Guinea during the Second World War. I found this a fascinating story about men who carried out very dangerous but extremely important intelligence work, monitoring the movements of the Japanese military forces in the Trust Territory of New Guinea, especially in such dense jungle as that around Lae, Salamaua and Finschhafen.

Soon after finishing the book I heard John Guise, then a Papuan political leader and one of the very few indigenous members of the country's Legislative Council, on the ABC radio program *Guest of Honour*. Guise told his Australian audience about the need for young Australians to come to Papua and New Guinea to help the country develop skills and administrative capacity as it moved towards self-government and independence. He spoke very movingly. So I sought a job in the recently created Public Solicitor's Office. I thought this would be a constructive way of making a contribution to the development of the country. I was appointed a legal officer in the Department of Law, based in Port Moresby, arriving there in October 1963. Six months later I was transferred from Crown Law to the Public Solicitor's Office, where I dealt with criminal and civil cases for six years.

In 1969 I became the first Counsel to the Speaker and private members of the House of Assembly, a position created at the instigation of then Speaker (Sir) John Guise MHA and a number of influential elected members of the Assembly. The aim was to enable the Speaker and the mostly indigenous private members to obtain legal advice and assistance, independent of the Administration's Department of Law. Taking up that role in 1970 brought me to the centre of political activity in the country at a time when the colonial era was concluding and dramatic changes, in various parts of the country, were beginning to be reflected at the national political level and to impact on Australia's policies concerning the Territory. My hopes of making a significant contribution to Papua New Guinean independence, kindled by Guise's encouraging words on radio eight years earlier, were about to be fulfilled.

Port Moresby

I arrived in the dusty capital of the Australian-administered Territory of Papua and New Guinea at 6.00am on a hot, October day. I had come overnight from Sydney on a Douglas DC-6B aircraft, which took about nine hours, including a refuelling stop at the very basic wartime Quonset hut that was Brisbane airport. As a legal officer, I was a member of a small but dominant minority group of white Australian colonial *mastas*. The society was a stratified one with white expatriates, including defence personnel, at the top of the pyramid. In the middle was a much smaller number of Chinese and mixed-race small business people, who typically owned and ran trade stores in Port Moresby and other significant towns, but also some larger businesses such as a coastal shipping company. The population of the country was about 2.1 million. Port Moresby was home to 60,000 people, including a significant number of 'squatters' living in makeshift shacks with very few services – Papuans and New Guineans who had come into town looking for work and other 'bright lights' opportunities. At the same time, there were educated Papuans and New Guineans – tertiary students, tradesmen and graduates from educational institutions – beginning to form an emerging new class. Villagers throughout the country, who comprised the bulk of the population, lived in traditional ways. Whilst women had a key role in traditional society as gardeners and homemakers, very few had significant roles in the more modern aspects of PNG society and many suffered domestic violence.

I settled in quickly at the small Department of Law. It comprised the Crown Law Office, which advised and acted for the Administration, and the Public Solicitor's Office, which independently advised and represented indigent Papuans and New Guineans in a range of criminal cases and in some land title and other civil cases. The Legislative Draftsman's Office was also within the Department but, like the Public Solicitor's Office, it had no statutory basis establishing its independence. Pubsol's Office, as it was known, comprised approximately ten expatriate (all but one male) lawyers and two administrative staff, one expatriate and one indigenous. A Papuan man was the well-regarded interpreter. There was a strong esprit de corps among the staff, who were headed by W. A. (Peter) Lalor, a *kiap* very committed to the independence of the office from the Administration. The office sometimes became involved in politically sensitive issues, such as restoration of pre-war land title cases and some criminal matters, several going on appeal to the High Court of Australia.

The lawyers socialised easily and frequently among themselves and at dinner parties, which were usually organised by one or other of their wives. Then 24 years old and married, I had arrived alone, owing to a shortage of accommodation for married Australian Administration officers. Within a month, I had been fortunate enough to arrange for my wife and me to occupy a 'leave house' overlooking Port Moresby harbour. Julie, who was pregnant with our first daughter, Karen, joined me in November 1963. After Julie arrived, we were fully embraced by the social group. I joined in the afternoon social tennis and squash matches, and in swimming at nearby Ela Beach, which had recently been desegregated. Although I had had no previous experience of a colonial situation, I soon realised that the Territory was very much in that mould. As expatriates, at first blush it seemed a very comfortable situation for my wife and me, but we both quickly recognised and disliked the injustice of the 'second class' situation of the Papuans and New Guineans. The training of indigenous public servants was at an early stage and so the public service was still dominated by expatriate officers in all fields – technical, professional and administrative. In private enterprise little was being done to provide greater training and employment opportunities for Papuans and New Guineans. For example, in the major department stores such as Burns Philp, Steamships and Carpenters, most of the sales staff were married expatriate women.

The country's future as a colony and trust territory seemed unlikely to change quickly, despite decolonisation proceeding apace in Asia, Africa and elsewhere. Even several years later, in March 1967, the Minister for Territories, Charles Barnes, confirmed this in an official statement by stating that he 'could not speculate what future generations might think on the independence issue: but the Territory would not achieve independence for many years, *if at all*' (Downs 1980, 378 – his italics).

The Highlands: defending in criminal cases

For the next two and a half years, most of my legal work comprised defending Papuans and New Guineans in the Supreme Court, on circuits to major towns and remote subdistricts. I travelled on light aircraft with a judge, his associate, the prosecutor and the pilot – sometimes through rough weather and landing on short, steep-sloping airstrips. There was little time to take instructions from my clients as the timetable of the touring judicial party was tight. In each case, defence counsel and the prosecutor had a copy of the transcript of the committal proceedings that had led to the trial. In some remote areas, two interpreters were needed – one from the local language to Tok Pisin and the other from Pisin to English and back. The trials

145

were by a judge alone, who wore the traditional British and Australian red, ermine-trimmed gown, which was an incongruous sight in bush materials courtrooms with bare-chested prisoners wearing only *laplaps*. In determining the sentences, the judges, all of whom were Australian, generally took into account the extent to which the convicted prisoner had been in contact with Australian law and administration, and gave lighter sentences to those who had little experience of that law. In such cases the prisoner generally had far more knowledge and understanding of customary law and practices than he did of Australian law. Nevertheless, many of the accused in the Highlands knew well that the relatives of the victim were likely to want to carry out 'payback' against them and went quickly to the local administrative patrol post to make a confession and be put into protective custody by the local *kiap* pending their court hearings.

East New Britain

In 1966 I was transferred to the post of Deputy Public Solicitor in Rabaul, the district headquarters of East New Britain. Rabaul, on the Gazelle Peninsula, was a striking contrast to Port Moresby. During the dry season from March to November, Moresby looked much like many rural parts of Australia outside the tropics – dry and with much of the scrub burnt by small grass fires, intended by Papuans to drive out wallabies to hunt. Rabaul, on the other hand, was green for most of the year and surrounded by spectacular volcanoes. The lush tropical vegetation growing in the volcanic soil gave the town its picturesque appearance. There was a constant smell of sulphur, and minor tremors (*gurias*) shook the earth on a regular basis.

The composition of the Rabaul population was very different from that of Port Moresby's population. There were fewer expatriate Australians and more New Guineans. Rabaul was a quiet but thriving town where the Tolai people had a major part in daily life, driving their Japanese 'hap cars' (small trucks), often with produce from their gardens for the bustling local market. They had a reasonably effective, though limited, political role through their participation in the all-Tolai Gazelle local government council. During the two years my family and I were in Rabaul, I learned tok pisin and felt much closer to the Tolai people than I had to the Papuans and New Guineans in Port Moresby, where the larger number of white Australians had a more dominant role and lived in a manner quite similar to that in some country towns in Australia. In Rabaul I came to know as friends several local leaders, one of whom, Julius Chan, later became an MHA and Prime Minister. Another, John Kaputin, a leading Tolai, also became an MHA and enjoyed a long parliamentary career. He co-founded, with John Momis Member for Bougainville, the Melanesian Alliance. In time, I would come to work with them both on the Constitutional Planning Committee, 1972–4.

In 1969 the loosely structured Mataungan Association (MA) was formed and became very active politically. It was founded and flourished on the Gazelle Peninsula because of deep resentment on the part of many Tolai about the loss of their traditional land to German planters and missionaries before 1914 and, subsequently, to Australian plantation companies and missions. Some of this land had been taken in reprisal for violent actions by villagers towards Germans, but much had been alienated, as many Tolais saw it, as a result of grossly unfair land dealings with local landowners. After the First World War, in accordance with the terms of the Treaty of Versailles, these lands were expropriated and became the property of the Australian Custodian of Expropriated Properties. Between the wars, the properties were made available to the Australian Administration, expatriate plantation companies, individuals and missionary organisations – with indefeasible Torrens system titles.

After the Second World War, some local villagers began to occupy rundown copra plantations owned by Australian companies such as Burns Philp, Steamships and Carpenters, which for years had failed to invest in them. Despite a recommendation in 1946 by then District Commissioner Bates that the Administration buy all the rundown plantation land and hand it back to dispossessed Tolais, the plantations were not made available for purchase or in any other way. The Department of Territories in Canberra had vetoed the recommendation. The Tolai also resented a controversial decision by the Administration, taken in the late 1960s, to replace the all-Tolai local government council with a multiracial Rabaul Council. The Tolai community was itself deeply divided over the council issue. The quiet, apparently peaceful township and surrounding area, in which there was already discontent about land alienation, changed rapidly to an environment where many felt deep anger and hostility towards the Administration and expatriate commercial interests on the peninsula.

In September 1969, just before my family and I went to London where I was to undertake postgraduate legal studies, John Kaputin, a leader of the MA, came to my house. He asked me, as Deputy Public Solicitor, to make a bail application on behalf of several MA leaders who had been arrested for allegedly stealing the keys to the Rabaul Council. The Administration's decision to make the council a multiracial body had enraged MA members and many other Tolais. Under pressure from the physically remote Department of Territories, the Administration was using the full force of the law to prosecute the MA leaders for theft of the council keys. Kaputin argued that the three arrested MA members did not intend to keep the keys; the act was not a theft but a symbolic protest, intended to highlight the sense of injustice that the MA members felt about the council issue. The situation was extremely tense: Kaputin thought that a substantial number of MA members would descend on the police station, where the leaders were being held in custody.

That evening brought me, for the first time, into close personal contact with Kaputin and the powerful sense of grievance that he and many of the villagers felt towards the Administration and the plantation companies. This was a turning point in my relationship with the indigenous people of the country, as well as a critical moment in Australia's colonial rule. By bringing in riot police, the Administration reacted very strongly to the situation, creating considerable tension in its relations with the Tolai people. The pressure that built up over the arrests was diffused when I was successful in obtaining a bail order for the release of the MA leaders, pending a later court hearing of the charges against them. Their argument about the substance of the charge, and the provocative nature of the arrest of the leaders, carried weight with the magistrate, Paul Quinlivan.

After I had left the country, tensions in the Rabaul area escalated. Helicopters hovered overhead in places where significant numbers of MA supporters gathered, and more riot police were sent from Port Moresby. In early 1970 the Australian opposition leader, Gough Whitlam, toured the Territory and spoke to a large, enthusiastic crowd of about 11,000 people at Rabaul airport. He said that if the ALP were elected to government in 1972, he would take all necessary steps for the country to achieve self-government and independence before 1976. This was seen as a controversial prediction. In July 1970 Prime Minister Gorton also toured PNG. He too addressed a huge crowd in Rabaul, but had a very different reception. The crowd was obviously hostile towards the government's conservative attitude to the Territory's political development, especially the multiracial council and the alienated land issue. The occasion became notorious for the fact that Gorton accepted advice to carry a concealed pistol for protection. Upon his return to Canberra, Gorton immediately pressed ahead with a carefully planned process of transferring powers from Canberra to Papua New Guinean 'ministerial members' of the House of Assembly.

I did return briefly to Rabaul on one occasion, to give evidence at the 1971 trial of those who were alleged to have murdered DC Jack Emanuel near Kabaira plantation, a tragic and highly significant event in the post-war history of the Territory under Australia's administration. Thirteen Tolai men were tried for the Emanuel murder, after several were discharged at the outset. Two were convicted of murder, three of conspiracy to murder, and eight acquitted. My evidence related to the frustrations and concerns of Tolai land claimants, who had come to my office in the late 1960s a number of times, over many months, to seek what they regarded as justice concerning the acquisition and retention of their lands by expatriates over many decades. Australian plantation companies had taken over the German-claimed land in the area where Emanuel had been killed. I had been unable to find an effective avenue for the Tolai to obtain redress for their grievances, as the title to the land was found to be legally secure and the plantation company concerned was not willing to give or sell any of the land to the claimants.

The House of Assembly and the CPC

After the 1972 general election there was a dramatic change in the composition of the House of Assembly, which had been established in 1964 on the basis of the first common roll and expanded substantially in 1968. My work changed significantly too. In the several years following the 1968 election, new political parties had been formed. In 1972, for the first time, a number of organised parties competed for votes and the right to govern, and a progressive National Coalition Government comprising three parties and a number of independents was formed, to the surprise of many political observers. Michael Somare, leader of the pro-self-government Pangu Pati, became the first Chief Minister of PNG.

In mid-1972, the Somare administration established a new committee of parliamentarians to advise on the establishment of a constitution in preparation for PNG self-government. The committee's genesis was in discussions between new minister Ebia Olewale and a political scientist, New Zealander Dr David Stone from the Australian National University (ANU) New Guinea Research Unit. I was aware that a specific proposal had been put to the government through Tony Voutas, an adviser to Chief Minister Somare and ex-Pangu MHA. Unlike previous

select committees of the Assembly for constitutional development, the committee comprised all Papua New Guinean MHAs.

The Constitutional Planning Committee (CPC) was nomi-
nally headed, *ex officio*, by Chief Minister Somare and included
Deputy Chief Minister Dr John Guise. Somare rarely attended
meetings, Guise did not attend any, and neither voted on the
CPC's draft proposals. The members comprised almost equal
numbers of government and opposition members. Among their
number was John Kaputin. In a masterstroke, the government
chose as deputy of the CPC (and de facto chairman) recently
ordained Catholic priest Father John Momis, the new regional
member for Bougainville. He was a staunch critic of many aspects
of the massive, highly controversial copper mine established in
the late 1960s at Panguna, Bougainville, by Conzinc Riotinto.

The CPC drew on the expertise of some highly qualified and
experienced academic lawyers from other recently independent
Commonwealth countries. They included Professor Yash Ghai,
two West Indian judges, and a Papua New Guinean lawyer,
Bernard Narokobi and expatriate political scientists David Stone
and Edward Wolfers who were employed as legal and political
consultants. I was appointed as legal officer, on secondment from
the House of Assembly. Together with the consultants, I participated in the committee's discussions on issues and proposals
for resolving them. Bernard Narokobi and I wrote several of
the chapters of the committee's reports. A crucial aspect of the
CPC's process was that the members, not consultants or staff,
initiated ideas for discussions on the various terms of reference
and made all of the decisions about their recommendations. As
Momis put it, 'the consultants are to be on tap, not on top'.

Consultation with the people was a vital component of

the committee's work. Public meetings with groups of CPC members were held in every sub-district, and the committee received hundreds of written submissions from individuals and groups. These submissions were made in response to six detailed CPC issues papers, facilitated by local officials and scribes. ANU Asia-Pacific constitutional lawyer Anthony Regan has said this was the first widely consultative and participatory constitutional process in the world, and later provided a model for constitutional reform in countries such as Uganda and Kenya. During extensive tours of the country by two groups of committee members, led by Momis and Kaputin, the very different views of people in various regions of the country towards self-government became clear. Broadly, island people were the most vocal in seeking early independence, although coastal Papuans were concerned about how independence could affect them adversely as a minority group. For their part, Highlanders and expatriate plantation owners and business people were very concerned about being disadvantaged by early independence. Most Highlanders felt they would be disadvantaged by their late contact with Europeans and relative lack of education, business skills and experience of the outside world.

Momis effectively led the deliberations of the committee, but in a very inclusive way with a visionary, human rights-oriented approach based on Catholic liberation and social justice theology. He gave considerable weight to the urgent yet longstanding demands of many Bougainvilleans and Tolais for a substantial degree of autonomy. Momis and Kaputin were convinced that there must be a substantial measure of political and administrative decentralisation of the country if the people were to have a real say in their government and PNG was to be a cohesive political entity post-independence. Without such devolution of power, Momis saw little prospect of disillusioned Bougainvilleans remaining within the new nation. Later events bore this out. Over time the other committee members came to agree with them on many issues, including six from the United Party (opposition) who contributed strongly. The CPC's final report set out comprehensive recommendations for the establishment of elected provincial governments in provinces that chose to have them.

The right to citizenship in the new state was highly controversial and given much media coverage. The CPC saw it as crucial to national identity. It wanted automatic citizenship to go only to indigenous Papua New Guineans (defined initially as those born in PNG who had at least three indigenous grandparents, and no foreign citizenship). To be eligible for naturalisation, the CPC proposed that a non-citizen must have eight years residence, post-independence. These measures were intended to give indigenes some advantages over expatriates, many of whom, they felt, had enjoyed unfair advantages over local people for much too long during the colonial period. With two cabinet members, the Speaker, and several other MHAs being Australian citizens, the CPC's proposals came under heavy fire, in Australia as well as PNG. Momis was accused by some Australian MHAs of being a racist, claims he rebutted in a powerful response in the House. After heated debate in the House of Assembly, the government and a number of United Party members were successful in securing more liberal citizenship by descent provisions. For example, two indigenous grandparents, and prompt relinquishment of a 'real' foreign citizenship (including Australian) became sufficient for a foreign citizen to acquire citizenship. As for naturalisation, eight years residence in PNG before or after independence, with certain other conditions, would suffice.

The CPC recognised the important role that PNG's future leaders would have in shaping the development of the country. In an effort to minimise the potential for corruption that had beleaguered other new nations, the committee recommended, and the government and constituent assembly accepted, a number of key provisions in the constitution. These included the establishment of a leadership code; a leadership tribunal to determine cases of alleged misconduct by leaders; and the establishment of an ombudsman commission to deal with investigating such matters (then a novel role for such a body but since followed in some African countries such as Uganda), as well as investigating errors and delays in administration by the bureaucracy. These provisions have been maintained and many political leaders have been found to have committed serious breaches of the code and punished accordingly.

The CPC made detailed recommendations about the legislature, the executive government and the judiciary – for a unified liberal democratic PNG – which were largely adopted by the House of Assembly members. The recommendations comprised a unicameral Westminster model of government, with a strong committee system in the parliament; emphasis on the independence of the judiciary and the rule of law; and the requirement that all members of the executive be MPs. The committee proposed there be no separate head of state, with those functions to be exercised, as appropriate but with no 'reserve powers', by the Prime Minister, Chief Justice, National Executive Council (Cabinet), Foreign Minister, Attorney General and Speaker. However, the government rejected this, and a range of other important recommendations, in a White Paper tabled in response to the CPC's final report.

In response to the Government's rejection of these major recommendations, most of the former CPC members formed a group, called the Nationalist Pressure Group (NPG), to support the Committee's recommendations during debates in the Assembly on them and on the Government's and the United Party's proposed changes to them. The Government became quite reliant on the United Party to obtain sufficient support for its own controversial proposals to be agreed upon. For example, with United Party support, the Assembly endorsed the government's proposal that there should be an indigenous head of state elected by Parliament. The Government and the United Party did support the CPC's key recommendations on provincial government – aimed at establishing, constitutionally, directly elected provincial governments headed by executive councils. These groups also supported the CPC's recommendations on the legislature, the executive and the judicature.

In the first half of 1975, decisions were to be made by the National Constituent Assembly (comprising all members of the House of Assembly) established to enact the new autochthonous, or home-grown, constitution. The intention was for the constitution to be firmly rooted in the 'needs and aspirations of Papua New Guineans', not handed down by the colonial power. Various other CPC proposals were rejected.

However, when the Assembly resolved itself into a Constituent Assembly, in early 1975, to adopt the constitution, at the outset of debate the government suddenly changed its position in relation to the provincial government chapter of the draft constitution. This was almost certainly as a result of serious disagreements in its dealings with Bougainvillean leaders about the Bougainville Interim Provincial Government's budget. Late on the last sitting day of a week of debates, Provincial Affairs Minister Olewale successfully moved, without having given notice of his intention, to have all provisions about provincial government deleted from the draft constitution. This was a body blow for the Bougainvilleans, and Momis in particular, who had put enormous faith and energy into the provincial government solution over several years. It was also a major setback for the other CPC members and leaders and people in a number of districts, especially East New Britain.

For the Bougainvilleans wanting to secede, this was the final straw. On 1 June 1975 a Bougainvillean leadership group, involving 200 (or so it was claimed) local government council representatives, declared independence for the new Bougainvillean nation they called North Solomons. Although PNG formally became independent as a united country on 16 September 1975, the Bougainville situation remained unresolved for many months. After a civil war was narrowly averted in December 1975 – January 1976, an agreement was reached between the North Solomons/Bougainville leadership, in which Momis was heavily involved, and the PNG government, which led to constitutional entrenchment of the autonomy of the Bougainville provincial government.

Earlier, when the first drafts of the proposed constitution were circulated in January and February 1975, it was clear that many key recommendations of the CPC which the government and the Assembly had formally endorsed had been 'turned on their head' by the government. These changes, apparently authorised by the Chief Minister through a small group of senior expatriate lawyers, transformed a modern, liberal demo-cratic set of wide-ranging human rights provisions and strictly constrained emergency powers, specifically endorsed by the Assembly, into authoritarian executive powers with little or no recourse to court remedies for abuses of power. According to Legislative Counsel Joe Lynch, the provisions had been inspired by the British emergency powers in colonial Malaya.

Similarly, the strong entrenchment of human rights and emergency powers protections and many other key consti-tutional provisions previously agreed to by the House were watered down in these early drafts to the point of being inef-fectual. The result amounted to a complete betrayal of trust on the part of the government. Momis and other former CPC members were stunned, as was the Leader of the United Party, Tei Abal. Abal and Momis immediately wrote strongly worded letters of criticism to Chief Minister Somare. In doing so they acted on advice from their respective legal advisers: former UPNG law academic Peter Bayne was brought back from Australia to advise the United Party during the debates on the constitutional issues, and I was appointed adviser to the NPG. On a current affairs radio program on the National Broadcasting Commission, Somare accused me of 'sticking my nose into PNG's affairs'. The following day, John Kaputin mounted a strong defence, arguing that I had acted in my professional capacity as a legal adviser.

After an intense meeting between the respective party and group leaders and advisers, the Chief Minister announced that an 'inter-party committee' was being established at the House of Assembly involving representatives of the three main parlia-mentary groups – the government, the opposition and the

NPG/Country Party – to resolve the issues. This was a major breakthrough. It brought together a range of senior Papua New Guinean legal and political advisers to the government. These included Buri Kidu, recently appointed Secretary of the renamed Department of Justice, later PNG's first indigenous Chief Justice; Rabbie Namaliu, senior adviser to Somare and later to become Prime Minister; Peter Bayne, United Party adviser; Bernard Narokobi and me, NPG advisers. The Papua New Guinean government advisers brought fresh, independent minds to the issues, judged these on their merits based on House of Assembly resolutions, and facilitated reasonably prompt agreement on the many major matters of concern to the non-government groups. As a result, eventually a fresh draft of the constitution was prepared which restored the provisions that had been drastically changed, though the two-thirds vote entrenchment requirement provisions were not restored until debate resumed on the floor of the Constituent Assembly.

When the fourth draft appeared, without any prior notice to non-government MHAs and contrary to the earlier drafting instructions set by the House of Assembly for an indigenous head of state to be established, there were provisions for the Queen of England to be head of state. A Papua New Guinean governor-general was to represent her in PNG. Suddenly PNG was to be a monarchy, not a republic. The government eventually had these provisions passed by the Constituent Assembly, with the support of the United Party. However, this was in the face of strong opposition from most former CPC members. Many University of Papua New Guinea students marched in the streets in protest, to no avail.

Gains and losses of the country since Independence

In almost four decades since 1975, the country has been through very substantial changes. The population has increased from 2.1 million to approximately 7 million, despite high levels of infant and maternal mortality and major weaknesses in the national health system. After substantial GDP increases between 1975 and 1988, the forced closure of the Panguna mine in 1989 resulted in a substantial loss of export income from mining, causing a considerable decrease in GDP and a serious diminution of government services.

During the Bougainville Crisis from 1988 to 1998, the Panguna mine and related port and facilities were shut down by the Bougainville Revolutionary Army and the island was blockaded by the PNG government. There were in the order of 12,000 civilian and military deaths caused by military action and lack of adequate nutrition and medical supplies. The war divided groups and families throughout the province and led to massive economic, social, educational and health losses. Before the Crisis, Bougainvillians had among the highest levels of education, health care, skills and economic development in the country. Afterwards they became seriously disadvantaged compared with people from other provinces.

Through remarkable and largely successful efforts to achieve reconciliation among the previously warring groups, in recent years Bougainvillians have been rebuilding their lives and their society, with vital assistance from Papua New Guinean, Australian, New Zealand, United Nations and some Pacific island authorities. Central to this recovery has been the increasingly strong role of the new, constitutionally entrenched Autonomous Government of Bougainville

(AGB). John Momis, who left the priesthood 21 years ago, was elected president of that government in 2010. He is now leading Bougainvillians toward his and his government's vision of Bougainville becoming a successful, largely self-reliant, autonomous province within PNG. Under the PNG constitution, amended under a peace agreement to encompass autonomy after the Crisis ended, there will be a referendum among Bougainvillians within five years of 2015 to determine whether they wish to remain part of PNG or become an independent nation. This will be a major challenge for the Momis-led AGB and Bougainvillians generally.

As for PNG's constitutional and legal structures, I believe it is remarkable how well the country has weathered massive pressures over the past four decades. Key features of the constitution have served Papua New Guineans well. There have been regular changes of government following general elections, and sometimes between elections. Each of these changes has occurred without violence, although serious violence has occurred during many elections. There has also been a number of challenges to the legitimacy of particular governments upon which the Supreme Court has adjudicated, and its decisions generally have been regarded as principled. The decisions of the court have been respected by political leaders, except for the most recent challenge by former Prime Minister Somare to the transfer of his prime ministership to Peter O'Neill in 2011. This situation was resolved ultimately by the outcome of the 2012 general election, in which O'Neill was able to form a majority coalition which the ousted Somare joined. Some commentators have suggested that this outcome accords with the so-called 'Papua New Guinean way' of resolving disputes, by accommodating very different perspectives in a practical way. I think they have a point.

References

Denoon, Donald, *A Trial Separation: Australia and the Decolonisation of Papua New Guinea*, (Canberra: Pandanus, 2005).

Denoon, Donald (ed.), *Hindsight: A Workshop for Participants in the Decolonisation of Papua New Guinea*, 3–4 November 2002 at ANU, Draft Record, (4 April 2003).

Downs, Ian, *The Australian Trusteeship: Papua New Guinea, 1945–75*, (Canberra: Australian Government Publishing Service, 1980).

Griffin, James, Hank Nelson and Stewart Firth, *Papua New Guinea: A Political History*, (Melbourne: Heinemann, 1979).

Gunther, J. T., 'Trouble in Tolailand', *New Guinea and Australia, the Pacific and Southeast Asia*, 5: 3 (1970), 25–36.

Regan, A. J. and H. M. Griffin (eds), *Bougainville Before the Conflict*, (Canberra: Pandanus, 2005).

Woolford, Don, *Papua New Guinea: Initiation and Independence*, (St Lucia: University of Queensland Press, 1976).

9

TELEFOMIN AND PANGUNA – A *KIAP'S* VIEW
Bill Brown

It was July 1959, and just five weeks earlier Pamela and I had been married in Sydney, Australia. Now we were the only passengers in a three-engined Junkers JU52, an old German-designed aircraft with corrugated duralumin sides, an undercarriage that did not retract, and a cruising speed of 160 kilometres per hour – and we were flying into the mountains of New Guinea. Twenty-five years earlier, Adolf Hitler had trundled around Germany in the same type of aircraft, but it was unlikely that his aircraft had the passengers sitting just behind a huge stack of sawn timber, and it may have been equipped with a toilet.

We had been flying for almost two hours and would soon reach Telefomin. The north coast, and Wewak, where we had spent a few nights, was now 275 kilometres behind us. 80 kilometres to the west in Dutch New Guinea, the snow-covered peak of

Mt Juliana thrust 4,750 metres into the sky. Our pilot would soon have to descend to find our destination, a grass airstrip hiding in one of the many cloud-shrouded valleys. Telefomin was one of the more remote Papua and New Guinea Administration outposts. At 1,500 metres above sea level it was cold, and it rained every day. It was where I would become responsible for the administration of 1,500 square kilometres of mountains and valleys that were inhabited by some unruly people.

I was an Assistant District Officer – a *kiap* – and a member of the *kiap* hierarchy. District Commissioners administered the Territory's 16 districts. ADOs administered sub-districts – such as Telefomin – and took the law to the people, visiting the villages on foot, but sometimes by canoe. They camped a night or two in each – sowing the seeds of law and order – then moved on. That was basic patrolling. The ADOs were the magistrates, the coroners, the police officers and the gaolers. They investigated crimes, arrested lawbreakers, tried people in courts, put the guilty ones in gaol, looked after them while they were in there, and sent them home when their terms expired. From their base, the Sub-District Office, they ran the bank, the post office and radio communications. Patrol Officers reported to ADOs, also patrolled, and some of them ran smaller stations called Patrol Posts, but they were not the all-powerful DCs, or the almost as powerful ADOs.

At Telefomin, the priority was to expand the area of control, and to impose a respect for the law. Less than six years earlier, the officer-in-charge (a Patrol Officer), a Cadet Patrol Officer, and two constables had been murdered – hacked to death – only a half-day's walk away. In the valleys to the north, the Mianmin people were still periodically culling (slaughtering and eating) their neighbours – saving only the comely females to be additional wives. The rugged country three days climb to the east, on the other side of the 3,000 metre high Victor Emanuel Range, and stretching 20 kilometres to the Strickland River Gorge, was home to the Oksapmin people, and it was overdue for attention. The Oksapmin and their neighbours had seen the pre-war explorers, but a patrol had visited only once, in 1951.

Telefomin was a dramatic change for my 22-year-old bride, fresh from a small close-knit family and a workplace full of young female companions. Now she was the only woman, of the six expatriates, on the government station. Two other expatriate women, the wives of Baptist missionaries, lived with their families on the other side of the airstrip a two-kilometre walk away. It was a lonely life without feminine companionship, until Patrol Officer John Tierney and his wife Margaret arrived in March 1960. Four months later, the two ladies would have plenty of time together when Tierney and I left for a 28-day patrol to the Oksapmin.

There would be other surprises and challenges for Pamela. They included my absences on patrol, generally for about two weeks but sometimes longer, and the need to learn to speak pidgin English to communicate – especially during my absences. There was no electricity, only kerosene pressure lamps, a kerosene refrigerator and a wood-fired stove instead of more modern electrical gadgets. Water came from a small tank on the roof, replenished from the rainwater tanks by a manual pump. The Telefomin men wandering around the station were virtually naked, with bare buttocks, penises sheathed in gourds of varying lengths and curvature, testicles in the breeze, and just a few strips of cane around the waist.

I had been a *kiap* for 16 years, in the Sepik District for more than ten (the last four at Maprik), and back from leave ten days, when, on 2 June 1966, DC Ted Hicks came on the radio to tell me that I had been transferred to the Bougainville District. The situation was urgent; as soon as we were packed, we would be flown direct to Bougainville by a Caribou aircraft. Director Keith McCarthy's letter arrived the next day:

> [because] of the possibility of large scale mineral development in ... the Bougainville District ... [and] various local factors and problems involved in this possible development which require ... an additional experienced and capable officer ... I have decided to transfer Mr W. T. Brown, District Officer, ... for duty in the Kieta Sub-District. (McCarthy letter)

We packed, and waited, and waited. A fortnight later, two single-engined Norseman aircraft began shuttling our household and effects to the Wewak airstrip, Boram, where they were manhandled into the waiting Douglas Dakota, the military version of the Douglas DC-3 aircraft. We were to have flown direct from Wewak to Bougainville, but mechanical failure caused a diversion to Madang, followed by an overnight stop at Rabaul, so we were a day late when we arrived; the grass airstrip, Aropa, was deserted, and the only shade was under the aircraft's wing.

Deputy DC Max Denehy drove us to town, but there was nary a mention of mining, or problems, as we bounced around for an hour over the 14 miles of water-filled wheel ruts winding through coconut groves, and the occasional stretches that were almost a road. The next morning, Thursday 16

June, at the Sub-District Office, I was interested to hear from Patrol Officer Andrew Melville that mining giant Conzinc Riotinto of Australia Limited's prospecting operation in the Crown Prince Range behind Kieta had been brought to a standstill by native landowners. Denehy declined to discuss it, and when he told me that my new task would be to update the Common Roll (the Electoral Roll), I rebelled. (Hereafter Conzinc Riotinto of Australia Limited, and subsidiaries Conzinc Riotinto of Australia Exploration Pty Ltd and Bougainville Copper Pty Ltd, are referred to as either CRA or 'the Company'.) I did not think that I had been flown 1,500 kilometres by special charter to undertake a mundane task related to elections that were not due until 1968, and that at Maprik, with three times the population, I had delegated to the cadets. I suggested that he refer my refusal to accept his instructions to the Director.

I do not know how the Administrator, Brigadier Cleland, became involved, but he ended the impasse with an instruction to the Bougainville DC, copied to Denehy and myself:

Mr Brown should spend as much time as possible in the field. This will give him the opportunity of establishing contacts with the people and help in disseminating information on Administration policy on mining matters ... The CRA problem is to be given priority over all other work in your District. Mr Denehy should maintain his good relations with the Kieta Council, and handle the CRA problem generally. Mr Brown was posted to your District to strengthen field contacts in the CRA area and his energies are not to be dissipated on Census and routine matters. (Administrator's memorandum)

DC Mollison added his comments, but seemed oblivious to the enormity of the problem:

> Neither of you are involved in the Census collection and Mr Brown, with advice and any assistance necessary from yourself, owing to his recent arrival in the Sub-District, should commence his field work without delay, and make every effort to achieve results ... One disadvantage [the CRA] may have is their Australian employees have come direct to the Guava and would have no understanding of the people or even be able to converse with them ... Perhaps interpreters could travel with such teams ... A lot can be gained by a friendly approach and good comradely relations in such outback parts. Care should be taken too, not to disturb any native property of value or significance to them ... In my view it is best to keep the immediate task in perspective and to work for the success of the exploratory stage, achieving harmony in relations, and ... enable the people to obtain the monetary benefits from the amended legislation. (Administrator's memorandum)

It would have taken me ten minutes to reach Guava village, near Panguna, by CRA's helicopter, but I had no intention of being viewed as a Company employee. Accompanied by two police constables, I travelled in an Administration lorry to the roadhead behind Arawa plantation, and then plodded on foot up the Bovo Valley. The hard climb began near the old mine site at Kupei, up the muddy steps cut into the almost vertical 900-metre-high bluff. We climbed in a forest of moss-covered, dripping trees, crossed the divide at about 1,300 metres, and slithered down the western slope to Guava village, just before nightfall. Guava village nestled in a hollow, but the rest house, isolated on a 900-metre-high ridge, was exposed to the west coast. The cold, moist wind blew up the valley from Torokina, whistled through the openings that served as doors and through the cracks in the bush timber floor. It rained every afternoon; cloudbursts of more than 100 millimetres an hour, and the nights were freezing.

We were not a welcome intrusion, but the next day the people gathered to hear, and reject, what I had to say about prospecting and the law. Only the *luluai* Oni, clan leader Mathew Kove, and one or two others were friendly. For days, I walked around the prospect with the people, and talked. I was harangued by Anthony Ampei from Guava, by Damien from Irang, and by Gregory Korpa from Moroni. CRA certainly had problems. They had acceded to Anthony Ampei's demand that they cease drilling on his land, and five of the eight drilling rigs now lay idle. Gregory Korpa, as spokesman of the large Moroni-Pakia group, was adamant that people had opposed the geologists' intrusion from the outset. He said he had told the geologists that they were trespassers. He and his people wanted the Company to leave – now!

After two weeks I needed a break. I wanted to see my family, and I needed to report to Denehy, even though I had no good news. The people were not interested in any promises of financial rewards, and their opposition to prospecting was intense. I predicted that there would be violence, and I thought there might even be suicides. Perhaps I surprised Denehy when I said that I intended to visit all the villages in the Guava Division on a formal patrol and that I would update the census in each village. At the rollcall, when all the people were present, I would be able to explain the law about mining, and I would be certain that the people knew about the changes to the mining legislation that provided for financial rewards to land-owners: an occupation fee of $1 per acre ($2.47 per hectare) per annum in respect of land actually occupied within Prospecting Authorities, and $2 per acre ($4.94 per hectare) per annum in respect of a Mining Lease.

At the time, I thought the changes to the legislation had been driven by altruism. In fact, CRA had been wooing the Department of Territories since October 1964 with the objective of changing the mining laws (which were designed for relatively small-scale operations) to permit the prospecting and mining of huge areas, and to guarantee a successful prospector the right to a mining title.

The Company's efforts were successful. On 7 December 1964, Secretary for Territories, Warwick Smith, wrote to the Administrator:

> It is considered that experienced and sound financial companies such as CRA should be given every encouragement to carry out large scale prospecting. Once minerals have been found in sufficient quantities ... The matter is considered to be of the utmost importance and every effort should be made to ensure that the Ordinances are amended at the next session of the House of Assembly. (Doran 2006, 36)

In November 1966, after five months in and around Guava village, I needed some helping hands, I needed company, and I needed to move into the area where the exploratory drilling was taking place. Patrol Officer John Dagge at Ambunti, and a Senior-Constable from Maprik, were plucked out of the Sepik

District to join me, and we moved to our new base, a disused, ramshackle house at Barapina in the Kawerong Valley. Dagge and I were the forerunners of a long line of *kiaps*, thrown into a situation that we detested, trying to convince the people that, even though they owned the land, they did not own the mineral rights. That we could live in Guava and move around the Guava Division, sometimes with a few police – sometimes with none – was a testament to the fortitude, forbearance and dignity of the Nasioi people. They maintained that discipline throughout, and they were respected by every *kiap* that worked with them.

Denehy departed on leave in December 1966, and I inherited the Kieta Sub-District and the CRA operation. Assistant Director T. G. Aitchison arrived from Port Moresby on 27 December, disturbing our Christmas–New Year break. At Canberra's behest, he had come to find out the facts: what were the real attitudes of the local people in the mining area, and were some Marist priests playing a part in the dispute? He talked to people in Kieta; I took him to Barapina to speak with Anthony Ampei (Guava), Damien Damen (Irang), Gregory Korpa (Moroni), and their supporters; and he travelled by helicopter around Bougainville, visiting some of the Catholic missions.

Aitchison told me that he thought the operation should be slowed down to allow the people to adjust. His report to Assistant Administrator (Economic Affairs), that he had told me to advise CRA that the [proposed] Kokorei operation should not proceed if physical resistance [was] offered, was not endorsed; the Assistant Administrator advising Canberra that:

(a) CRA to be encouraged to proceed to the next stage of prospecting, including the location of drills and roads to Kokorei land, and any other land to which native land owners wish to deny the Company access.

(b) The Administration to be prepared to protect Company personnel carrying out these operations, if necessary, with an adequate Police detachment. (Doran 2006, 258)

On 8 January, when CRA resumed after the New Year, John Dagge, myself and some native police provided the 'Administration protection' as a drill rig was moved on to the 'entry forbidden' Kokorei land to the south of Panguna. The movement of the first drill on to the 'entry forbidden' Moroni land on the right bank of Kawerong River was seen as a more hazardous exercise, and we were accompanied by the Deputy Crown Prosecutor, Norris Pratt, who was flown in from Rabaul for the event. Led by Gregory Korpa, the Moronis screamed their protests and ceremoniously impeded the move. Perhaps overawed, Norris Pratt stumbled and fell into the stream, and the opposition faded.

The obligatory renewal of the Prospecting Authorities at Warden's Court hearings in January 1967 seemed designed to further annoy and provoke the people. Newspaper advertisements advised of a series of public hearings; the first at Kieta, then sequentially at Daratui, Pakia and finally at Barapina, where objections could be made. The hearings at Kieta, Daratui and Pakia had prepared the people for the open-air Barapina hearing, where they crowded around Mining Warden

McKenzie to demonstrate their wrath. We onlookers had a nervous day as they screamed their opposition to the prospecting, to CRA's intrusion, and their rejection of the law – and of the Government. A journalist covering the event reported that Dagge and I saw ourselves 'as educators not trouble shooters' and that we claimed 'continual education and liaison work' were 'the only way to counter … the opposition of the people' (*South Pacific Post*).

In late February 1967, Canberra produced a bemusing instruction:

> Each move to a new area is to be preceded by patient and perse-vering attempts by Administration officials over several weeks if necessary … to explain what is involved … the benefits … The actual commencement of operations in a new area will be preceded if necessary by a formal attempt to explain the forgoing in writing, by loud speaker, and by word of mouth. If after these steps have been taken there is reason to think that new mining operations are likely to result in violence … a final effort by a top-level group … (e.g. the Director of Lands, the Secretary for Law, and one or both the Assistant Administrators) to go through the procedures of explanation, advice and consultation again. The possibility is not ruled out of the Administrator himself visiting the area with such a group … . (Doran 2006, 266)

We wondered what we had been doing for the past eight months and whether time would stand still while we called for, and awaited the arrival of, the 'top level group'?

It was to become more confusing. In mid-1967, I was called to Canberra, perhaps, I thought, to be 'stiffened up'. It was probably the first time that anyone of my rank had been summonsed to Canberra. A group of senior officials sat around the meeting table expounding on the prospecting problems on Bougainville, but only one of them, Gerry Gutman, had ever been there – and he only for two nights, when he accompanied the Minister in February 1966. They reminded me of my responsibilities; that as a public servant I had to do what the Government said, and that as an Officer of the Royal Papuan New Guinea Constabulary I had a responsibility to see that the laws were observed. I thought I might have lost my job when I abruptly rejected the advice given by one senior officer, said to have had a British Overseas Civil Service background, who said that when I returned to Bougainville, I should issue ultimatums – and enforce them.

CRA had been pushing Canberra and Moresby to arrange access to mineralised areas at Mainoki, Karato and Atamo from where it had been ejected. Those areas had to be evaluated before the Company committed to Panguna, and ADO (a new title for those formerly known as senior Patrol Officers) Chris Warrilow and Patrol Officer John Gordon-Kirkby had the job of escorting the geologists to the sites. Warrilow was responsible for Mainoki and Atamo; Gordon-Kirkby for Karato, and they had their unwritten instructions: there was to be no violence. Warrilow and his colleague Ross Henderson had been transferred from the Highlands to Bougainville in 1967; Gordon-Kirkby had been drafted from Boku – a Buin Patrol Post for a one-off event.

District Officer Ross Henderson took over at Barapina in October 1967 and was given a multitude of tasks: to try and explain the Company's continuing changing plans to the

people, to protect the people's interests, to organise the deline-
ation of land ownership boundaries before landmarks were
destroyed, to prevent violence, and to keep the peace in a
burgeoning – almost Wild West – township. Henderson spent
over three years with that horror, supported variously by Mike
Bell, Mike D'Abbs, Brian Dodds, Noel Mathieson, Chris
Warrilow, Jim Wellington and Peter Wohlers. They each experienced the opposition to stream sampling, drilling, surveying
and the mine.

The people from the villages around the mine were overwhelmed by the destruction. The trees in their forest were
poisoned, and then felled by a giant hawser dragline. The
undergrowth was sprayed with herbicide, and then every vestige
of vegetation burnt in fan-forced fires, accelerated with dieso-
line. The ash, soil, rocks and huge boulders were hosed into the
streams by a battery of six monitors (water canon), each 'fed'
by three bulldozers. One hundred and twenty million cubic
metres of soft overburden, followed by the waste rock, were
flushed into the Kawerong, thence downstream to destroy the
Jaba River environment.

The Guava people were left first with desolation, then with
a void: a gaping oval-shaped hole more than 300 metres deep,
2,000 metres long and 5,000 metres wide. A huge part of their
heritage had gone forever. Ross Henderson, recorded by Film
Australia in July 1969, said:

It did not surprise anyone that the Moronis were angry over the land
situation. It is not just a block of dirt to them – it is part of the
body and the soul. Their whole social system is based on land. The
land is owned by the ancestors now dead, the present occupiers and

by the unborn generations to come. The occupiers have the right to use the land, to lease, but not to destroy. From as early as 1966 we have been telling all the villages as much as we knew of the project ... It was difficult even for us to envisage what was going to happen. You can imagine how bewildering it must have been for the Moronis. (Martin-Jones and Beckett 1970)

John Wakeford, who had replaced Mollison as DC in March 1967, was also concerned about the CRA problems. He visited Kieta once a month, told Headquarters that mining was going to destroy communities, and was replaced by Des Ashton in January 1968. Ashton thrust himself into the CRA activities, and moved district headquarters from Sohano to Kieta in August. Ian Downs said that Ashton 'was not easily disturbed by violent situations ... not an imaginative man ... unimpressed by the awesome political and commercial power of Conzinc Riotinto ... prepared to do his duty in any situation to which he was called' (Downs 1980, 357).

I had attended the monthly Port Moresby meetings between the Company and the Administration since May 1967; Ashton attended two or three, decided he was being disdained, and did not attend again. Those meetings were where CRA discussed their progress and their projections, made their demands, and were the scene of solo battles for me until Tom Ellis was appointed Director and came to my support. Chaired by an Assistant Administrator (Economic Affairs), they were attended by the Treasurer, the Secretary for Law, the Directors of District Administration, the Director of Lands & Mines, someone from the Department of Territories, and by CRA's Frank Espie and his team from Melbourne.

In August 1968 the company tabled their 'urgent survey proposals' covering a band of country stretching from the east coast to the west coast: town site, access road, power transmission line, tailings flume, quarry sites, siltation study and water supply. Those operations would cover an enormous swathe of land, including villages and gardens. We were allowed eight weeks to explain the proposals to the people, but there were no certainties to explain. The planners, surveyors and all manner of engineers would intrude on the land, cut survey lines, drill soil and rock, take samples, and conduct all sorts of tests – but all to what end? The company had yet to decide if the project was viable, and, even when the decision was made to go ahead in early 1969, they still did not know where the roads, powerlines and other facilities would be located.

New areas of concern were outside the prospecting area: in the Pinei Valley on the east coast, and the Jaba River valley on the west coast, where the tailings would soon become a hazard. Some of the villages in the Pinei Valley had already put up with the construction of an access road through their land. The new activities would disrupt all the villages as survey lines were cut through their gardens and through their small plantations of coconuts, coffee and cacao, as they would be inspected, and surveyed, in the search for a town site, and as rock outcrops were drilled and blasted in the search for materials.

Five officers were involved in visits, attempting to explain those intrusions, and to dispel distrust. In March 1969 I moved John Russell-Pell to Pakia so that he would be immediately available to the people. Mike Bell arrived on transfer from the Eastern Highlands in August 1968, and, after a three-day briefing period, moved to the Jaba River headwaters where he lived in a tent for almost 12 months. Bell's neighbours, the Darenai, first endured him, then threatened to burn him out, and finally accepted that he was there to help them.

The so-called Agreement between CRA and the Administration had a similar trajectory to the amendments to the mining legislation; negotiated with Canberra, endorsed by Cabinet in April 1967, and pushed through the House of Assembly in August. From the Bougainville perspective, the most significant implications were that it obliged the Administration to provide mining leases over any areas applied for by the Company, and to provide reasonable land requirements for the mining operation. The Company tabled their requirements at a meeting on 11 February 1969; a staggering area totalling in excess of 57,000 acres (23,000 hectares) for the mine, pipelines, powerlines, port, roads, tailings and the town.

In the Pinei valley, the proposed townsite, an area of 1,000 acres (405 hectares), encompassed Pakia village and gardens. The new two-lane highway would cut a swathe through the coconut, coffee and cocoa groves, while nearby land was said to be required for a garbage dump and industrial waste. At Rorovana, CRA required 2,000 acres (810 hectares) of native-owned land for loading facilities, an overseas wharf, oil storage, a 135-megawatt powerhouse, and a beachfront recreation area. (In August 1968 CRA had said that 'Loloho plantation and a small additional area' would be sufficient for the port, and I had relayed that to the village.) I was certain that a town could not be located at Pakia without bloodshed. I had said so the previous year, and I said so again. I could not see why Guava village, not even in the Panguna valley, was to be encompassed by the mining lease, and I thought the land grabs at Rorovana, and for the garbage dump, were an outrage.

At the May 1969 meeting, CRA said, 'delays in the project were now becoming critical and extremely costly and strongly pressed that the Administration should endeavour to remove indigenous oppositions a little more forcefully ...' (Doran 2006, 801). That pressure was the prelude to the troubles on the east coast, firstly in the Pinei Valley and then at Rorovana. The Company also failed to recognise its own failings; on 21 July 1969, we were given a map that showed the centre line of the route of the two-land road to be constructed to the mine. The map had arrived from Melbourne that morning, and pegging would start the next morning, allowing no time for further explanation to the landowners.

Despite continuous negotiations, we *kiaps* had failed to convince the Rorovanas to sell the land at Rorovana, and following the Canberra prescription of a 'final effort by a top level group', Assistant Administrator Newman took a delegation from Port Moresby. When his ultimatum for the sale of the (reduced) area of 1,200 acres for $105 an acre (485 hectares for $260 a hectare) was rejected, the Administrator, as threatened, granted the Company a lease for mining purposes on 31 July. I was with Ashton, in Administrator Hay's office in Port Moresby, when he was given his instructions. A police group would accompany CRA's surveyors, but Ashton would have ultimate control, and, true to his style, when the operation began on 1 August, he was in the vanguard with Deputy Police Commissioner Brian Holloway. Three riot squads, each under the command of an officer, made up the police detachment. All wore helmets and carried gasmasks, and had Ashton not done the same he could have been a soft target, but his photo in the news offended the Administrator, and may have contributed to subsequent events.

The operation ended in a stand-off; CRA's entry to the land was delayed, and on 30 November, following Prime Minister Gorton's involvement, the Administration and CRA entered into a formal agreement with the Rorovana people – the Rorovanas would be leased 140 acres for 42 years for $7,000 per annum.

On 6 November 1969, three months after the Rorovana affair, the entire area associated with the mine, port, tailings, town and construction was removed from Ashton's control and excised from the Bougainville District, to become my responsibility as DC-Special Duties. This was to coordinate the Administration's activities, and have 'the normal functions and responsibilities of a District Commissioner in this small area of Bougainville … [with] a direct channel of communication to the Assistant Administrator (Economic Affairs)' (*Bougainville Progress Report*, 3). That arrangement continued until February 1971, when I took over from Ashton completely, and moved District Headquarters from Kieta to Arawa.

In 1973 it was my turn to be replaced. Chief Minister Michael Somare's newly appointed personal advisor on Bougainville matters, Leo Hannett, called for 'the deportation of the Bougainville District Commissioner, Mr. W. T. Brown, the managing director of Bougainville Copper Mr. Ray Ballmer and a leading member of the Napidakoe Navitiu, Mr. B. Middlemiss', and on 18 May 1973 the Chief Minister announced, on the front page of the *Post Courier*, that a Bougainvillean, Dr Alexis Sarei (one-time Father Alexis Hollyweek) would replace me when I took leave.

My wife and I left Bougainville very early in the morning on Thursday 14 June 1973. There were lots of people to say goodbye, and it was too early to be drinking hot beer, but the Pakias, the Rorovanas and the people from Arawa brought cartons with them. We clinked bottles together, and I took an obligatory sip with each farewell handshake.

Reflecting on the *kiaps'* complex and totally new role, we knew that the Commonwealth and the Administration were determined that the exploration and evaluation be completed; a successful mine would contribute to the Territory's economic viability; and we knew that most Bougainvilleans wanted CRA to proceed, but only where they were not affected – at Panguna. The Bougainvilleans wanted employment, they wanted training, they wanted infrastructure development and they wanted money.

Many of us had reservations about CRA's operations. It seemed that the more CRA evaluated the ore body, the hungrier they became. And we saw the attitudes change, and harden, as the workforce increased dramatically (from a few hundred in 1969 to peak at 10,233 in June 1971), as immense financial loans had to be serviced and as deadlines tightened. (The Bank of America became lead bankers for a $200 million loan in February 1969. $A200 million in 1969 has an estimated relative buying power of $A1.27 billion in 2013.) We became the unintended buffer between the people and the three forces: the Company, the Commonwealth and the Administration. It was a balancing act that sometimes went awry. We tried to provide CRA with access and a safe workplace, and we were successful. Our attempts to provide the villagers with protection, advice and assistance would have been more successful if there had been more cooperation. Whether we were better than the many other harsher alternatives might be measured by the things people said and wrote: in 1968, CRA's consultant, Professor Douglas Oliver, suggested to CRA that I was not on their side (Oliver 1968, 29); in August 1969, when attempting to negotiate on Rorovana, CRA authorised their Area Manager, Colin Bishop, 'to enter into joint discussions with Lalor [the Public Solicitor] and W. T. Brown, not separately with Lalor' and required 'Bishop to advise [them] of his recommendations and those of Brown' (CRA Melbourne telex); and in 1971, an entry in John Russell-Pell's Field Officer's Journal records that Councillor Teori Tau was 'confident that between the DC [Bill Brown] and the Public Solicitor's office an effective solution will be found that will put the Company in its place' (Russell-Pell 1971).

Perhaps the giant fig tree that still stands on the roadside verge in the Pinei Valley is a testament to our endeavours. The people said it was of enormous cultural importance – a spirit tree of great age, sacred to their ancestors – but it stood directly in the path of the newly designed highway; the Company and the construction managers, Bechtel, wanted to cut it down. We could not prevent the mine, but I could save the tree; the road was given an unplanned curve.

References

Administrator's Memorandum 35/1/19, DC, Sohano, Bougainville, 27 June 1966. Consolidated Zinc–Rio Tinto Prospecting Activities. (Bill Brown collection.)

Bougainville Progress Report, September–November 1969, (Port Moresby: Government Printer, 1969).

CRA Melbourne Telex 691, August 1969. (Bill Brown collection.)

Doran, Stuart (ed.), *Australia and Papua New Guinea, 1966–1969*, (Canberra: Department of Foreign Affairs and Trade, 2006).

Downs, Ian, *The Australian Trusteeship: Papua New Guinea, 1945–75*, (Canberra: Australian Government Publishing Service, 1980).

[J. K.] McCarthy letter to DC, Wewak, Sepik District. (Bill Brown collection.)

Martin-Jones, John and Roland Beckett (producers), 'My Valley is Changing'. Film documentary, (Screen Australia, 1970).

Oliver, Douglas, *Some Social-Relational Aspects of CRA Copper Mining on Bougainville: A Confidential Report to Management*, (Unpublished typescript, 1968). (Bill Brown collection.)

Russell-Pell, John, *Field Officer's Journal*, 24 March 1971. Folio 95. (Bill Brown collection.)

South Pacific Post, 15 February 1967.

10

INTERVIEW WITH HIS EXCELLENCY
MR CHARLES W. LEPANI

Interview conducted by Seumas Spark at the PNG High Commission in
Canberra, 30 July 2013

SS   I would like to start by discussing something of your background. Where are you from and where did you grow up?
To what extent did the decisions of the Australian administration affect your childhood and upbringing? Were you
conscious of the Australian influence in PNG?

CWL   I was born in the Trobriand Islands. My father worked for
the colonial administration and he knew a lot of Australian
patrol officers and doctors in the Trobriand Islands. He was
then transferred to Port Moresby and we came with him in
1952. First he worked in Treasury as a clerk. At the time,
opportunities for PNG children to attend schools in Port
Moresby were limited, so a gentleman named Tom Dietz,
who worked for the Education Department, started a small

school at Konedobu for about six of us PNG kids. We lived at Three Mile, where the present Port Moresby General Hospital is, and every morning my father used to walk me all the way to Konedobu where he worked. I went to school with Mr Dietz's class of six, my father went to work, and at about five o'clock we'd walk all the way back to Three Mile. That went on from 1952 until we moved to Kaugere and then I went to school at Kila Kila Primary T-School from 1957–61. [At this time indigenous children usually attended T (Territory) schools. A (Australian) schools served mostly expatriate children.] In 1961 I was awarded a scholarship. It was Australian administration policy to send the top 20 grade six primary students to Australia for high school. That program started in 1954 and had already seen a lot of Papua New Guineans go to school in Australia. In 1961 I was in the group of 20. We went to school in Queensland mostly. I went to Thornburgh College in Charters Towers. That policy stood most of us in good stead at the time of Independence, when we took up the reins of running the country.

When I departed for high school in Australia I flew from Port Moresby to Townsville in a Fokker F-27. When I landed in Townsville I continued to sit in the aircraft. I couldn't believe there were no black people coming to do the manual work. I thought that if I stepped out I would be arrested by the police, so I waited until all the passengers, white people, had left. The stewardess said, 'This is the end of the flight, you have to get out here.' 'I'm waiting for some black people to bring the steps for me to step on to', I said. 'No, no', she said, 'this is Australia.' I got out and was looking around for police, expecting to be arrested, but nobody came. And there was the bus waiting to take me to high school. That was my first encounter with decolonisation – going to high school in Australia for six years.

SS   So you completed all your high school in Charters Towers?

CWL   Yes, it was wonderful. I had the greatest experience and I met a lot of friends, many of whom I still have. I must say I never encountered racism, or at least not blatant racism. I was more in fear of encountering racism in my own country, PNG, during those colonial days.

        After high school I went back and was enrolled at UPNG on a government scholarship: I entered the preliminary year in 1967 and the following year commenced studies for my degree, a Bachelor of Arts majoring in Economics. At the end of 1968, I won a scholarship, sponsored jointly by the PNG Public Service Association, the Australian Council of Trade Unions and the Australian Public Service Association. The scholarship provided for me to study for a Bachelor of Commerce degree (Industrial Relations) at the University of New South Wales (UNSW), and on holidays to gain work experience with Australian trade unions. Working with the PSA in PNG, and briefly with the ACTU in Australia, I came across some wonderful expatriates who became very good friends: Rod Madgwick, Secretary General, and Paul Munro, Industrial Advocate, for the PNG PSA. When they left their replacements at the union were Graham Delaney and John Hawks, respectively, to whom I was understudy for a year and a half or so. As a unionist with the PSA I undertook some cases for Papua New Guinean blue collar workers. I did a couple of public sector cases for technical officers in the health department – lab technicians, Health Extension Officers and Health Inspectors – but not a big public service-wide salaries case. That case had been advocated by Bob Hawke when he came up in 1966–7. In fact, the idea of a trade union scholarship for a Papua New Guinean was mooted by Bob Hawke, along with Rod Madgwick and Paul Munro, when Hawke was in PNG in those years. A few years later, while studying at UNSW in Sydney, I spent a week working with Bob Hawke at the ACTU offices in Melbourne to gain some practical experience. I stayed with Hazel and him and their kids in their Sandringham home. Bob Hawke was president of the ACTU at that time.

After UNSW, at the end of 1971, I went back and finished my degree at UPNG part-time because PNG self-government was fast approaching and political imperatives meant the public service in PNG was being localised. Most Australians around that time were leaving. The PNG PSA successfully negotiated a 'golden handshake' with the Australian government, and most Australian colonial public servants left the country. Localisation was also taking place within the PSA. Jacob Lameki was appointed Secretary General and I was appointed Industrial Advocate. I did this for a short period only because the government – it was self-government by then – asked me to take over the newly formed Bureau of Industrial Organisations, which looked at harmonising industrial relations between employers and employees. I was in this role for 16 to 18 months before I was asked to move to the National Planning Office (NPO) in 1974.

Originally I was the deputy there, and after Independence in 1975 I took over from a Canadian, David Beatty, as its head. There were only about five Papua New Guineans among the staff: three or four others who had come from UPNG and me. I had completed my degree by 1974.

Working with that cadre of expatriates in the PSA and the NPO was an enriching experience. There were one or two from colonial times who chose to remain and moved to agencies such as the NPO from the agriculture and forestry departments. But most were young, newer expatriates from Africa, England, Australia, Canada and America. There was quite a contrast between the long-established expatriates and those who came to PNG immediately before Independence – including from places such as Tanzania, Kenya, Ghana and Nigeria – to work in government and in academic circles at UPNG. In that group of expatriates there was a lot of excitement about independence and the political future of PNG. Ross Garnaut was there as a researcher and First Assistant Secretary in the Treasury Department, and there were others including Peter Drysdale. There was a wonderful air of optimism and euphoria about the country's potential and future. When I took over as head of the NPO, I had staff from Canada, the USA, England, Australia and New Zealand, as well as one Indian and several Papua New Guineans, of course. We had a good working relationship and they put their full confidence in me. They were technical advisors, while I was responsible for interpreting the policies put to the Cabinet and Prime Minister. The political atmosphere was full of optimism; the work relationship between the political and technical levels in PNG has never been as good since. These expatriates – in the NPO, Treasury and Finance – were more enthusiastic about the future of the country than most of the long-term expatriates, whose attitude generally was that Gough Whitlam gave independence too early – 'watch the country get screwed up'.

It's probably true [laughs]. On reflection, things probably didn't go as we had expected and hoped. I have questioned whether delaying independence would have bought time for PNG to develop in a stable manner without the challenges that we are facing today. But my view is that a delay would have made things worse. For one thing, the relationship between Australia and PNG would have developed differently. It probably would have become volatile, as are some relationships between Britain, France, Germany and their former African colonies. So timing was not the issue: PNG avoided an explosive decolonisation process. In running our country Papua New Guineans have messed up in some ways, and we are still facing challenges, but these are things we have to go through ourselves and learn from. In a lot of ways it was the expatriates who were there around Independence who were instrumental in bridging the gap between Papua New Guineans and Australians and in preventing what could have happened. Most of the enthusiastic Australians, who arrived in the late 1960s and 70s, left at Independence because they recognised that PNG belonged to Papua New Guineans and it was up to them to run the country. In essence, that is how I see the relationship between Papua New Guineans and Australians, or most Australians anyway.

My father didn't experience much racism in his workplace because most of his bosses, like Mr Ritchie, Director of the Treasury Department, and Mr Burke, my father's immediate boss, were very good. Mr Burke, as my father called him, married a Hanuabada woman. He used to drive one of those vintage cars around Port Moresby in the early days, and his son, Clarrie Burke, was my teacher at Kila Kila Primary T-School. Clarrie played for Kone Tigers in Port Moresby and John Kaputin also joined that team. I have never stopped following Kone Tigers, and in Australia I follow Wests Tigers, formerly Balmain Tigers. In Aussie Rules I follow St Kilda, because at UPNG we wore St Kilda uniforms. These were donated by St Kilda because of our coach's connections to that club. After breaking my collarbone playing rugby league at high school in Charters Towers, I spent a season playing Aussie Rules at UPNG. We were the first Papua New Guinean team to thrash an all-Australian team in Port Moresby. All of us in the team were students studying at UPNG or the Admin College – hence the Aduni name for the team – except for our fullback, a tall patrol officer from Victoria named Willensky. It was a great grand final. I can remember it still. The late Dr Hank Nelson used to talk about it because he was our assistant coach. The coach was Father Dillon, a Catholic priest who was chaplain of the university. A wonderful coach, Irish as you'd expect.

This kind of experience and the many friendships we made with expatriates at UPNG decolonised us and transformed our world views. To this day Rabbie Namaliu, Mekere Morauta, and the historian Bill Gammage tell stories and reminisce about their days as players in the Aduni rugby team, as did the late Anthony Siaguru. They played in our rugby union team when I was playing for the Aussie Rules team. After their matches they would get into the university bus and make haste to the Boroko Hotel. They would walk into the hotel in thongs and be told that they were not allowed to come in wearing thongs and that 'natives' were not allowed. They would all go out, put on shoes, and walk in again, the expatriates with the 'natives'. Eventually the Hotel management would run out of excuses to exclude the PNG students, and all the players, white and black, would be allowed in.

I tell this story because many, many years later, when I arrived in Canberra as PNG's High Commissioner, I met up again with Dr Hank Nelson and Professor Bill Gammage. On occasion we would reminisce about those years at UPNG. Bill would trot out photos of the great Aduni rugby team. Hank and I did not have a photo to brag about, but we held our own. As I mentioned at Hank's funeral in 2012, while the rugby players were decolonising the Boroko pub, we were performing the more important act of decolonisation – thrashing an all-white Port Moresby team in Aussie Rules.

SS   What did you study at UPNG?

CWL   I did my preliminary year there in 1967 and studied history, maths, English (literature mainly), geography and one or two other subjects I cannot recall. I was lucky enough to be dux of the preliminary year, sharing this award with another student, Tony Deklin. He went on to distinguish himself as an eminent PNG constitutional lawyer and taught at ANU. Once I started first year in 1968, I studied history, economics, English and maths.

As I mentioned earlier, at UPNG I came across Bill Gammage and Hank Nelson. I had a bit to do with Hank in particular because he was my history tutor, while Professor Ken Inglis lectured us in history. In retrospect, you cannot ask to be taught by better historians. History was my best subject, which is why I am so happy to look back on that time [laughs]. David Hegarty, John Ballard and Dr Ted Wolfers were other academics there around that time.

On the political front, I must mention people like Tony Voutas, Cecil Abel, John Yocklunn and the late Barry Holloway, all of whom contributed a great deal to politics and moves towards PNG independence. They influenced the older leaders such as Sir Michael Somare, Sir Albert Maori Kiki, Sir Peter Lus, Sir Ebia Olewale, Sir Paul Lapun, Gavera Rea and Dr Reuben Taureka, and others – all members of the Pangu Pati – and then those of us who came later, the younger generation. We were very happy that people like Tony Voutas and Ross Garnaut were there to mentor us in public policy, public administration, economic policy and other key policy and development issues which we were left to grapple with after they left. Let me clarify here that the PNG leaders I mentioned were the pro-independence advocates and members of Pangu that I personally had much to do with. The so-called moderates around the time of self-government and Independence, such as Sir Tei Abal, Sir

Julius Chan, Paulus Arek and Matthias Toliman, along with many others, made just as significant a contribution to the life and development of PNG.

SS   So learning from these people and your time at UPNG were of great benefit?

CWL   Yes. There were still some expatriates left from an earlier time, from the days of the colonial administration. Not all the white academics and expatriates saw eye to eye. The expatriate academics and some new public servants were nicknamed the baubles, bangles and bandanas brigade because of the way they dressed – some walked around like hippies. But they were good people. And that is not to demean, in any way, the contribution of expatriates who were in PNG during the time of the colonial administration. I still meet these people and go to their gatherings and Christmas lunches here in Australia. The PNG Australia Association is the biggest grouping of them. 'You are part of PNG's history', I tell them. 'Please write your memoirs of your experiences. Please go back to PNG and see what it is like. You are still part of PNG, whether you like it as it is now or not. You are part of what PNG is today. Your experiences contribute to the world knowing why PNG is what it is and where it has been.'

So in talking about colonialists, in no way am I being negative. They were there to contribute as best their generation saw fit. Patrol officers and people who made great contributions in the field of research. The historical records show what they achieved. They laid a solid foundation for

PNG in medical science, agriculture, forestry, fisheries, Ross Garnaut in economic policy. We cannot blame the Australians who were in PNG before Independence for whatever is happening today. That is our creation. We got our country to where it is and if there are problems they are ours and we should and we will fix them.

SS   To continue with the UPNG theme, Bill Gammage has written that the first UPNG students 'knew that some whites would judge not only them, but all their people, on how well they did'. The earliest UPNG students were thus representatives of their people. Did you feel the pressure of this responsibility?

CWL   Of course we did. It was a mixed feeling – responsibility but also euphoria and expectation. I was in the second university intake in 1967. The first group was [Rabbie] Namaliu, Tony Siaguru, [Mekere] Morauta and others in 1966. Of course we were interested in politics, and we took it upon ourselves to debate things seriously. The Waigani Seminars were very popular. We saw those seminars as a boiler room for the exchange of ideas, learned from international experiences. We recognised that we were the future leaders, but not in a boastful way. We felt the challenges. It was a very humbling experience and that's the key issue. We sensed we were the pioneers, taking the country forward to the next phase of independence and running our own country. That kind of pioneering spirit did not lead to a gung-ho mentality or approach. Rather, we took responsibility and in many ways I think did well, in part because of the people we had around us. The expatriates we had working with us and academic friends like Bill Gammage were always with us, always encouraging. They never showed any negativity. There was a sense that together we will get the country there.

SS   So in the late 1960s you were conscious that you were in the vanguard of those moving the country towards independence?

CWL   Well, I was at UNSW in 1969 and the ABC asked me to a debate with Gough Whitlam and Charlie Barnes at the University of New England in Armidale. I think there was a Teachers' Federation conference and they invited Charlie Barnes, then Minister for Territories, and Gough Whitlam of the Labor Party. I think it was January or February 1969, the first year I was at UNSW, or 1970. The debate was broadcast live on television. Gough Whitlam was very pro-independence and Charlie Barnes was against independence. So I was talking about independence in 1969–70, and not just with Whitlam and Barnes but in other debates at the university campus. But I was with the Public Service Association at that time, being groomed to take over from my expatriate colleagues, and I had no plans to enter public service more directly. Nonetheless, of course we felt a sense of responsibility even then.

SS   At that time did you ever anticipate that independence would be achieved within five years?

CWL Oh yes. I think most of us did, Somare's generation and mine. My father, Lepani Watson, was a little reluctant. [Lepani Watson was a distinguished and respected figure in the Papuan community. In addition to working as a Treasury clerk, he later won election to the Legislative Council and the House of Assembly. In 1955 he founded the Methodist Welfare Society, which catered for the needs of Papuan Methodists and provided services for indentured Milne Bay labourers in the Port Moresby region.] He was of the moderate view and thought there was still a lot of work to be done before we achieved independence. But some of us thought PNG was ready. The economy was strong enough. By 1972 production at Bougainville Copper was under way, and utilising the latest technology it was mining and selling large volumes of ore, to the extent that the mine was able to repay its original 15-year loan in two years. The PNG government considered the original agreement signed by the Australian colonial administration was inadequate and, to this end, formulated a Major Resources Policy which stated that 'PNG's resources belong to the people of PNG'. On the basis of this policy, and because of the massive profits Bougainville Copper Limited was generating, the PNG government renegotiated the mine agreement, introducing the Additional Profits Tax. The APT allowed for a more equitable share of revenues from the mine to flow to the new self-government of PNG. Both the Australian government and the self-government in PNG envisaged that the Bougainville mine would provide the revenue base for PNG's future independence. Copper, however, was not the sole driver of the economy at the time. In fact, there were four 'COs': copper, as well as coffee, cocoa and copra. Plus Ok Tedi was coming on-stream, although no significant government revenue was generated in its first ten years. We thought there was a bright future for the country. And we had wonderful people providing strong leadership: Sir Michael Somare, Sir Albert Maori Kiki, Sir Ebia Olewale, Sir Julius Chan, Sir Tei Abal and others.

Politics and policy had a happy confluence for 10 to 15 years after Independence, with politicians and bureaucrats working very well together. I do not agree with those who, when discussing the challenges PNG faces today, make sweeping declarations about the country since Independence. These people have no sense of history and a loose grasp of the facts. They should say 'Since the late 1980s ... ', for that is when the development problems and challenges facing PNG arose. In the years after Independence bureaucrats weren't too scared to offer their views for fear they would be sacked. We offered our views whether or not they went against the political grain. If we thought the politicians were going to spend too much money, Mekere [Morauta] in Treasury and me in Planning would tell them you can't do that, there is only this much left in the budget basket. They would bargain with each other in Cabinet about which projects should proceed and which should be delayed; about which provinces or electorates to fund. They listened to us in those days, unlike now where the answer is no, go find more money [laughs]. Politicians respected advice from bureaucrats, knowing that it was their responsibility if they did not. The politicians knew they were fully responsible for the decisions they made and would be judged by the electorate, the people of PNG, accordingly.

SS   Along with Mekere Morauta, Rabbie Namaliu and Tony Siaguru, you were a member of the Gang of Four, so-called because each of you headed central government agencies after Independence. In addition to working as a civil servant, you have worked as a trade unionist, consultant, and now as a diplomat. The other members of the Gang of Four entered politics, with Sir Mekere and Sir Rabbie serving as Prime Minister. Why did you choose the direction you did? Did you ever consider a career in politics?

CWL   I did. In 1982 I stood at the same time as Rabbie and Tony Siaguru. Mekere didn't, he came later. But we stood and they won. I lost in Trobriands, in an electorate I was expected to win. I don't want to whinge about it but I know I should have won. Suffice to say, an internal Trobriand politics – Rolf Gerritsen has written extensively about Trobriand politics – was at play. I was involved on one side as leader of a group. My electoral opponent was the brother-in-law of the returning officer. They used to take the ballot boxes to the returning officer's house at night and tamper with the ballot papers. If this is politics, I thought, I want nothing to do with it. Since then Trobrianders have urged me to stand again and again at each election but I have refused. No – I've had my bit [laughs]. I've never looked back or bothered to think about standing again, even though there has been a lot of pressure, including from people in Moresby who have encouraged me to stand for them. I just gave up on the idea, and eventually they did too.

SS   I am interested in your thoughts on the provision of foreign aid, a subject on which you have expressed strong and decisive views. You are on record as stating that PNG should decrease its reliance on Australian aid. Earlier this month the Australian Prime Minister, Kevin Rudd, announced that asylum seekers endeavouring to reach Australia would be taken to PNG for assessment and settlement. Peter O'Neill, the PNG Prime Minister, has stated that the money that PNG will receive from this arrangement will be spent on roads, universities, hospitals and suchlike. How does this tally with observations you have made that Australian aid to PNG benefits neither country and does not contribute to a long-term, strong and friendly relationship between Australia and PNG? Is the arrangement consistent with the Port Moresby Declaration, signed between Australia and PNG in 2008, which asserted that the two countries were equal partners in PNG's development?

CWL   It's a complex issue. I have dealt with the issue of Australian aid since Independence, when I was head of the NPO. The first package was given by Gough Whitlam's government – $300 million over three years. When he left [Malcolm] Fraser offered $500 million over five years. We were happy with the longer term, and since then there have been regular negotiations with Australia. I have seen the evolution of this issue. In the mid-1980s I was asked by the PNG and Australian governments to review Australia's aid to PNG and initiate the trial of a tied aid program. In 2003 a colleague and I reviewed all aid coming to PNG. In 2004 both governments hired me along with Alan Morris, Commissioner for the Commonwealth Regional Fund, and Epa Tuioti, former treasury secretary in Samoa, to review Australian aid to PNG. So I have an intimate working knowledge of Australia's aid program to PNG.

My concern is that it's a fragile arrangement for both our countries. We are offered a lot of cash but it is very difficult to see the impact of this Australian money. AusAID will tell you otherwise, but our review found there was no monitoring of how aid money was spent up to 2003–4. When we interviewed Australian treasury staff, one said, 'It's like benign neglect. We just give you the money and that's it.' After that we insisted that Australian aid had to be monitored according to the terms and administrative arrangements of the Development Cooperation Treaty, which sets out performance benchmarks that PNG has to fulfil before funds are released each year. We set up schedules for adhering to benchmarks and monitoring those areas where we need to see improvements – infant mortality rates, maternal deaths in childbirth, literacy, et cetera. This tallied with the MDGs [Millennium Development Goals] and Kevin Rudd's 2008 announcement of a Pacific-wide development partnership. So this is good. I'm not against that.

But in the long term, with regard to aid, there is an undercurrent of politics that we have to answer to and reflect on which is not conducive to long-term friendly relations between our two countries. It's a dependency relationship. In the Moti affair, Downer – not so much John Howard as Prime Minister but Alexander Downer – had no qualms about threatening to cut off Australia's aid to PNG. He was angry that Moti was spirited away to the Solomon Islands and he blamed the PNG government for that. [Julian Moti, an Australian citizen, was arrested in PNG in 2006. The Australian government wanted his extradition to Australia. Moti was flown to the Solomon Islands by the PNG Defence Force.] Then last week, Julie Bishop, the deputy leader of the Opposition, standing next to Tony Abbott, looked at the cameras straight-faced and said, 'Kevin Rudd has promised to sign a blank cheque to Peter O'Neill.' This is inaccurate. There was no mention of a blank cheque in the meeting. In fact I arranged for Tony Abbott, Julie Bishop and the shadow minister for immigration, Scott Morrison, to meet with our Prime Minister [Peter O'Neill] straight after the announcement on asylum seekers by Kevin Rudd in Brisbane. We met with them at the Sofitel Hotel. And I was there. There was no mention by Peter O'Neill that Kevin Rudd was signing a blank cheque for PNG to use however it wanted.

Let me explain. When Julia Gillard went to PNG earlier this year, she made commitments and accepted Prime Minister O'Neill's request that Australia's aid be realigned to address specifically some of the crumbling urban infra-structure. In this regard, Prime Minister Gillard agreed, and Prime Minister Rudd later affirmed, that Australia would fund three urban projects as a priority: a scoping study for the repair of the Lae to Madang highway; a design study for the repair of the courthouse in Port Moresby;

and the design and reconstruction of Angau Hospital in Lae, to which PNG has a recurrent funding commitment. Both Gillard and Rudd also agreed to fund the recommendations of the Garnaut/Namaliu University Review team on a kina for kina basis, as well as some sports projects and a 'women in business' project. This funding, totalling A$420 million, is additional to the A$580 million of funding that is part of the existing aid program for 2012–13. Further, when Rudd visited PNG in July, he agreed to fast-track the three major urban projects by six months. And it's not only Australia's money: PNG has a budget commitment to fund the recurrent costs, maintenance, staffing and so forth. Indeed, the arrangement made with Gillard and Rudd is not the usual one. Australia funds existing programs in primary health care and primary education, and pays for some infrastructure maintenance. It maintains the section of the Highlands Highway from Lae to Goroka. Otherwise Australian aid is focused purely on capital works. Generally PNG pays maintenance costs.

Manus asylum seeker funding is a different package altogether. This is where I think Julie Bishop, Tony Abbott and Scott Morrison got the idea of a blank cheque, which doesn't exist, although Julie Bishop has returned to me and clarified their position on this matter and I have accepted it. Australia is committed to building a new facility on Manus for processing asylum seekers and to developing the existing temporary facility into something permanent. Again, it's not just Australian money. PNG money will fund the building of roads and the improvement of utilities' infrastructure – sewerage, water and so on. That's PNG's commitment. So there's no such thing as a blank cheque. AusAID officials in Australia and Port Moresby sign cheques so that the contractors can build the new facility on Manus. We need better temporary facilities than tents. We've asked Australia to stop sending us the tents as there are so many criticisms of the temporary facilities and living conditions for asylum seekers on Manus.

I return now to the question about my views on Australian aid and why it should be reduced. There is an undercurrent to aid politics in Australia. Australian politicians, particularly on the Liberal/National Coalition side, use the subject of aid to whip PNG whenever it suits them. They make an issue out of it. My view, which I've expressed in lengthy discussions with AusAID people and politicians, including Julie Bishop, is that we should move away from an aid treaty, the Development Cooperation Treaty, towards a trade and investment treaty, the Economic Cooperation Treaty. We would deal with each other as friendly sovereign nations and equal partners. Australia will think twice before threatening us with trade and investment sanctions, unless of course we have breached our human rights obligations in very significant ways. Aid is certainly important in terms of expressing Australian support for PNG. But it's very easy for Australians to turn and use it to whip up a lot of anti-PNG sentiment, as is evidenced in Australian media commentaries about PNG: 'Ah, don't waste our money with that lot, those cannibals.' Aid just doesn't work well in the long run. With regard to the LNG project [a multi-billion dollar Liquid Natural Gas project in the Southern Highlands] and the resulting benefits stream setting up the sovereign wealth fund, we should look at phasing out Australian aid, reducing it over a period of 10 or 15 years. This should start five years from now, once LNG revenue flows are in place and we can do it in a responsible way without destabilising PNG's fiscal policy. We can then move to a trade and investment relationship. That is the essence of my view. We are not ungrateful to Australia and its taxpayers for their support all these years, but as it stands the aid arrangement does not promote good relations between our two countries or allow us to be equal partners in a sustainable way. The ever-present idea that PNG is dependent on Australia, an idea which underlies our relationship, results in negative politics and the poisoning of bilateral relations.

SS   Do you detect an element of paternalism or colonialism in the Australian attitude?

CWL   Well, yes. I mean you can make an argument for that: we're giving you all this money and we expect something in return. Aid is supposed to help and should not be conditional on receiving something in return. Based on aid flows, it could be argued that Australian aid is paternalistic. And yes, it can generate misunderstandings, such as Australia is pushing its barrel down a track; that PNG should kowtow because of the money it receives. But this aid can also be seen as a serious act of generosity from Australians to Papua New Guineans. And the good thing is that Australian and PNG leaders usually understand each other in these matters. An example is the Pacific Solution, which Howard implemented when Mekere Morauta was Prime Minister. Australia lent PNG A$60 million for balance of payments support. That was the payment made for Manus to be opened. Now there is a similar arrangement, and O'Neill and Rudd understand and support each other. There are no problems here. It's the Opposition reaction – the idea that Australian taxpayers are handing over money in the form of a blank cheque – that irks most of us in PNG. There is no such thing. [Charles Lepani added the following sentence on 24 October 2013: 'Since the election of the Abbott government in September 2013, it has fully supported the commitments made by the Rudd Labor government.']

SS   Was that what was behind your statement issued last week? [On 24 July 2013, several days after the Australia-PNG asylum seeker arrangement was announced, Charles Lepani issued this press release: 'The High Commissioner of Papua New Guinea to Australia today warned Australian politicians to observe international protocols and courtesies when discussing relations with other friendly sovereign nations and not impugn the dignity of our leaders who are attempting to assist Australia in this very complex regional and international issue of Asylum Seekers.']

CWL   Yes, that's it. I'll give you the original copy. In brackets I said, High Commissioner Lepani was referring to a statement by Julie Bishop, deputy leader of the Opposition, on blank cheques for Papua New Guineans. The blank cheque comment was repeated by shadow treasurer [Joe] Hockey two days later. On television he said: 'We will never sign a blank cheque to another country.' It's very frustrating. This is inaccurate. There was no mention of a blank cheque in the briefing room. The asylum seeker arrangement was organised in a very friendly way. As we wanted to play things in a bipartisan manner, our Prime Minister also met with the Opposition and told them about the arrangement and what had been agreed with Kevin Rudd. But a blank cheque was never mentioned.

I've described to you exactly what is happening with regard to the existing package of aid, the additional package, and the Manus Asylum Seeker Processing Centre package. Cheques will be written here and paid to Australian contracting companies to come and build a Manus facility. There is no blank cheque from Australia to PNG. Australia provided budget support aid for a few years after Independence but that stopped in the early 1980s.

SS   More generally, how do you assess the Australia-PNG relationship at the present time? What are its strengths and weaknesses? Has the relationship changed since Independence in 1975? If so, how? What role would you like to see Australia play in PNG's future?

CWL   I'm very optimistic, despite these sporadic family fights. We are the best of friends. We look at Australia as a friend and most Australians see PNG as a friend. We enjoy bipartisan support in your parliament which is good. Julie Bishop, deputy leader of the Opposition, goes to PNG regularly. She has walked the Kokoda track, like most Australian politicians. The Australia-PNG relationship is still very vibrant, very buoyant. We have very good relations, except for these occasional disagreements.

With regard to the future, I see a relationship based on economic cooperation rather than aid. I believe Australia, PNG and Indonesia should form a trading bloc, a trilateral regional or sub-regional grouping for trade and economic integration and organisation to bring the Pacific and Asia together. This idea has potential, as Kevin Rudd acknowledged in one of his press briefings. I have been mentioning the potential of this idea since 2006–7. A dynamic economic grouping such as this is the future for Australia, Indonesia and PNG, and the Asia-Pacific region generally.

SS   Have there been discussions to this end?

CWL   It's still in the thinking stage. It's certainly not at the policy stage. But Prime Minister O'Neill has gone to Indonesia and has moved to have annual Indonesian-PNG ministerial meetings, just as Australia and PNG have annual ministerial forums. Kevin Rudd mentioned the prospect recently, so it's starting to gain momentum, I'm happy to say. To me it's something we can all look forward to, something for the well-being and prosperity of the peoples of our three countries.

SS   Many Australians and Papua New Guineans look back at the 1960–75 period with great fondness, as you have in this interview. The future for PNG was bright, full of hope and promise. Do you think that hope and promise have been realised, or are being realised? What are the gains and losses PNG has experienced since Independence?

CWL   In terms of the expectations of expatriates in those days, perhaps PNG hasn't matured as they expected. But for those of us who were there and who played a part, I don't think it can be said we failed. There's no measure of failure or success in this work in progress. PNG has 800 linguistic ethnic groupings and rough terrain for development efforts, though we should have learnt from other developing countries and how they emerged from independence. We had this opportunity, and we did send a lot of our leaders to African countries. I went to Tanzania to look at political systems, workplace relations, and business.

SS   When Julius Nyerere was leader?

CWL   Yes, in 1974. So, you can only say that PNG is a work in progress, rather than that it has failed or succeeded. PNG people are also a work in progress. As a Trobriander, I'm still learning what Highlanders do, what Sepiks do, what people from other parts of the country do, about their cultures and so forth. Not too much is made of this, but more and more marriages are between young people from different parts of the country. I think they are the people who will deal with the issues arising from the different cultures in PNG. The homogeneity they bring will help to resolve problems and overcome the daunting task of building national unity, a national identity. These are the people who will do it and they are coming in great numbers now: a woman from Milne Bay marries a man from the Highlands; a Tolai marries someone from other parts. The children from these unions are the hope of the country because they will identify more as Papua New Guineans than previous generations.

SS   Rather than as Tolai or Trobrianders?

CWL   Yes. To the question 'Where are you from?' the reply might be, 'I'm mixed – I'm Tolai, Manus.' I think that's the unspoken positive – demographic change will help to tackle the issue of national unity and national identity in PNG. From there we can move to politics and policy making. Stability in politics and stability in policy development must go hand in hand. Where there is instability in politics, policy will not be effective.

        I'm not pessimistic. PNG has a bright future. It is a work in progress, but over the next few generations I think we'll see a happier and more prosperous country than it is today.

EDUCATION, RACE AND SOCIAL CHANGE

11

INTERVIEW WITH PROFESSOR KEN INGLIS

Interview conducted by Seumas Spark in Melbourne, 24 September 2013

SS   You went to PNG in 1967 as the inaugural Professor of History at UPNG. More so than a number of other Australian contributors to this book, you had already forged a successful career in Australia. What prompted you to put your career in Australia on hold and head to PNG? What did you hope to contribute or gain from living in PNG?

KI   I should preface my answer by reminding you that it's a long time ago. Old men forget and even remember things that didn't happen. 1967 is 46 years ago. I could be an unreliable witness.

When I applied for the job it was late 1965, so I was 36 or 35. I had been a widower with three children and that was a way of life that didn't leave much time for anything beyond teaching and a bit of research. But in 1965 I married

Amirah and we merged our two families – she had three kids and I had three kids. Suddenly, in 1965, we had six kids. The world seemed to be opened up by my marrying Amirah. Partly that she was so full of life and joy and verve. And I think I felt I had withdrawn from life a bit in the years after my first wife died in 1962. By 1965 I was ready for something more adventurous than what I was doing. I was a Professor of History in the department run by Manning Clark in Canberra and very happily placed there. Whatever has been said about Manning in more recent years, I found him a wonderful colleague and I owed it to him that I had a chair of history. He had a second chair created in his department and made it clear that he wanted me to have it.

So what was I going to do with my life? The big issue around campuses then was Vietnam and I didn't find myself wanting to get involved in the politics of Vietnam, the campus politics of Vietnam. I'm not proud of this but I didn't have any sympathy with either side in Vietnam. Many of the people closest to me were supporters of the VietCong and I wasn't. I wasn't anti-North Vietnam or VietCong. In fact I didn't take any part in campus poli-tics. I shared the quite common hostility – I was going to say contempt but certainly hostility – to the govern-ment of South Vietnam, but I didn't feel that I wanted to be involved in what was the big issue of the time. The other big issue in which I might have become involved, and with which I had been marginally involved, was Aboriginal affairs. I don't know why I didn't become more active in Aboriginal matters. I felt a sort of pent-up frustration as I wanted to be doing something in the wide world and I knew it wasn't Vietnam. In 1964 or 1965 the Australian government, responding to nudges from the United Nations and the World Bank, decided to establish a university in PNG. And the more I thought about it the more it appealed to me as a likely place to work. When I asked Amirah what she thought about it, she responded with characteristic enthusiasm. So I decided to apply for the chair of history. I was appointed on the understanding that I wouldn't go up for another year.

Before deciding to apply I had made a tour. I went to Port Moresby – I forget whether I went to other places too at that stage – to see what it would be like for family life. My children and my wife reckoned that when I took photographs of Port Moresby and its surroundings I deliberately chose beautiful scenes to accompany my supposedly impartial judgment that it'd be a good place for us to go [laughs]. It turned out to be a very good place for us to go.

The only regret concerns the oldest of our children, Deborah, Amirah's older daughter, who was 15 when I applied for the chair. At that stage it looked as if she was going to do engineering. She could go to school up there for a year or two, or go to school in Australia. And while the schools in PNG were good enough up until the middle years, the high school couldn't offer good teaching in science. And there was going to be no engineering at UPNG. We realised that if we went she would have to stay behind and go to boarding school in Melbourne, to leave open the prospect of a degree in science or engineering. So when we ultimately went to PNG, she went to school in Melbourne and came up in vacations. Eventually all the kids went down to boarding schools in Melbourne, at public expense. This was the common thing then for expatriates in PNG – they received heavily subsidised access to boarding schools.

So here was I, not yet 40 and not wanting to spend the rest of my life going round and round, and there was this interesting, mysterious, attractive place. I wasn't on a treadmill – I enjoyed my teaching and was always fortunate in my colleagues – but I felt that there was something more I could do, some more adventures I could have before I settled.

SS   Did anyone decry your decision to move to PNG or attempt to dissuade you from going?

KI   Professor John La Nauze was head of the history department in the Research School of Social Sciences, and I was in Manning Clark's department in the School of General Studies at ANU. But I had a spell in the Research School of Social Sciences. Bob Gollan kindly agreed to swap with me for half a year to help me do some writing. I was probably in La Nauze's department about the time the PNG job came up. He didn't exactly try to dissuade me, for he knew that I'd made up my mind. He was an Anglophile Australian with an affable, Oxonian manner. La Nauze said, 'Well, you have my blessings. Of course it will be the end of you as a historian, my boy' [laughs]. I don't know whether he remembered that scornful advice, but when I decided to return to Australia, and as I hoped to ANU, he was kind enough not to treat me as a ruined case. I should say that in those days it was very easy to get jobs in Australian universities. Once Menzies had been converted to higher education he poured money into it. I look back with wonder to realise that you could leave a job in Australia confident that you could get it back if you went away for many years. You wouldn't dare think of it now.

SS   In 1967 R. J. Turnbull, Independent senator for Tasmania, visited UPNG. He was reported as saying: 'I still believe that the University is a gross extravagance, 10 to 15 years before its time and poor window dressing for the United Nations. No country can afford a University which contains 38 undergraduates. With each succeeding year this will increase but in view of the fact that these 38 students cause the employment of at least ten professors each drawing more than $10,000 it would have been cheaper to have sent all these students to Australia.' What did you make of Turnbull's visit and this comment?

KI   I don't have to trust my memory here because I've just looked at an account that I published at the time. I always wanted to be a journalist and I enjoyed practising journalism wherever I was. As a fun thing to do, I edited a little newsletter called *UPNG News*, which came out about once or twice a semester. I've just had a peep at the story we ran on Turnbull's visit and it reminded me of how important the ABC was at that stage in PNG. There were very few forums for free expression. It wasn't that the Territory administration was tyrannous, but that there wasn't the demand – or possibly supply. I don't know how much it was supply, how much demand. There was one newspaper and the ABC was almost the only outlet for serious discussion. After Turnbull made those remarks, an ABC bloke who ran a current affairs program, a chap called Philip Satchell, interviewed a number of students as they came out of lectures. What impressed people a great deal was how articulate the students were and what good arguments they put up against Turnbull's assertion that it would be much better to educate them in Australia. He had added that it would be better in general for the students to be educated in Australia because then they would adjust to Australian ways of thinking and talking. Well, of course they would. This was one reason why the students, who didn't deny their education was very costly, preferred what had happened, as they explained in their interviews. Turnbull's visit was probably the first time that students had been quoted in public discourse, and their response was calm, somewhat ironic, and much more articulate than a lot of their critics – a lot of our critics – had expected.

SS   To what extent were you and your staff conscious that you were preparing the future leaders of an independent PNG? Was there resentment of the role played by UPNG scholars in this regard, both within and beyond the university?

KI   I don't know about resentment. There was scepticism among the old time expatriates – the 'befores' (they were there 'before'). Some were sceptical of the university and, like Turnbull, thought it was 'window dressing'. And there was the almost flat earth scepticism of some planters who didn't believe that the sons and daughters of bush *kanakas* were fit candidates for higher education. But among expatriate administrators, mainly Australians, the nearest that I can remember to any hostility was that they thought that we had it easy compared with them, the people who'd been on the job in PNG for a long time. They were a bit envious of the resources which the university seemed to be getting. As for our students, I must not generalise. There was one thing that surprised everyone about the university and that was the number of Australians working in the territory who chose to go to the university. It simply wasn't part of the plan. We had part-time students who were expatriates. A lot of fresh thinking had to be done about this.

Among the indigenous students, who were in the majority, I didn't detect any ill will towards the university. The people who were our indigenous students knew that they were a privileged elite. To get to university you had to have had unusual exposure to the English language. And that meant that you had to have a father who was a policeman or a mission worker or in some occupation which exposed him to English because the education system, and this remains so all these years later, takes in a small and diminishing fragment of the school-age population. The pool of talent for the university was pretty small and people in it knew that they were privileged. And they knew that by the time the university started they were going to be running the country, or at least that their generation was going to be running the country sooner than they may have wanted or been ready for. One course I taught was American History. I began with two lectures on the making of the American Constitution. The lectures were pretty much the same as lectures I'd given in Canberra. In Canberra I could hardly keep students awake because constitution is a soporific word in Australia. When I gave the same lecture in PNG the students hung on every word because the word constitution was connected with nation-making. To have a close look at how the great American nation had been constituted was a very different experience in PNG from what it was in Canberra or Melbourne.

SS   Were you conscious of tailoring your lectures and activities at university to suit those indigenous students who would become the leaders of PNG?

KI   I think we knew that's what we were there for. We decided, before we had any competence to teach it, that PNG history would be the first course we put on. And it was our good luck that we happened to have a genius to teach it – Hank Nelson. He had done a little work on Aboriginal history in Australia when working at RMIT, and he was the core teacher of our History of Papua New Guinea course. Papua New Guineans, like Africans, were scarcely visible in the history books, except as objects of colonialism. We were resolved to teach (and before that to learn!) a history in which the antecedents of our students were actors, in their relationships both with masters from elsewhere and with each other. The Second World War presented itself as an obvious candidate for a new history, connecting the lives of the students' families with the great occurrences of history. When we started in 1967, it was 25 years after the Japanese invasion. We got the impression that for a long time the generation to which our students' parents belonged wasn't ready to talk about anything to do with the war, except possibly the myth of the fuzzy-wuzzy angels. It was one thing if you had lived in an area that the Japanese hadn't occupied, another if you had been in an area that they had. What were you to say about it 25 years later? People had to make all sorts of accommodations and compromises if they had been in Japanese-occupied areas.

It turned out that the students were the first generation that was prepared, willing and able to talk with some frankness about the experience of the war. The war became a central event in our teaching of PNG history. One student in the History of PNG course came from near Madang. In 1944 Madang had been contested territory between the Japanese and the Australians. This student said his father remembered waking up each morning, looking out of his house, and putting on a Japanese hat or an Australian hat according to what he thought he saw. That was really quite a shock to Australians.

I got a personal shock one day when talking to a student from the Sepik, an area which had been occupied by the Japanese. (Michael Somare, a Sepik man, had his first schooling at the hands of the Japanese.) I asked the student a corny, chalky question: 'What did your family say about the Japanese occupation?' He said: 'Towards the end it was terrible as there was no food and they were eating people, but for a long time it was okay. They were the only white men who would ever sit down on the floor of the house with us.' I had to prevent myself from saying, 'White men, what do you mean white men?' It was a very instructive moment for me to realise that Sepik people regarded all Japanese, Australians, British and Germans as varieties of white men.

SS   In 1972 you replaced John Gunther as vice-chancellor of UPNG. Did you enjoy this role? What were your main priorities and policies as vice-chancellor?

KI   I didn't enjoy it all that much, though I enjoyed it more than I expected to. I never wanted to be an administrator and I took this on with misgivings. Again I think John La Nauze might have made a waspish remark or two about it. But I remember gratefully advice from two people. One was Anthony Low, who was a historian of Africa and a vice-chancellor of ANU, and the other was Hugh Stretton, my head of department at the University of Adelaide. They both encouraged me by saying it would be good for a historian to have a keyhole view of momentous change in a nation. And it was. To have good professional reason to go and see the Chief Minister or the Minister for Finance was something to cherish. There were ludicrous aspects too. The Boy Scouts Association asked me to be chief scout. As a boy I'd lasted one week in the Scouts before I was knocked over by a medicine ball and never went back. By my being vice-chancellor my wife and I got to spend an evening dining with the Queen on her yacht the *Britannia*. A mere professor of history wouldn't have scored that. So there were experiences that the job opened up for me.

As for what I wanted to do ... John Gunther was a great man. He thought there was a great deal of bullshit in academic notions of democracy, and who's to say he was wrong about that. But he would always listen, and he had an open mind on many things which I wouldn't have expected a senior administrator in a colonial regime to have an open mind on. When he was Director of Public Health he was a great help to scientists and to scholars, including my sister [Shirley Lindenbaum] who is an anthropologist. There were a number of academics who thought he was a tyrant. When I took over from John Gunther – and it was he who pressed me to take the job – I thought my first task should be to work out ways of decision-making that were more consultative. I think some would say I overdid it. In his history of UPNG, *A Thousand Graduates*, Ian Howie-Willis reports people being critical of me for overdoing the consultation business and occupying too much time that could have been better spent. That may well be right.

I saw the job as being a transitional one and what I wanted to do was prepare the role for the first indigenous vice-chancellor. I was succeeded by an indigenous vice-chancellor [Dr Gabriel Gris] who hated the job. He died young of a heart attack, possibly induced by stress. He wasn't comfortable in the job. Since then there have been both indigenous and expatriate vice-chancellors. We were all for what was called localisation, where indigenous people filled as many responsible jobs as possible. Perhaps we overestimated the need for that, I don't know. I remember a Papua New Guinean saying, 'We can live with expatriates doing jobs like vice-chancellor, so long as they do what we want them to do.'

Localisation began in my time as vice-chancellor when the first of our graduates began to move into government and administration. One of the most admirable and lovable of the first wave of students was Mekere Morauta. We wallowed in the pleasure of having, so we thought, brought up the first Prime Ministers. Two Prime Ministers, Sir Rabbie Namaliu and Sir Mekere Morauta, were among our favourite students, and the national airline was run by another favourite, Bart Philemon. Sir Mekere and Sir Rabbie. Some of us thought, quite wrongly, that Papua New Guineans wouldn't want the imperial rank. A lot of them were quite happy to have it, without any sense that it diminished their integrity.

There are two kinds of administrators: those for whom it is the fulfilling work of their life, and those who mentally mark off each day. It's very difficult for one sort of administrator – I was the latter type – to understand the other. I was blessed with having a wonderful chancellor, Sir John Crawford, who at the same time was vice-chancellor of ANU. He found it very difficult to believe that I would only take the job for three years. He couldn't understand why I wouldn't want longer. When we first met, he said, 'We should talk about the role of the vice-chancellor and the chancellor. I think it is the job of the chancellor to support the vice-chancellor.' Well, good, I thought. After a pause, he continued: 'And the job of the vice-chancellor is to earn that support.' Isn't that a great statement? When we went to PNG we were not expecting to stay more than three or four years. My three years as vice-chancellor were unexpected. We thought we would see the first generation of students through, but in the end we stayed eight years, with 18 months out at various times during that period. We left just a few months before Independence. As someone joked, we fled Independence.

SS   How much understanding did you have of the broader context in PNG given that your experience of the country was confined mainly to the particular environment of UPNG? Did you travel extensively beyond Port Moresby?

KI   I certainly only had glimpses of the world beyond Port Moresby. I was on a body called the National Education Board which used to meet in rural or provincial areas, sometimes even in villages. Charles Rowley, who was Professor of Political Studies at ANU and at UPNG, wrote a marvellous book called *The New Guinea Villager* which was the first book to put the Papua New Guinean at the centre of the story. Just about all our students went home to villages. They lived in two worlds, chronologically and spiritually. I remember a remark on that subject by Tony – Sir Anthony – Siaguru, possibly the ablest of students from the Sepik district. Between important jobs in PNG, he became Deputy Secretary General of the Commonwealth in London, and alas died young of cancer. I remember him saying that what he had to work at hardest when he went home for vacations was to set aside western notions of the passing of time in order to live comfortably in the place where he'd grown up. He had to think in a different calendar. That must have been a common experience.

We could at least go and visit places from which our students came. Amirah was writing a book about a notorious

Papuan character of the 1930s and she went to stay with Mekere Morauta's family in their home on the Gulf of Papua. On her return, Amirah told me that Mekere's father had said to Mekere: 'My son, you tell me many things which I find difficult to believe about what you do. I have done my best to believe. But this I cannot believe – you've gone too far.' And he held up a kina note on which the name Mekere Morauta was signed. [Mekere Morauta was the first Papua New Guinean to head the country's Finance Department, the equivalent of the Reserve Bank in Australia.]

So we had these glimpses, just enough to remind us of what was out there. I cherish a photograph of me in the vice-chancellor's office surrounded by scary-looking people from the Highlands carrying weapons. They had come down for a cultural festival and a young man from their group, a student, had brought them into my office to say hello. It's the kind of experience you wouldn't have in the course of an ordinary day as vice-chancellor in an Australian university. But no doubt, it was a Port Moresby-centred view that I had.

SS   You left the vice-chancellorship, and PNG, in 1975. What prompted your return to Australia?

KI   As I said earlier, the question is why we stayed as long as we did. It wasn't that we made a decision at that stage to leave; it's that we had deferred earlier decisions to leave. And by 1975 nearly all of our kids were at school or university in Australia. Deborah, the only one not to go to school in Moresby, was teaching at UPNG, having opted for a degree in social sciences.

You asked before was there any hostility to my going to PNG? I remember a lot of people saying what a challenge we were going to face in PNG. Our 'challenges' were quite pleasurable compared with those faced by my colleagues left behind in Australia. All our students, or nearly all of them, regarded UPNG as I had regarded the University of Melbourne in the 1940s – as a benign place that I felt privileged to be in and loved and enjoyed everything about. That was the case for me in PNG too. Back in Australia the campuses were exploding with anti-Vietnam and anti-authoritarian protest movements. That's where the challenges were.

SS   Since leaving in 1975, have you visited PNG? If so, what were your impressions?

KI   Only once, in the mid-1990s. We had an institution called the Waigani Seminar which was an annual conference about things of the moment. It started in 1967, disappeared for a while in the years after we left, and was revived in the 1990s. Amirah and I went back to one of the Seminars, I think in 1995. There were two main impressions. We knew that PNG had been a golden age in our lives, but we hadn't realised fully that it was a golden age in the lives of our students, such a time of hope, such a time of excitement. That was one thing. The other impression was that times had become very difficult indeed – there was so much violence and corruption. I could hear questions behind many of the conversations we had: did Australia leave too soon? Did independence come too soon? To know how to answer those questions we have first to imagine the alternatives. In the late 1960s there were movements with considerable potential for violence; those tendencies were subdued by the granting of independence. Would there have been terrible violence if PNG independence had been delayed? Who knows? Did the country have enough skilled and highly educated people, public servants and politicians – not that the politician needs to be highly educated – to run a country? Perhaps not. But was the alternative thinkable? Who knows? Someone who's written very well about this is Donald Denoon, who succeeded me as Professor of History at UPNG. He writes in one of his books that Australia declared itself independent of PNG. One of Donald's books, about the Australia-PNG relationship, is nicely called *A Trial Separation*.

SS   You speak of hope and promise. Do you think that the hope and promise of those years has in any way been realised, or is being realised?

KI   I think the violence is more terrible and more pervasive and less evidently curable than anybody expected; at least as bad as we'd feared, perhaps worse. But there are still dedicated people. When we went up in the mid-nineties we were enormously impressed by the dedication and bravery of many indigenous academics, public servants and business people.

      There has been deep disenchantment with the regimes of Michael Somare. [Sir Michael Somare was Chief Minister from 1972–5, and Prime Minister from 1975–80, 1982–5 and

2002–11.] He was briefly a law student in 1972 or 1973 while he was Chief Minister. In every way Somare was a friend of the university and greatly admired by students. Later, there was increasing disenchantment. People wanted so much to believe that Somare was an admirable leader, but they were forced to realise that he went in for a great deal of what we would call corruption, as did a lot of people who had been our friends. Not all of them, by any means, but a lot of them.

SS   How has the experience of living and working in PNG influenced your life and career?

KI   Amirah once said that it's made her sceptical of any general remarks about the human condition. When she hears any remark about what people are like, she finds herself asking herself whether or not it applies to PNG. The experience of living there gave us a temporary foothold in a world that wasn't our own – a glimpse into a world that was exciting, alien, and constantly challenging our understanding. And that continues even to this day. That sense of having lived on the edge of another world has stayed with all our kids, as with us.

SS   Do you have any thoughts on the role Australia should take in PNG, now and in the future?

KI   I'd like to think we had things to do that aren't as shonky as the PNG solution to our problem of boat people. Otherwise I don't have anything beyond platitudes – of course we

should realise that Australia and PNG have compatible
interests, of course we should be good neighbours. We're
always going to be close neighbours.

SS   Charles Lepani has expressed the opinion that Australian
aid ultimately does not help PNG because it creates a
dependency relationship. He has suggested that Australian
aid to PNG should be gradually phased out. Do you have any
opinions on the provision of foreign aid?

KI   That is now a common view of aid all around the world. I find
myself thinking in a contrary way about aid projects, some
of which must be doing good. My friend Jan Gammage, who
worked with AusAID, was with the peacekeeping group in
Bougainville. She found that when you asked women what
they wanted by way of aid, you got very different answers
from when you asked men. What women most wanted was
pencils. Now it seems to me that a society without pencils
can only benefit from aid which isn't corrupting or creating
a new dependence. Perhaps it's creating a dependence
on foreign pencils? I suspect the view that aid creates
dependence is often an excuse or a pretext for meanness or
economy rather than anything more admirable. That is not
fair to Charles Lepani, however, because he's speaking as
someone from a recipient country, not a donor country.

I haven't talked much about what matters most to me
about my time in PNG. John La Nauze might have teased
me that my brain would turn to pudding in PNG, but I found
it intellectually most stimulating and exciting. Our next-
door neighbours in the university village were Ralph and

Sue Bulmer. He was Professor of Anthropology and she was an archaeologist. They both did fieldwork in a place up in the mountains behind Madang called Kaironk. Ralph was studying how the locals of that area classified birds and nature generally, and Sue was digging. I have known anthropologists and archaeologists in other places but I have never been so close to other people's work. We would hear boisterous laughter coming through the louvres from the Bulmers' place. Some famous anthropologists would be enjoying their hospitality. Margaret Mead might be there. My head was in a more interdisciplinary world in PNG than it has ever been anywhere.

On a slightly different tack, we were all much younger than the people we had worked with previously. We came from universities where our seniors made the rules. In PNG we could make our own rules. They weren't all that revolutionary, but the point was no-one was stopping us. For example, when we wanted to introduce a semester system there wasn't an aged English-born professor to say otherwise. We could just go away and do it.

My first visit to PNG was when Gunther invited those who had been appointed to UPNG to go up for a look before we moved with our families.

SS   That was in 1966?

KI   In 1966, yes. When the first preliminary year was going but degree studies hadn't yet begun. 'What will the students want to talk about?' I asked the librarian, who had gone up before me. 'They will want to know if you are a proper professor', he said. 'They wanted to know was I a proper librarian. They're so used to getting the second best fobbed off on them, or believing that to be so, and they have so little idea about a university, that they will want confidence that you are a proper academic.' I remember a colleague of mine mentioning he'd gone up to an Anglican mission station where he had spoken with people about the university. They had asked, 'What happens at a university? Do they make bicycles at a university?' A perfectly intelligent question. They were in a world innocent of that knowledge. I asked the preliminary year students what they would want to know most from history when it came time for their degree studies. One said, and the others agreed, that they would want to know how it was that all the peoples of PNG came to be so different from each other. How did a country with hundreds of different languages and different cultures get to be? I don't know what the status of the relevant scholarship is now, but it's a good question, particularly when it concerns your world.

Students were admitted to the preliminary year at UPNG after four years of high school. In Australia students were admitted to first-year university only after six years of high school. A number of our critics and the [Australian] government's critics thought we were fooling ourselves or the students if we thought we could get them to degree capability earlier than in Australia. Four years, plus one [preliminary year], plus the three-year degree was one year fewer than in Australia. People questioned whether we were offering inferior degrees, and whether we could get our students to the same point as students in Australia one year sooner. So we devised course structures which assumed that the average student, without failing, would get through in four years. We held our breath to see whether the government would finance a four-year degree. It did. There would have been a mighty conflict if it hadn't because a lot of people who took up jobs at UPNG would have felt short-changed or misled if they hadn't been given the resources to provide comparable education. I mentioned the Australian expatriate students who turned up in unexpected numbers as part-timers. They were able to get their UPNG degrees recognised when they returned to Australia. We had other critics who said we shouldn't be hung up on Australian degrees; that we should be thinking of the country that the degrees are being created for and not looking nervously over our shoulders at imperialist Australia. But that's another story.

There are two other things I haven't spoken about, both of which I've written about. [See K. S. Inglis, 'Education on the Frontier: The First Ten Years of the University of Papua New Guinea' in Stephen Murray-Smith (ed.), *Melbourne Studies in Education 1980*, (Melbourne: Melbourne University Press, 1980).] One is the deeply embarrassing salary structure that was in place, at UPNG and elsewhere. That was an insoluble problem and whatever you did had consequences that you wished it didn't. [Expatriate and local staff were paid at different rates. In the 1970s expatriates teaching in the same university department as Papua New Guineans were paid approximately twice the salary of their local colleagues.] The other was the relationship between male and female students. PNG is a deeply masculine society and a lot of our male students really didn't want the women to be there. The women were always a minority because so few girls had the opportunities which led to university. I think it was a hard thing being a female student in those early days. And it remains so. When we went back in the 1990s the women's dormitory had protective razor wire all around it.

The proudest moment of my time at UPNG was in 1970, when we were hosts at an ANZAAS Congress which enabled scholars from and beyond Australia to inspect us and to take part in a ceremony honouring our first indigenous graduands. I remember one visitor saying that this was one of the most convivial events of his working life. 'Convivial' is a good word for the UPNG I remember. We had a staff club which was open to all, including pidgin-speaking gardeners. I remember a student looking around the club, probably in 1973, and saying, 'This place is getting too big. There are people here I don't know.' There were 1,500 students by 1973–4, and 300 graduates by the time we left in 1975.

12
MORESBY 1966
Bill Gammage

Out Lockhart way, in the Riverina, the weed called bindii is *Tribulus terrestis*, the one that punctures bike tyres. When it dies, its prickles are the same colour as the dirt, so the best way to pick them up is to pat your hands into the dust so the spines stick, and when both hands are full, scrape the prickles into a bucket. In February 1966 I had both hands nicely loaded when the boss sang out, 'Bill! You're wanted on the phone. Trunk call from Canberra.' We scurry when technology commands, so I raced in and grabbed the phone, holding it delicately between thumb and finger, and shedding prickles.

'Hello Bill, Ken Inglis. Would you like to teach at the university in Papua New Guinea?'

'There isn't a university in Papua New Guinea.'

'There will be when you get there.'

I thought about it for a few days. It was only for a year, until Ken could get there as the first professor of history, it'd beat teaching high school, and Ken must be near the bottom of the barrel to be ringing me. I said I'd go.

Quicker the better, Ken said: next week? On the way get some history texts. Don't know how many copies, say 50. Pretty soon, wearing prickle scars and a smallpox scab, I was in Sydney, looking for multiple copy textbooks. All I could find were two on Europe since 1789. I got about 30 of each.

The bloke next to me on the Golden Orchid flight was a carpenter, full of stories and jokes about native incompetence. I think he could see I was crook from the smallpox vaccination so was trying to cheer me up, but let's say it didn't work. After a night flight, we came over the morning coast southeast of Moresby. The land was the most brilliant green I'd ever seen, far from the gold wheat stubble I'd just left. 'Gee it's green!' I exclaimed. 'Of course it's green, mug', the carpenter's look said. The plane door opened, I stepped forward, and a blast of warm, humid air rocked me back. Crikey, I thought, I hope it cools down. It heated up.

Peter Biskup met me and took me to Ela Beach Hotel. My bed was on a verandah, under a mosquito net, next to a companionable crocodile shooter on his third bottle of rum, he thought, without much obvious effect. He asked if I'd like a nip, but I said he seemed to be managing, and for hours he told yarns about crocodiles and 'natives', mostly sympathetic. I should have had a tape recorder, but they were flash items then.

Next morning it was time to find the university. Alas, Peter said, there isn't one. No teaching materials, no office, no class-rooms, no buildings in fact. There will be pretty soon: David

Chenoweth at Adcol [Administrative College] HQ in Konedobu is knocking things together. To Kone. Tavern across the road, Chenoweth's office past a room of Papuan girls learning to type to music – click, click, click, click in 4/4 time called by a white lady up the front. This got familiar in the weeks ahead. Chenoweth explained that pretty soon a university would be set up at June Valley showground, and I'd share a house further out, in a part later named Waigani, after a swamp. Nice rural area, lot of wallabies, but alas not all that near the showground, so I'd need a car.

Turned out I was the first university teacher to come from overseas, and since I'd arrived suddenly, small things like money, food and board had been overlooked. But a car? I'd just paid off my honours year with my farm money. 'Any chance of some pay?' 'Ah, we'll get to that pretty soon. But there's the Adcol bus, and we'll have a timetable for it pretty soon.' Could be worse, I thought, though I was stretched to think how. Pretty soon I bought a second hand Holden ute with Pete Metcalf from Adcol. It was handy for shopping, taking half the Rugby team to matches, and at night dodging two-metre Papuan Black snakes stretched almost the width of the dirt track out to Waigani. I didn't know snakes so deadly could be so big. Pete is a New Zealander and took even less kindly to them. Perhaps that's why pretty soon he drove the ute over a cliff, and that was that.

No-one was sure how a university should work, and I wasn't sure what history to teach. The Preliminary Year offered four compulsory subjects, English, History, Science and Maths, at matriculation level but via uni-style lectures and tutorials. I could use those Europe since 1789 texts when they turned up, but already the crocodile shooter and the typing pool made them seem a bit incongruous. I decided the course would ask, 'Why was I teaching PNG students in Port Moresby, rather than one of them teaching me in London?' I would start with the Renaissance, when European global expansion began.

Pretty soon I met the students, one from Samoa, 53 men and four women from PNG, mostly sons or daughters of village officials, police, clerks, or mission workers. Some had grown up in Moresby; most had never been there till now; all lived in places I'd never seen. Most had finished Australian or Territory high schools; others had left school at junior level but had been chosen from clerical jobs for their ability. I doubt any had been to a lecture, or knew how things were done in a university.

If things were a trifle disorganised for me, they were a shambles for them. The men were housed first at Adcol's 6 Mile Annex, later in the June Valley workers' quarters, four to a room, pressure lamps and no tables initially, and so many mosquitoes that one wipe turned an arm from black to red. 'Mosquito nets proved futile', Rabbie Namaliu recalled. 'In the morning there were always bloodstains and dead "mozzies" stuck to one's pyjamas.' Every morning students waited for the bus, to escape, but the showground was only comparatively better. Its buildings were meant for the annual show. History was in the Tutt Bryant shed: tin roof, paper walls open at top and bottom, dirt floor, not enough seats at first so a few men sat two to a seat. They lived by the bus. Unless it broke down or the driver was drunk, it rescued them from their dorms but marooned them at the showground all day, and it brought out their food. Breakfast and tea, Martin Buluna wrote, was 'bully beef and rice or bread smeared with an unpalatable grease', while lunch, if it came, was 'sandwiches containing the same "grease" and jam, vegemite or corn beef brought out in an enormous garbage bin' which arrived about the same time as the sanitary truck.

Except for an odd trip to Ela Beach library, whatever people got in class or from the two texts and handouts was all they were going to get. They battled to write essays and prepare for tutorials, and some battled with writing English and note-taking. One day Tony Siaguru interrupted a class to ask me to explain something I said, not because he couldn't follow, but because he knew others couldn't. One or two students were uneasy that the land opposite was to be a cemetery; many were dismayed when it was proposed to change teaching breaks from terms to semesters; and often they made clear that the food was inedible. Yet they complained very little: not enough I thought, even about the food.

They did brilliantly. In the bush behind the dorms men hunted *magani* (wallaby) and explored downed planes or empty belly tanks or piles of mortar bombs or ammunition left from the Second World War, although the Papuan Blacks, as common as flies on a carcass, made that a bit chancy. They formed sports teams with Adcol and battled to get to games. They formed a Students' Representative Council and contacted the Australian National University (ANU) SRC and no doubt others. They found ways to get to the Teachers' College or Kone Tavern or the back of the Drive-In. Only one student dropped out early.

They wanted to succeed. They knew that some whites would judge not only them, but all their people, on how well they did. They made a community bonded by adversity, and across a great variety of language and background they helped each other. The end-of-year exams came with the Wet, but they waded through the deluge up to a house converted to a library and study centre, or sat on their beds studying while a torrent of water 20 centimetres deep flooded across the floor. Thirty-six matriculated, including all four women. How so many students did so well still has me bluffed, especially since everyone had to pass both science and arts subjects. Not many in Australia try that. They look back on 1966 with pride. 'The good old days', Rabbie declared in 1970.

No thanks to me. About mid-March I was told that someone else was to help teach the course. I bristled. Who says? I never did find out who said, but pretty soon the new man turned up: Hank Nelson, to teach at Adcol. Decades later I found out that until he got to Moresby he didn't know he was to teach with me either. We met. I told Hank the question my course was pivoting on, but privately I was beginning to flounder. Three lectures a week plus six tutorials plus administering the course plus helping students was heavy going. Worse, with the Renaissance I had started too far back, and too far from what students knew. I could see that I might not get to PNG 1966. This, as the man falling off Everest said, was not good.

Hank saw it straight away and had a solution. What if I continued with European expansion, and he gave a lecture a week on PNG history? Saved. Pretty soon we were getting along very well. We were country boys, we played in Aduni [combined Adcol-university] teams, and we formed a common front in defence of student interests. We double-marked everything, and amazed each other at how close our marks were: if not the same, within a mark or two. Pretty soon we could each tell what the other was thinking, which led Hank's wife Jan to dub us Mutt and Jeff, after two comic strip dills. Hank became a mate for life, and began that extraordinary journey which made him the world authority on PNG's history and people. In 1966 the few books he could find mostly dealt with PNG's administrators, but he began reading laws, reports and statistics, contrasting Papua with New Guinea, and learning from what residents and students said about their parents, people and places in war and peace. He made PNG history a discipline, and ensured that it would focus forever on the experiences of its people.

The Prelim Year's success raised a troubling question. Here was Australia setting up a university in Moresby, but doing nothing like it for Aborigines in Australia. Australia had been edging towards a PNG university for a long time. Papuans had graduated from Fiji Medical College since before the war, and from 1946 a steady trickle of PNG children, mostly boys funded privately or by the government, went to Australian schools. The 1962 United Nations report (the Foot Report) recommended a university and other reforms at the prompting of senior Moresby public servants like John Gunther, who became UPNG's first vice-chancellor. I thought reform came too slowly. Only belatedly did I see that for Aborigines it wasn't coming at all. Even now the contrast jars. Why hadn't I seen this earlier? With less excuse than most, I shared a national blindness.

Dress codes were a fetish everywhere. In Australia I was told to bring shorts, black shoes and long white socks, length just below the knee. I actually bought the things, and still have them lying around, museum items. A dress code was forced on public servants, but a university should never buckle to that. I wore thongs. That did not amuse, but it was suffered, which hinted that most whites accepted that uni students couldn't be treated like 'boongs'. Almost all dress rules were aimed at whites. Once Ken and I went to the Boroko Hotel for dinner. The dining room doorman wouldn't let us in. Ken was wearing shorts and long socks – not acceptable. 'Why not?' Ken asked. 'Part of your leg is bare.' Annoyed, Ken pointed to his socks. 'So this part of my leg is acceptable, but [pointing above his knee] this part is not?' 'Yes', said the champion of moral standards. Luckily he never got to me. We left.

By then some students and me had cracked the Boroko Hotel's bars. 'Natives' had legally been allowed to drink since 1962, but Territory hotels still had a 'white bar' and a 'native bar'. I invited some student friends for a drink at the Boroko Hotel's white bar. They didn't think it could be done, but steeled themselves. We sat quietly in the beer garden. I bought a round. Tony Siaguru went to order. He returned. 'They won't serve me.' We went back.

'Why won't you serve this man?'

'He's not properly dressed.'

'What's wrong with his dress?'

'He hasn't got proper footwear.'

'He's wearing sandals. I'm only wearing thongs, but you served me.'

Tony was served. So was Bernard Sakora. Pretty soon I was sorry for the Boroko Hotel. Most whites had promptly retreated to clubs which were almost all whites only, while day after day it had to battle dozens of drunk locals.

Cracking the Boroko Hotel was a symbolic but small expression of a big question: PNG's political future. Independence? Or independence for New Guinea, a UN Trust Territory, but a seventh Australian state for Papua, an Australian Territory? In 1907 the seventh point of the Australian flag's federal star was added for Papua, and on Ela Beach oval in October 1966 C. E. Barnes, Minister for Territories, announced that statehood was Papua's probable future. Standing in the crowd Hank and I heard that, but the snorts of derision around us said what PNG's future would be. From then on I thought that Papua Besena, which argued for Papuan separatism well into the 1970s, had as much chance as a snowflake in summer.

Independence faced big challenges. Several times I was abused for starting a Mau Mau factory, after Kenya's violent independence movement. A Dutchman kicked out of Indonesia at independence said it would serve me right if I was butchered when the 'boongs' took over. In 1967 the Moresby magazine *Black & White* warned, 'There will evolve in the Territory a clique of half-baked idiots who, by virtue of their attendance at university whose degrees mean nothing, will set themselves up as intellectuals and social leaders of their own people.' Awful prospect! I got plenty of this, but it couldn't last, and pretty soon it mostly went underground.

The Prelim Year signalled another challenge, for it breached a policy of advancing all PNG children evenly through a basic school system, instead creating an elitist few, skilled in Western ways but de-skilled in village ways, and in this sense sacrifices to nationhood. Today, unemployed school leavers trained for offices which aren't there, but unable or unwilling to return home, often form criminal gangs which are among PNG's major problems. On the other hand, there were no Highlanders in the 1966 Prelim Year, though Joe Nombri was at Adcol. There was no-one from some other districts either, but so large and populous a region was not represented largely because the oldest Highland schools had not been going long enough, while some parts had no schools at all, and others had never seen an outsider. How to balance that against coastal areas which began getting local government in 1962, and which had good roads and schools though not enough, a better telecom system than Australia, flourishing rural industries and the first undergraduates?

But to ask if is to ask when. Once an independence movement emerged, it was wise to meet its cutting edge rather than wait for those who had never heard of it. In 1975, as Hank observed, many Highlanders became independent without ever being dependent, post-colonial without ever being colonial. Without ever being national either: the notion that the state might own their land, or even have a say in it, is still preposterous, and not only in the Highlands.

Enter Tony Voutas. We knew each other at ANU, and now Tony was planning for independence. In October Pete Metcalf and I walked with him out from Menyamya patrol post in Morobe Province while he contested a by-election for Kaindi, a House of Assembly seat. We walked village by village to the edge of uncontrolled country, and at nights Tony called meetings, or we would go to a prayer meeting, wait till the missionary finished, and Tony would explain what a parliament, a vote, a candidate was, and ask for their votes. What is Moresby?, people asked. If you're going there, how can you be helping us? Will the *kiaps* vote for you? What does the missionary say?

One day, as Pete and I were resting on a grass hillside (Tony didn't need rests), I asked Tony how he could work for independence without a political party. He answered that pretty soon he was going to Moresby to talk to Papua New Guinean trade union leaders, hoping to form an independence party.

'How much to join?'

'About $2. We must get Papua New Guineans to join.'

'Here's my money.' Ever since, I've been under the delusion that I was the first paid-up member of the Pangu Pati, formed early in 1967.

On another grassy hill I asked, 'When do you think independence might come?'

'I don't know,' Tony said, 'perhaps by the turn of the century.'

'That's soon. We might live to see it.'

It came in less than a decade. Tony's dogged and skilful strategy and tactics, Michael Somare's charisma, and Australians aware that it was better to give independence than have it taken, achieved the miraculous.

From Menyamya, pretty soon we were back in Lae. Horrie Niall, Morobe District Commissioner, heard of it, and sent a *kiap* to track us down. He found us that night, and in a friendly way asked Pete and I when we were leaving. As it happened we were off to Moresby the next day, so after a beer he left, but Niall's threat was obvious. Tony said that was nothing to what he sometimes copped, but also that many outstation *kiaps* helped him, and some supported his quiet, determined crusade.

I made only one other trip out of Moresby; to walk the Kokoda track with Wayne Fitzherbert. We travelled light: blanket, bandaids, torch, toilet paper, tins of meat to trade for fruit and vegetables. From Kokoda we walked up to Isurava rest house, with beautiful views across a valley to houses which seemed next door, but even for local people were a day's walk away, down and up. The night seemed so cold that I left a tin of meat open for breakfast, and got food poisoning. I must have passed out above Templeton's Crossing, but Fitz shepherded me along. War relics were everywhere: Jap helmets, piles of cartridges, green signal wire threading the trees, neatly squared Jap ambush pits, the metal of an Owen gun with a live bullet in the breech, in the villages plane parts. Parts of the track were overgrown, and wading creeks was tricky: we got through OK, but heard later that an army team out at the same time got lost, and a man died. The village men were wonderfully hospitable, typical country people, making sure we had water and tucker, inviting us to church meetings, showing us war relics, yarning in the rest houses at night. We had only four days, and by Ioribaiwa Ridge we were behind time thanks to me, so two men agreed to carry our packs up. One twisted his knee and it swelled up, but he wouldn't turn back. He got a switch of stinging-nettle tree and whipped his injured knee. All the way up that ridge he grabbed a fresh switch whenever he passed a stinging tree, whipping his knee constantly. Thought nothing of it. I tried it years later, though not nearly for as long; it doesn't ease pain or swelling, but it stops stiffening. From the bottom of Imita Ridge, Fitz pushed on for Ower's Corner, but night caught me short of the top. I sat under my blanket in pouring rain on a giant tree root, brilliant fireflies of different colours bobbing through the jungle. Unforgettable.

Both trips were short and late in the year. This was a pity. Public servants and uni staff appointed after me got a 'famil' – a trip to somewhere else in the country. Until October 1966 all I did was to go to every roadhead out of Moresby: Idler's Bay around the harbour, Kwikila down the coast, Lea Lea up the coast and by canoe across the river to the village, Vanapa and Brown Rivers past rubber and teak plantations inland. None gave an inkling of the rest of the country. For someone teaching

PNG students this was not good, but I fell between a 'famil' policy gap. Price of pioneering.

In November I left Moresby, and pretty soon was back patting bindiis. I didn't say goodbye to the students: some were still doing exams, and I didn't want a fuss. But I didn't forget them, and some are still my friends. Most would be important to an independent PNG. Rabbie Namaliu and Mekere Morauta became prime minister, Bart Philemon became a minister, others became department heads or ambassadors or church leaders, many did valuable work for their country in Moresby or the bush. Back at ANU I raised a few funds for Pangu and distributed publicity, and kept in touch as Hank and Ken steadily promoted PNG history and UPNG flourished. I went back to teach in 1972, free-loading off Hank for the first semester, and in 1973 replacing him in teaching PNG history. I kept his main tutorial method: distribute notes on the broad context, ask a student to tell of the experiences of family or clan on the topic, then ask the group to relate this to their own districts. I have never learnt so much in class, never been in a happier department, and never been so certain that Tony was right in 1966, when he argued that the key task was to persuade white and black that Papua New Guineans could run their country.

13

NOT A *MISIS*

Christine Stewart

It was the racism that got to me most. Soon after I arrived in 1968, I found myself in the bar of some Highlands hotel, sipping a glass of excellent red wine while an officious young (Australian) man offered me his opinion of the country and its people. 'They're all rock apes', he slurred, 'just bloody rock apes, still not down from the trees.'

There didn't seem much point in taking issue with the assertion that rock apes lived in trees. He was wearing a sparkling clean white shirt, and for a few moments I entertained the highly satisfying vision of reaching out and gently pouring red, red wine all over his head and down the front of that white, white shirt. I didn't do it though, just wandered away. It would have been such a waste of good wine.

I went to PNG to get married. Simple as that. Not to a clerk, not to a missionary or a doctor or a teacher or a businessman. And *of course* not to a 'native' – in 1968, only the bravest of white women were prepared to risk community ostracism and try that, and very few of those unions lasted. No, Tony Voutas was a patrol officer, a *kiap*, with some thoroughly unpatriotic ideas about the colonial enterprise. He was supposed to be 'sorting his head out' through degree studies at ANU when I met him at some intervarsity do in 1964. I was dumbfounded. I couldn't believe someone could think such things and live in such ways and places.

I grew up longing to escape the unbearable boredom of Sydney suburbia, where I had been raised on a diet of *Women's Weekly*, dreams of 'going home' to England, rope petticoats and rock'n'roll. Girls of that era were supposed to become teachers, nurses or secretaries. A few of the more capable were sent on to higher education, mainly to enable them to catch a better class of husband, but at Sydney University I accidentally stumbled into anthropology. Okay, I thought, what's to study? People the world over are basically the same, aren't they? Doing the same things (though in various National Geographic settings, some may have quaint and colourful marriage ceremonies and the like)? By the end of first year, however, my mind was blown. Okay, we might do it this way, but almost everyone else every-where else does it differently, and in many instances, far better. There were other ways to live and other goals to reach for. I wanted out of this future, this country. I had no idea what else lay out there, but I wanted to find out. This is what saved me. This, and meeting Tony. He was the answer to my ill-formed dreams.

Unfortunately, he didn't think so at the time, and after a brief romance conducted mainly by mail between Canberra and Sydney, he dumped me and headed back to PNG where a timely by-election shape-shifted him from a *kiap* to a Member of the House of Assembly, the colonial version of a parliament. Seems I would have to make my escape alone. The backpacker, overland-to-London movement hadn't yet begun so, pretending to gather material for a Masters degree which I never completed, I took myself off to Indonesia, proudly independent for nearly two decades and steeped in millennia-long traditions of urbanisation, monetary trade, hierarchical societies, exotic religions and culture. I might have stayed in Indonesia, might have become an academic specialising in Indonesian literature, but then out of the blue Tony wrote me a letter, in essence proposing marriage. But, he warned me, don't rush in. You should come and see the place before you make up your mind.

A new general election was looming. Tony was campaigning all over Morobe District, which in those days meant light plane to some remote outpost followed by days of walking and talking. He didn't have much time for a prospective wife. After I extracted myself from Jakarta and home to Sydney, he emerged from the jungle and called me with detailed travel instructions before disappearing again. 'Fly to Port Moresby', he told me, 'then on to Bulolo. Then catch a "passenger truck" to Mumeng, where you will stay with my friend John and his wife. I'll get in touch with you there.'

For one who had gaily traversed Java and Bali by train and bus as well as on the trusty Vespa, encountering no more difficulties than having to locate decent two-stroke mix or to bargain hard with *betjak* drivers, these instructions posed no problems.

I alighted from the Bulolo-bound DC-3 on to an airstrip miles from anywhere, to be met by an airline agent who was dumb-founded by my request to be pointed in the direction of the nearest passenger truck.

It must have been such a shock for him. Of course, I didn't realise at the time that I was breaking all the rules in the unwritten book of Good Colonialist Conduct. He dropped me at some intersection where one bush-lined dirt road met another, and there I waited, trusting. Before long, a truck hove into sight and pulled up with much scrunching of gravel. I was rapidly established in the front seat with the driver and *boskru*, brightly trying out my very recently acquired and minimal Tok Pisin (courtesy of teaching tapes borrowed from a friend at Monash University). Everybody aboard clearly knew Tony, and I made my first linguistic mistake of many, saying no I was not his wife, just a friend. *Pren tasol* (just a 'friend'). I didn't realise, then, that this term had semantic overtones of the most lascivious kind. People didn't usually live in sin in PNG, or even in Australia, in 1968. I didn't realise, either, when I was installed in a little administration house at Mumeng station, with John the agricultural officer and his wife – who both just happened to be Papua New Guinean – that a white *misis* (a term used only for colonial women whether married or not) stayed with white people.

By day Tony and I discussed whether or not to get married, as we slithered up and down impossibly steep tracks, through leech-ridden beech forests, over ridiculously high mountains. I began to appreciate the subtleties of *longwe liklik* (a fairly long way) and *klostu tasol* (fairly close) and learned how to avoid freezing when river-bathing at 5,000 feet. In the evenings, I went with Tony to watch and listen at campaign meetings around a campfire. My Tok Pisin improved in leaps and bounds. So did my understanding of the place and its people.

I started to realise that there was a black-white divide, but I still attributed it to the utter remoteness of those mountain villages. I had seen similar in Java. Anthropologists pitched their tents in places like these and drew up kinship tables, didn't they? I came from a social set which protested the White Australia policy and partied with Indonesian Colombo Plan students, but our main cause was the war in Vietnam, not racism in the colonies. We believed in equality, peace and freedom, Bob Dylan sang to us of the death of the establishment, and we truly thought that if we protested loudly enough, those stodgy over-thirties people would eventually see reason, the bombs would cease falling and everyone would be free, rich and happy.

Even when we married, in a civil ceremony conducted in Lae in the office of the District Commissioner, the fact that Tony's *manki masta* (*kiaps* did not have *haus bois*!) was the only Papua New Guinean present at the ceremony did not tell me much.

We were staying at the time with a couple from the Buang area, in the mountains south of Lae, in what was known as the 'Admin Compound', where 'native' government employees – the drivers, the cleaners, the petty clerks – were housed in tiny fibro two-roomers with hot wood-burning stoves inside and bucket toilets outside. I thought nothing of these conditions – I had encountered far worse in Indonesia, particularly in the toilet department – and this house was often our lodging in Lae until we built our own in a new 'mixed' suburb. From the lady of the house I learned about ways to cook local vegetables and the efficacy of love magic (the stories she told!); and from a teenage son who was appointed my guide and companion, a whole new geography of the walking routes around the town. Another rule broken – whites were not supposed to walk, they drove.

At the time, I was too caught up in a daze of wonder. We whisked ourselves away from the champagne to head up the Bulolo road back to Mumeng, where not one but two wedding feasts awaited us – one at John's household, the other further up the hill at the house of an amazing 'old-timer', a wartime coastwatcher, and Aid Post Orderly, Eric Robson, who had recently married a tiny young woman from the nearby Buang area. I think that at some stage Eric had an Australian family, or ex-family, somewhere, but they had long vanished from the scene, and Lakeli had recently been presented to Eric upon his request for a bride to manage him and his household. I was told how the resident missionary had steadfastly refused to perform the ceremony, until Eric threatened: marry us or we'll live in sin!

In a year or two the happy couple produced a baby boy, who died tragically of pneumonia only a few months later. Eric's medical experience told him that the baby needed antibiotics and oxygen, fast, but he could not leave his duties at Mumeng, so he sent Lakeli and the baby posthaste to the hospital in Bulolo, with all the necessary paperwork. But when she arrived at the white wing of the hospital (all hospitals were segregated then) she was ordered away to the 'black' wing. While she stood there at the foot of the steps arguing, the baby expired in her arms.

In Mumeng we enjoyed all the amenities of a bush materials house with the bathroom by the front door, and a stunning view of the surrounding mountains. But we soon realised that we had to leave. Tony's new electorate took in the entire District, and Lae was its centre. We built a house in a new 'low-covenant' suburb, which was open to all; it was one of the first integrated areas of the town. I hadn't lived there long before I started realising plenty. There was official and unofficial segregation. The town of Lae at the time boasted two movie theatres, in the classic Australian design of front and back stalls downstairs, and the more expensive dress circle upstairs. In 1968, whites sat upstairs in the circle, blacks sat downstairs in the stalls. Everyone seemed happy that way, except me and Tony. He told me how he had tried to make a point by taking his erstwhile Buang hosts' daughter on a date to sit upstairs, but she was desperately uncomfortable. When we later made friends with three other Australian couples living in Lae, we finally discovered the secret of integrated movie-going. We sat in the back stalls, along with a handful of like-minded whites and a growing number of working, English-speaking Papua New Guineans.

Moresby was the territory's administrative centre, in close contact with Canberra and obliged to follow the 'official' rules. But Lae was a company town and made many of its own rules. Picture theatre seating wasn't its only issue. When he was elected as the Regional Member, Tony urged me to go along to the monthly Lae Women's Club luncheons. I demurred. The *Women's Weekly* had taught me all about the Australian society cult. This time, the local newspaper came to my rescue, and I triumphantly showed Tony the write-up of the most recent of these events. 'Mrs A, the wife of the manager of B company, in oatmeal linen,' it read. 'Mrs C, the wife of the manager of

D company, in pale blue crimplene … '. 'But this is all about clothes!' my emancipated spouse exclaimed in horror. 'Shall I go in my denim culottes and jungle boots?' I asked sweetly. No more was said about the luncheons, and I explained to the wives-of that I was usually out of town 'patrolling' with Tony, though one determined soul did ask me when we met in the street one day whether I would distribute some Girl Guide materials next time I headed out. Umm.

When Lae became too stifling, and even the lure of the bush patrol palled, we would fly off to Moresby for a House of Assembly meeting. I became the fledgling Pangu Pati's typist, translator, speech-writer, researcher and general factotum, and was even granted special permission to install myself at Tony's desk in a tiny shared office in the old Parliament House Members' wing. Too bad about the anthropology! Too bad about Indonesian literature, too. I eventually discontinued the MA. Instead, I learned plenty about colonial politics, an enormous amount about parliamentary processes, and very little about economics (no matter how patiently Tony tried to explain the principles to me). Most importantly, I came to realise that there were more ways of being a lawyer than standing up and looking good in court. I discovered legislative drafting.

I steadfastly refused to be a good colonial *misis*. I refused even to be a wife-of. When I visited the immigration office in Moresby after marriage to change my visa status, I was told that my occupation would henceforth be 'housewife'. Just like everyone else, I was told reassuringly, that's what we do. Again I demurred, and eventually we settled on 'student' – that MA program had to be good for something.

And then there was the dress code. By this time, the late 1960s, Papua New Guineans were legally allowed to drink, and their entry into bars and hotels was, in theory, unrestricted. But hoteliers had ways of keeping out undesirably-coloured patrons. Dress codes, for example requiring men to wear long trousers with shoes and socks, or shorts with sandals and long socks (the standard *kiap* garb), ensured that only the most highly-placed people patronised expatriate watering holes. Even that didn't always work. The Pangu Pati leader Michael Somare was caught out once, when he came through Lae to stay with us. We gathered up one of our friends, the Lae-based *Post-Courier* reporter, to go to dinner with us at the Melanesian hotel, but the future Prime Minister had on only sandals and trousers, and we were all turned away. We dined at the local Chinese, got very drunk, and rolled home in our battered VW singing loudly and composing tomorrow's indignant press statement.

I still claim to be one of the first white women to appear at an official function in a *meri* blouse. Towards the end of that second House of Assembly, Canberra tried to initiate proto-nationalism by devising a 'National Day'. All the MHAs, and their wives if they were in town, were invited to lunch by the Administrator in the Government House gardens. National Day? Hmmm. I took myself off to the Koki store of Luk Poi Wai, the town tailor, and selected a bright cotton hibiscus print fabric for a made-to-measure blouse. It made quite a splash, with Honourable Members rushing up one after the other to congratulate me and tell me how good I looked. Officialdom was stupefied. One *misis* actually got up the courage to say: 'It must be very ... er ... cool?' 'Very', I responded sweetly.

In 1972, four years after my arrival, we left Lae and the rugged wonder of the mountain ranges which cradled it, rising 13,000 feet to Mt Sarawaged to the north and 8,000 to Mt Shungol to the south. Tony passed the stewardship of the electorate to a young Papua New Guinean successor. We came to Moresby, he to teach politics at the university and me to work for the newly elected Chief Minister Somare. After only one semester, Tony ended up in the Chief's office and I, inspired by what I had learned working for the Pangu Pati and determined to draft legislation, started a law degree at UPNG.

The university then was a cutting-edge scene of assimilation. It was brand-new and staffed by hand-picked academics from all around the world, determined to bring tertiary education (at last!) to the country. I found myself, utterly terrified, in a class almost entirely composed of this new generation, the few rare individuals who had succeeded in battling their way through the various levels of school and the tight selection process to end up in the university. It was especially hard for the girls, most of whom had to contend with parental disapproval of schooling for girls and the ever-present threat of pregnancy.

By second semester, my classmates and I ceased being strangers and started becoming friends. We studied together, partied together, and each vacation I would beg someone to take me home to their village if I paid the airfare. This is how I found my family, in a village down the coast to the east of Moresby. A classmate invited me to visit, along with one of our teachers, and I fell in love with this cluster of houses built in the water at a river-mouth. I became my classmate's 'brother', and his family became mine. I studied the language, performed my clan allegiances and joined ineptly but enthusiastically in the dancing and singing at Christmas time. In town, I networked with a host of new relatives, both resident and visiting.

In 1972 the Pangu Pati confounded Canberra by forging a coalition with other leaders and political parties to take over the third House of Assembly and install Somare as the first Chief Minister. Thanks to this 'bloodless coup', racial barriers began to collapse. We law students did our bit, taking on the dress code. When a bar opened at Jackson's Airport, with the usual nitpicking requirements as to trousers, socks, sandals and so on for the men, a dozen or so of us headed out there one afternoon in September 1975, men in trousers, women (Papua New Guinean and expatriate) in *meri* blouses, all with thongs or bare feet. The story and photograph made the front page of the newspaper the following day.

Somewhere along the way to that law degree I lost the marriage, and after the usual trauma Tony landed in Canberra working to help set up what eventually was to become AusAID. I stayed on to complete my studies, moving into the girls' dorm on campus, sharing a room with my classmate 'sister'. She told me one day, laughing, that some of the girls had asked her: 'What's it like sharing with a white girl?' She shrugged. 'Same as sharing with any other girl', she replied.

But it didn't last. In 1976 I left PNG for a life in rural Australia. Jumping ship was commonplace for expatriates at the time. Independence had arrived and the terms Mau Mau and Kikuyu were being bandied around. Others simply felt it was time for them to bow out and hand over the reins. My reasons were a little different. One important motivation was that PNG had shown me how incompetent I was at basic survival. It seemed to me that civilisation was only a veneer available for the lucky few. I felt that if I were to be a complete citizen of this world, I had to learn to hew my own wood and draw my own water.

When I returned, more than a decade later at the end of the 1980s, I thought nobody would recognise me. I thought I would recognise nothing of Moresby. Instead, I felt instantly at home, and my classmates, now all grown up and running the country, welcomed me as if I had been absent for just a few months. I told them how much PNG had given me. They told me in return that I should restore the balance and give something back. Jobs were offered, there was plenty to be done.

There were changes. The first I noticed was that all the trees we had planted in that dust bowl of a town were now full-grown, casting green, leafy shade. No longer did we 'expatriates' get to choose whether to live in a comfy bungalow in Boroko or 'Town', or to make a statement by heading for Hohola or Tokarara. By the 1990s, we were being herded into apartment blocks and compounds with security guards at the gate.

I also noted a significant shift in attitudes – now it was PNG villagers who were surprised at my behaviour. I still wanted to visit the villages of my family and friends, still wanted to be absorbed into whatever was going on, to dress, eat, perform as they did. I stayed one Easter with a very dear friend in a Rigo village, not far by road from Moresby. We were entertained on Good Friday evening with a special treat: the village *peroveta* choir – word had got out that I loved this Central Province LMS (London Missionary Society)-inspired style of hymn-singing, with its weaving melodies and heavy bass counterpoints. So to reciprocate, my friend and I spent one afternoon baking scones in a camp oven and preparing huge pots of tea. We invited the *peroveta* singers and served them where they sat in a huge circle in front of the house. My friend was scolded afterwards for letting me 'work'.

I started to wonder what had happened during those intervening years to make villagers marvel at my unplanned demonstrations of equality and anti-racism. It seemed I was still fighting the same battles – but now I wasn't trying to persuade white colonials but Papua New Guineans. It seemed as if they had absorbed the myths of colonisation. There was the self-deprecation: we've had so many changes of government; women can't get ahead in the Public Service; there is so much corruption now; and worst of all to my mind: we weren't ready for Independence, the time of the *mastas* was better. Maybe some of the sentiments were genuine apologies, maybe sometimes they were simply attempts to curry favour or wheedle a *haus meri* job out of me. Whichever, I went to great lengths to try to explain how many of these issues were commonplace worldwide, and yes, in Australia too.

Many decades have passed since I stepped off that DC-3. The big change, from my point of view, is in the now openly-expressed aversion to foreigners meddling in internal affairs. A kind of reverse racism on the part of Papua New Guineans? But still the unease persists in Australia, fanned by media reportage which tries to scare up fear of damage to Australia, whether it be from fallout from the Rabaul volcanic eruption in 1994 or the threat of disease spreading insidiously throughout the country via Torres Strait and northern Queensland. Now PNG has been through its latest political crisis, the government change of 2011 and the elections of 2012, and as usual, has survived. Some may take this as proof that 'they still can't govern themselves'. For me, it shows how, after all this time, Papua New Guineans are truly taking charge. They're just not necessarily playing by our rules. And who am I to say what is right and what is wrong?

14
INTERVIEW WITH DAME MEG TAYLOR

Interview conducted by Ceridwen Spark in Melbourne, 25 June 2013

CS   Meg, I know you were a child at the time, but I wonder if
        you could tell me a bit about your recollections of the roles
        played by Australians in PNG during the pre-Independence
        decade?

MT   Living in the Highlands at that time was an elegant life-
        style, and Goroka was a very beautiful town. It was a well
        laid out town with trees and gardens and amenities for
        a good life. There was a distinct difference between the
        lives Australians were living and the lives of the Papua New
        Guineans. And because we were Jim's daughters, we had
        access to parts of the Australian community, but not to all
        of it. We had our lives with our extended family and friends.
        We had our world of the Asaro valley and the Wahgi valley

and we belonged to it. Our interaction with the Australians in our community was different. When I think back it was clear that we were always on the edges. I always felt that I was on the edge watching. I was going off to boarding school in Australia and when we came back for school holidays, it was fabulous, because the Rotary Club in Goroka put on all sorts of interesting activities for the young people, so it was a busy time, very active with lots of sporting activities. This, of course, was for the children of Australians who had gone away to school and I was part of it because I had been away as well. I had good friends growing up. I grew up with Australians whose whole lives were in the Highlands and this was their home: families that settled and whose lives were entwined with my family, families like the Greatheads that still remain an intrinsic part of my life.

CS   Discussing expatriates in PNG, people often talk about missionaries, mercenaries and misfits. Does that ring true for you? Or do you have another perception of the types of people who were in PNG at that time?

MT   There were some fantastic personalities. When I reminisce about some of them, I remember with great humour how life was lived. There weren't any inhibitions. I mean the personalities that used to hang out at the Goroka Hotel, the Gillies brothers and Danny Fleck, their view of the world, the way I watched them live their lives. They were completely oblivious to all the norms of a society that in many ways in Goroka was pretty straight-laced. And then of course you had the missionaries. You had people who'd come there to spread the gospel. You had the Catholic Church, the Church of England, the Lutheran congregation and their work at Asaroka, and the Seventh Day Adventists and their establishment at Kabiufa. There were also missionaries living in the community, in villages. There were distinct groups: government people, private sector people, people who were on coffee farms or plantations, and missionaries. And then there would have been people who came to the university, the Teachers' College when it was established, the medical institute [Institute of Medical Research (IMR)], and they were a very different kind of people because they actually had relationships with Papua New Guineans. And, as I observed, this was a different interaction.

CS   Prior to that most of the Australians had lived in their own enclaves almost?

MT   There were those of my father's friends who had either married or had Papua New Guinean women in their lives, and I think that wasn't ... people turned up their noses against men who had taken Highland women as wives. Jim actually didn't encourage us to socialise a lot with people, with society in town. He could never understand why I wanted that interaction. But when you've been away at boarding school, and you've got a lot of energy, you want to be doing things with other young people. Growing up as a teenager, was it easy in Goroka? Yes, it was an easy place to live and it was a wonderful place to be alive and explore. Did I have a social conscience about it all? No. That came later. Did I know I belonged to a different world? Yes.

CS   Apart from his own group of friends, did Jim pretty much keep to himself?

MT   Yes, on the whole, though he had very good friends who shared his interests. Jim also wanted his space and time to read and think. He was busy with the coffee and he was busy up in Porgera. He had his close Papua New Guinean friends and his family, of course. He had friends who were missionaries, tradesmen, farmers, aviators, academics and retired administrators. His close friends until the end were George and Nell Greathead, Marie and Bill O'Brien and Joe Searson, and of course he maintained his friendship with the Leahys [with whom he explored the Highlands in the 1930s]. He was very close to a lot of the Catholic priests, those that he knew in the early days of pioneering, and later the bishops who had come to head the Diocese of Goroka. On the whole he was a man who had made choices in his life that had ensured his exclusion from Australian society in PNG and in Australia. So he became a self-contained person and I think he thought that we should be the same.

CS   There was also an element of protecting you too, wasn't there, an element of protecting you from people's prejudice perhaps? Is that one of the reasons he wanted you to remain separate?

MT   I think so, but he never articulated it. He spoke to us, to me and my sister, Metahe (fondly known as Daisy) of how our lives would or should evolve. I am sure he worried for us. He need not have. Our lives have been rich beyond measure.

CS   What are some of the things that you think Australians gained from being in PNG in the period 1960–75? There are lots of different ways to consider this question.

MT   The interesting aspect for me is this. Many of my friends in Australia are those Australians who grew up in the Highlands of PNG, and then left because their parents left or they had opportunities that they pursued in Australia. For many of them there is a tie to PNG that will never be broken, and it binds them to each other. So what is it that binds them? It is a sense of an identity from the country that wasn't in the long term theirs, but one that emotionally they still belong to, and that still holds them all together. It is where they grew up and it is where they belonged at an early age. Many still go back to the Highlands. It's interesting to see that children of my friends have now gone back to work there, and to start businesses there. They've got relationships with the people who were in their households when they were children and who worked for their families, and they still have that link. Some of them have family that are buried there, and they go back to visit their family graves, and show a keen interest in the country. And it's almost as if they never left. The question for me is when they went back to Australia, where and how did they fit in? Their identity was not derived from Australia; their identity was derived from PNG. So what they got out of it was a sense of who they were, in a country that gave them opportunity, life, and for some, deep friendships they still nurture.

CS   You've spoken about that in relation to your friends in Brisbane and Sydney specifically, but do you think that you would extrapolate and say that's the case for many of the people you know who have spent a lot of time in PNG?

MT   Absolutely, absolutely. PNG gets under the skin and it holds you to her.

CS   That it gave them a place they didn't find in Australia, a belonging maybe?

MT   Yes, but sometimes it's important to remind them that their memories should not be caught in a time warp. The country that was their home has changed and it's moved on and it's got challenges, and I think the braver souls accommodate that change, and know that there are challenges. For others, particularly for friends who worked at the IMR, it was a deep relationship in terms of a rich professional experience, but also in allowing rich relationships with the communities they were working with, and invested in. I think it was and is a different dynamic for them.

CS   Yes, PNG certainly seems to occupy a very special place in the hearts of many Australians who've lived there.

MT   I remember when the country was on the verge of self-government and independence, amongst some groups of people in the Highlands there was real resistance, and a concern, particularly about the future, that Papua New Guineans weren't ready for it. When I went to the University

of Papua New Guinea, I got very involved in the self-government movement and the Pangu Pati. I got a letter from a
family friend in the Highlands who was not pleased with
my activities. Jim, on the other hand, had a very different
view. You see, we came from a situation where our father
was always encouraging of Papua New Guineans being
educated and to be preparing to run the country, and that
was something Jim espoused in the 1940s. And for him, the
arrival of self-government was no threat. It was the transition from a country under Australian administration to one
moving to find its own destiny.

CS   He welcomed it?

MT   He did. I then went to work with Michael Somare, who
      was Chief Minister at the time of self-government and
      Independence. When Papua New Guinean citizenship
      was offered, Jim was one of the first in the Highlands to
      become a citizen of PNG. Others chose not to, because
      they didn't want to be second-class citizens, and that was
      their choice. Jim didn't see it that way. For him this was
      the completion of the commitment that he'd made. Does
      it mean that he denied his origins? No, not at all. But it
      was his adopted country, and the country where his wife
      came from, and I think he was very clear about that. And
      there were young people that he spent time with, young
      men from the university, that became his friends who were
      Papua New Guineans, like Rabbie Namaliu and Leo Hannett,
      and they would come and visit and stay when we were at
      university and spend time with our family. His friendships

with the leaders of an independent PNG endured till his death when Rabbie and Leo stood with us to bury him in Gahuku soil.

CS   So what changes in that Australia/PNG relationship have you observed since Independence?

MT   I think one of the biggest concerns I have is the lack of understanding of PNG. For Australia, it's almost as if the horizon is over that island to Bali, then to Hong Kong and beyond to China. Or it is across the Pacific to Fiji because it's a tourist destination and then to the USA or to the UK? Do Australians care about what happens in PNG? I think some people do. I think the majority don't. So I would say that there is a lack of an honest and close relationship with the people next door.

CS   Do you think that that's shifted in the last 30 or 40 years? Do you think Australians used to know a lot more about PNG than they do now?

MT   I think there was a whole generation who had fought there during World War Two and they had deep and profound memories. I remember when I was a student in Australia, and people would ask me where I was from, and when I said PNG, they'd reply, 'Oh I was there during the war', and you'd have conversations with all these men who wanted to talk to you because it was part of their history. That doesn't exist any longer. I think it's fantastic now that there is a resurgence of interest through young people coming to

Kokoda, because I think that's a way of building bridges again, a way in which groups of Australians can understand what Kokoda meant for their fathers and now for them, and hopefully build relationships with Papua New Guineans. There were also Australians who had worked in PNG or had settled there. They knew the country.

CS   But you feel generally that we've really moved away from Australians knowing much about PNG?

MT   Yes indeed. Just look at the press reports. It's always the things that go wrong that get the press coverage, but the positives of the country are never looked at, or rarely looked at. Look at all the negative commentary about PNG when the issue of asylum seekers, boat people, is raised. People in PNG are interested in Australia, and we [Papua New Guineans] should know more about our neighbour as well. But it's hard to get to know your neighbour when it has been so hard to get a visa for the average person in my country. I realise that there are efforts to make the process easier so we will see how it goes. I often think Australia takes PNG for granted. Things are changing with China now in the picture in PNG.

CS   It will be interesting to see if the visa situation does change.
       Sometimes when I go to PNG, people I meet say, 'It was better when the Australians were here'.

MT   That's true.

CS   What do you think that's about? Can you comment on that?

MT   I think it's about governance, about services, systems that work, that you could get medicine, have access to schools, the primary schools, and in the villages, the system of administration. When there were problems somebody would come and deal with it. During the time of Australia things were better because there was a structure and a system that worked. It's not about the laws, it's about the order. Most people thrive when there's a structure that they can work within, and I think now it's who knows whom and who can do something for somebody else. I am interested in what has been happening in the Papuan community. There are many people who believe that their citizenship as Australians was taken away from them by the declaration of Independence, and they have a right to be Australian citizens. So there's been a real movement there. I've been living away quite a time so I think a lot of the pains of the last decade I've not felt as much as others, but you pick it up in conversations, and you also see a lot of women moving to Australia to live, because it's about their security in PNG.

CS   So do you have any comments on the current Australian government relationship with PNG?

MT   Well, I was surprised it took Prime Minister Gillard so long to visit PNG. Quite disappointed actually. That's what I'm saying. One looks over this island nation to the next bit of land, and it's taken for granted that the country right next door will always be an ally. I don't think that anybody should take anyone for granted. Other powers in the region have interests now in PNG, and Australia is no longer the biggest investor. So it will be interesting how we both manage those relationships over the next decade. I think that what ties my generation to Australia is the fact that we were educated there, we made friends there, we share an interest in the same sports, cultural activities. But there are generations after us who've never had that experience. Yes, everybody will watch the State of Origin tonight, between Queensland and New South Wales, and that takes on a whole life of its own in PNG, and it gives people something to be interested in, and it does tie Australia to the people of PNG, which is really interesting. It's quite a phenomenon, I think, because a lot of those people have never set foot in Australia, but it's this love of the sport, and the heroes are those who are playing rugby league. It's fascinating. And building stronger ties on a shared love of the sport would be worthwhile. I think the Australian Rugby League Federation has been doing a lot in PNG. And now there's the cricket. There's been a real interest in cricket again, which is really great. It is important to rebuild these relationships that were there pre-Independence, and for 10 to 20 years after, which then started to deteriorate. With this current government, I'm not privy to the intimacies of the relationship. Like every other Papua New Guinean, I see the diplomatic interchange and read of the officials that come to visit. So I'll be interested to see how the next government does things.

CS   Politicians say all the right things, don't they, about their special relationship and the unique ties?

MT   Yes, and I think Papua New Guineans know the support that we get from Australia financially. We're not oblivious to that, and there is an understanding of it. But I think there was concern a couple of years ago that with this large contingent of consultants coming into the country, a lot of the money was going to pay Australian consultants, and questions were asked about the impact of Australian aid. I think that was a bit of a shake-up, which was good.

CS   So what role do you think Australia should take in PNG, now and in the future?

MT   Both our countries should be constant in our engagement and focused on the long-term relationship that we share. Greater respect from Australia for the challenges PNG faces, and from our side a respect for the taxpayer who contributes to Australia's financial support for our country. It has to be as human as that. The diplomats will find the language to craft the shared interests, but it is people who share values. There are new players in the Pacific region: China, Malaysia and the USA. China is paying much greater attention to the region.

CS   And is now more present?

MT   And is now more present.

CS   So Australia's probably got a role to play between PNG and China as well?

MT   Yes, to some extent, but PNG is establishing its own relationship with China.

CS   I wonder if you could reflect on some of the gains and losses that PNG has experienced since Independence?

MT   There is a strong current of nationalism in PNG but also a realisation that we have greater challenges than we anticipated. We gained our independence. That in itself is a great achievement. The right to self-determination is an achievement. For the first 20 years after Independence the country ran efficiently. In the later years I think the challenges have been much tougher. The gains are harder to account for when you have social indicators showing very poor results on health and education. There remains the challenges of poor delivery of services, lack of infrastructure and lack of good governance in some of our institutions. The reality of governing ourselves gives opportunities for developing our resources, but it also presents challenges in ensuring a better life for our people. So gains versus challenges. We are in the challenge box right now.

CS   Did you ever identify with the Australian side of your family?

MT   I think some of my personal feelings were that there were and are racial overtones with my English and Australian family, no doubt about it. Were there racial overtones in Goroka and the Highlands toward bi-racial children like me, and Papua New Guineans? Yes. Independence gave me my public identity. I always knew where I came from and my place in our mother's tribal society. I think we've always felt our identity was very much ingrained with our people in the Highlands and as Papua New Guineans. I have many good friends in the Aboriginal communities in the north-west and with settler Australians, but Australia is not my country. There is much about your country that I care about. Members of my family have settled in Australia. I want the best for our countries and would hope that we foster better and enduring relations.

CS   Did you feel that there were divisions in the Goroka community that you grew up in?

MT   Yes, of course. In the early days of settlement the town was divided. We had the ability to move in between because we came from two worlds, but it wasn't as if Jim was a serious part of the Australian community. John Gunther, the first vice-chancellor of UPNG and former [Assistant] Administrator, told me that Jim was ostracised by the Australian community for his views and his decision to marry my mother. So when Jim left the government, and shared a life with Yerima, they made it very difficult for him, so he virtually kept away from them and his life was pretty much removed from that society. He kept to his friends. Recently I was looking at old photographs in the J. K. McCarthy Museum in Goroka, and there's a photograph of the Australian Catholic community gathering after Sunday mass in front of the Goroka Hotel, and it was very interesting that our family was absent from that gathering. And to me, when I saw that picture, it said it all. It just said it all. It brought back a lot of memories.

CS   Were all the other people in the photo, people that you were ...

MT   That I went to the same church with?

CS   I wonder why you were absent?

MT   I'd say because of Jim and Yerima. A lot of those people, even though they were Catholics, wouldn't have accepted that.

CS   When UPNG and other institutions like the IMR in Goroka were established, did that bring into the country a different kind of Australian?

MT   Definitely, and a new dynamic was established between Australians and Papua New Guineans, at least for those of us who were students at UPNG. And as Australians worked for the PNG government we saw the strong personal and professional relationships that were developed between Papua New Guineans and Australians which have endured to this day. Many of my good friends are those Australians who were our lecturers and those that worked with us through self-government and Independence, and colleagues who are still involved in working with us. The relationship is on an equal footing. My concern is the future and how young people from my country and young people from your country see and know each other.

Chapter 15
INTERVIEW WITH DAME CAROL KIDU
Interview conducted by Ceridwen Spark in Port Moresby, 13 March
2013

CS   Dame Carol, can you please say a little about when you first
came to PNG and how that time was for you?

CK   My first visit was during the Christmas and New Year period
of 1965–6 on a university volunteer work camp. I had previously met the man who was going to become my husband in
1964 at a school holiday camp in Tallebudgera, Queensland.
He was a student from PNG on a colonial scholarship.

CS   So when you came on the work camp, did you have in mind
that you wanted to see him again?

CK   Certainly, that was a reason why I came. I came with my
sister. I was not a university student at the time. I was

in grade 12 and going into university. She was a university student. It was organised by the National Union of Students – a student volunteer visit. And so we came together. I had met my late husband the year before, 1964, in my grade 11 year. It was very progressive of my parents to allow me to come, knowing that I was friends with a young man from PNG during that time of the White Australia Policy.

CS   So what are your personal recollections of the role played by Australians in PNG in the period 1960–75?

CK   I had no contact with them.

CS   With Australians?

CK   Yes, or should I say very little contact, because when I came back in 1969 as a married woman and then back again in 1971 permanently when all our studies were finished, I never lived in the Australian community. I lived completely in the Motu society. Basically my only interaction with Australians was at school as a teacher.

Early, the only real interaction I had was negative. In the holiday work camp time (1966), we were billeted with families and, unfortunately, I was billeted with an extremely racist family. And when Buri came to the door to say, 'I've come to see Carol' – he was a student and school captain from Toowoomba Grammar School at the time, going into university – he was told, 'Get out, you're a native, you go to the back door.' So my first impressions of Australians in PNG were not positive. These impressions were from the perspective of a person who was in a permanent relationship and close to marriage with a Papua New Guinean man, which was extremely unusual in those days. Relationships the other way occurred, between an Australian man and a Papua New Guinean woman, but between a Papua New Guinean man and an Australian woman, it was very rare. I think it was the second such relationship at the time. So some of my experiences were quite negative. But on the other hand, some were wonderful, with people such as the late Dr John Biddulph and Professor Ian Maddocks, who was then Dr Maddocks and lived in my husband's village with his wife and children. So there was an unusual balance.

CS   Would you have seen people like Dr Maddocks as exceptional and the more racist Australians as the norm?

CK   Biddulph and Maddocks were exceptional in many ways. Then the people I was billeted with were exceptional in the other way, extreme racists, and I think there probably was a mass in the middle that kind of vacillated, depending on their circumstances. I remember when my sister and I came as university volunteers, some young Aussie pilots thought they'd take these Australian students out for a trip flying over Fisherman Island. And again, it was to me a very distasteful experience, because they got one of the elderly men there – he was probably from Goilala, judging by his stature – and they had him climbing up to the roof of the plane hangar and then swinging across the rafters to the other side and coming down again, which was very degrading. They were laughing and saying, 'This is why we call them monkeys'. And I didn't know how to handle it at the time, because I'd never experienced such things. So I had very mixed experiences.

Once I came back permanently in 1971, I was a teacher, mostly at Port Moresby International School, but for some time at Kila Kila High and also Boisen High School in Rabaul (which was later destroyed by the volcanic eruption). In my profession as a teacher, I was interacting with a lot of really genuine, good, committed Australian teachers (or mostly Australian in those days – a few from England, but mostly Australian). So they were very positive. I think they saw me as a bit of an enigma, but they were very genuine.

CS   An enigma, in what way? Because you were married to a Papua New Guinean?

CK   Yes, and that I was, by choice, living the Papuan life, because it's not like his village was somewhere else. The village is in Moresby, so that was a unique circumstance and our whole social life involved the village activities. At that stage, Buri was a young lawyer. He was not part of the upper echelons and our total social life was tied to the village, the Motu way of life. My only interaction with Australians was when I was teaching, and of course, that was positive. I'd go to school with my burnt banana and smoked fish when we'd run out of money and I think my co-workers perhaps pitied me. Really I don't know what they thought.

CS   Reflecting on that time particularly, what did you feel or observe that Australians were bringing to PNG?

CK   I don't think I can really reflect much on this. My whole life became immersed in learning to live in a completely different culture. I don't think I even reflected much on that. We didn't have a vehicle. We walked with babies and shopping and the PMV (Public Motor Vehicle) drivers would pick us up and give us a free ride because they felt for us. I didn't feel antagonism, but there was no interaction. Our total social life was with Motu society, because Buri's village was right here in the city. What interactions I did have with the Australian population were in general very pleasant, because those who didn't agree with my chosen way of life would not have interacted with me anyway, so I didn't have contact with them except when, as a student, I was billeted with a family. I don't know what I can say, because all the ones I interacted with certainly made huge contributions and I think made a good effort to adjust the lens by which they were seeing the world. Certainly Dr Maddocks did that. That's why he went and lived in the village, because he wanted to better understand the people who were his patients. When he was working at the Port Moresby General Hospital, he soon realised that he could never minister as a doctor when he didn't understand how people lived and where they lived. And so that's when he went and lived in the village, with the support of a young doctor from Pari, Isi Kevau (now Professor Sir Isi Kevau), and learnt the language and really got completely immersed, possibly in some ways more than I did, but in other ways not so. He became completely immersed in the whole village life, including reciprocal expectations and obligations (something that became daily life for me also).

CS   So did you experience any kind of direct opposition or criticism about your having married a Papua New Guinean man?

CK   No, not after we became married, but I think for those people we were not part of their social scene, we were not on their radar. I always reflect on when I was billeted and that man who refused to speak to me from the time he knew I was friends with a Papua New Guinean man. I just lived in the house and didn't speak to him. It was very interesting. His daughter used to come and sit on the back steps with me. It was clear that she was not of the same inclination. She was questioning her own parents' ethics. And I always remember as he drove me to the airport, he said, 'My best advice to you, young lady, is to get that monkey off your back.' And then years later, I saw this man at the airport. I was with Buri, who at that time was the Chief Justice. And Buri and I kept looking at this fellow at the airport and thinking, 'Who is that?' I went and looked at his luggage ticket and I realised it was the same man. I really wanted to go up and say, 'Can I introduce you to that monkey on my back?' Buri, of course, wouldn't let me do it, and told me to forget it. It was quite funny, but no, I wouldn't say I experienced overt anti-feelings of racism. I think people just …

CS   Found it puzzling?

CK   Yes, and the fact that we made a conscious choice that our children were going to grow up in the village with their grandparents and learn the Motu way of life. Whether that was the right choice or not, I don't know, in retrospect, but that was the choice we made. I think it was, but it leaves them with an enormous burden now, in their lives and expectations.

CS   Because you've got such a long personal history in PNG, as well as a political history, you're in a unique position to comment on the developmental changes in PNG since Independence. So perhaps if you could just reflect on the gains and losses that PNG has experienced since Independence. I know it's a huge question.

CK   Yes, a very difficult one. It's really very difficult to rate this. We look at PNG, we look at Motu society. I'll look at Motu society first, because that's been my life. I'm conscious of the fact that I married into a very proud, dignified society that was not a perfect society. I'm not trying to talk about the rose-tinted glasses view of traditional life, but it was a proud, dignified society. It had purpose, it had intent. Our life was built around the seasonal cycle of traditional liveli- hood activities and even when I first came, the clan leaders would announce, 'This is the time for such and such', and we followed the season and cycle of events, which was a 13-month lunar calendar. And I spent all of my personal time as part of that, over 44, 45 years. I would say in the last 15 probably, I've seen a disintegration of the society that I find very distressing. But I think it's not only Motu society. I think it is happening right at the base in PNG, from what Papua New Guinean friends who have been home to their villages have said to me. One young friend married to a Papua New Guinean said people live in a 'bubble' in Moresby, away from the reality of village life. One friend spent a two-month period in his village after he had some issues with his health, and said he was quite distressed about the social breakdown he saw in his village in East New Britain. I thought that was a society that was holding together, but he said, 'No, it's the same there'.

A lot of it is a result of the introduction of the cash economy: greed, the desire for cash, the pressures that cash puts on your life, and from the inability to share, as was done with garden produce, because it becomes impossible sometimes to satisfy the expectations of relatives.

I think this change is one that's inevitable. I find it really distressing, I find it hard to cope with, but I know it's bound to happen. But one would hope that out of it eventually can come something that's still uniquely Motu, rather than some bad photocopy of another culture. And sometimes I feel that is what we will be creating if we're not careful.

It's too difficult to talk about. How can you write anything about this? It's so hard, because customs in themselves are not static, culture is not static and perhaps the reality is that many of the customs of PNG are now abused. They're not what they were originally and they haven't evolved into a better way. They've become abused, sometimes to the detriment of women and family cohesion. So this type of thing distresses me. But on the other hand, the new generation is there. This young generation will redefine the new Motu society, I would hope. It can't be what it was, but I would hope it could still be proud and have some identity. I struggle with all of that because I'm very conscious of this social breakdown that is occurring, although people may have progressed economically. Not all have, there's inequity, although many people now have cars and the trappings of modern life. Whether it balances out some of the social breakdown, I don't know. The social breakdown is inevitable because young people have to disengage themselves from their traditional obligations because they cannot fulfil them with their limited cash income. There are too many people without money, more than the ones with money, to fulfil the expectations, and I see my own children struggling with this and the stress they're under. Mum's income can help save face, and they keep saying to me, 'Mum, stop pushing it out. You're just making it harder for us, because when you die, we don't have enough to satisfy all expectations. So let it happen now gradually.' And it's not only me. This is just what Papua New Guineans are going through in general. It's nothing to do with me as an Australian in PNG. It's what Papua New Guineans are going through on how to disengage and how to re-engage in new ways. It's really hard and some people are more analytical than others. I don't know how you can make anything out of that, because this is too complex. One day, I'm going to sit down and actually write and illustrate with examples what I'm talking about here.

So that's the Motu side, which has really been my life. This is what a lot of people don't understand. When I leave the office of parliament, or when I leave you now, I go back to my extended family, all my children and a couple of other families there that may be dependent on me. I do not live in the main village, but if I'm quite frank, if we had built in the main Pari village, which was our original intention, it would have been very difficult to live in such a crowded, closed environment. We were going to build over the water at the back of the line of houses of the clan that we belong to, and people challenged our right to be there. I'm so glad now that Buri said, 'To hell with it. We'll go out to Taurama', and we went and found original bush on traditional land. Elders walked the boundaries and said, 'Yes, you have rights here and we say this is for you.'

Mind you, we're now getting challenged on it. Those things are very painful. After 44 years contributing to a society, to now be challenged about where we are living is quite painful. But if we had lived in the village there, I don't think I could have stayed forever the way I have. I would have been overwhelmed, financially and psychologically. Living on traditional land a little bit outside the village means that for people to come and get help, for sugar or whatever, they have to actually get in a dinghy or in a car and come around. If we had built our house in the village, without Buri's income after he died, it would've been ... I just can't imagine how I would've coped, because there is an assumption that people of foreign origin have money. It was a good decision to build on customary land, but outside the village, because I have a tendency to want to give, especially when I see people are very poor. But there comes a time when you just have nothing more to give. And in the early years, we experienced that quite a bit. We'd be at the end of our food and we'd be relying on the tapioca and things that Buri's mum grew in the garden. He was on a native wage and I was on an Australian wage as a teacher. Sometimes we would not last the fortnight with all the people we were supporting.

So my whole life was, and still is, built around that. I go to social events, but it's purely role-playing in a way. I go to dinners and things, but then I'll go back to someone dying, or someone sick, or a discussion of a bride price contribution, or a funeral feast, and my kids say to me, 'Mum, you can't keep doing this. You can't be worrying about dishes of food and packets of rice for people until the day you die. It's unfair.' But how do you deal with it when there are people with no rice and no sugar? So I'm having a reality check in my own life as to how I can balance it out. I have a daughter in Cairns and I probably have to move to and fro and work it that way. I think that can be more effective, because otherwise I'll just go under, or I'll become a different person and become very hard and say, 'Sorry, there's no more. Finished. Go. Leave me.' That's very difficult when you've spent 40 years in a society and your children have grown up knowing we always helped. So it's very difficult.

To be quite frank, I think there are very few Australians who can truly understand the depths of these struggles for ordinary PNG people living in contact with their clan and village. It's an inner gut thing. It's not just in the mind or in the heart. It's in the gut as well, a feeling of guilt, and the society here is very good at putting you on guilt trips. So I became a Motuan; I was no longer an Australian in PNG. I'd never be known by this, but my roots determined so much of me. How do you define who I am now? But it's that persona that made it possible for me to win elections without having a lot of money, those relationships and all those things. But will that continue in PNG? That you can win an election through hard work, or will money become more the determining factor in the outcomes of elections? And if so, what does that say for women in politics? It's hard for them.

CS So perhaps putting on this persona, your political hat, could you comment on what role you think Australia should take in PNG now? What do you observe and what do you think should be happening?

CK One would hope that what Australians have done in PNG has, in general, all been done with the best of intentions. I don't mean individually. There are people here who have come as one of the three Ms – missionaries, mercenaries, misfits. But I think, in general, Australia as a nation and Australians as people, what they've done in PNG has been with the very best of intentions. But quite often too, they are very willing to admit that what they've put in has not produced the results they would have hoped for, given the amount of funding that has come into PNG.

I think it came out in the Pacific dialogue in Timor that Pacific nations in general have to deconstruct their thinking to some degree and take themselves out of a colonial mentality. Development is hard. I think the most important thing is patience, listening and allowing and ensuring and fostering ownership, which is very difficult. And that's very difficult not just for Australia, but for all countries that are development partners. Development projects are driven by timeframes and outcomes. That's not the way society here operates – timeframes and outcomes. So quite often you'll do the timeframe, you'll do the outcome, but there won't be any sustainability. And it's partly to do with ownership, and partly to do just with the way things are done. It's not like we're a poor country. Of course, there are positives and incremental gains being made. But too often with these things the timeframes are too short and it's the end of the project when it's just starting to gain traction. Moving from the project mentality into a systematic comprehensive program will take commitment and ownership from the nation too.

CS   So you're sensing a bit of a shift?

CK   I think so, yes, and it's got to come from ownership. What my former secretary did was excellent, because we were a department that had very little money from the national government. Basically we were working on bones, and yet we were working really solidly to get policy frameworks and legislative reform done.

Because of these reforms, we did get a lot of development support. We found that there were lots of offers of support coming from development partners, but in the end it meant that the senior officers were project managing the development partner projects and they had no time for their own core business under the corporate plan. So the secretary would call the development partners together twice a year and basically say, 'This is the corporate plan. We can use your help with our corporate plan. If you don't want to do it, we don't want you.' This integration between development partners and government plans and priorities is improving constantly.

CS   What do you hope for the people of PNG?

CK   What one would hope for any nation, I think. Justice, peace, prosperity for the majority, not the minority. By prosperity, I don't necessarily mean enormous wealth, but sufficiency. Let's have sufficiency for all, rather than absolute prosperity for a few and destitution for others. One would hope that we could manage that. We will certainly have enough money. There's no doubt about that, but whether we can manage it is another matter. And that's not a criticism of any particular government.

Getting our system working is critical – delivery systems – and in some ways, we've tended to decimate the public delivery mechanisms and not fund them enough and not build them enough. I guess my basic hope is that all this wealth that is there, and that should be coming in the future, will materialise because the rest of the world wants our resources. My hope is that it will deliver improved education, health, and livelihood opportunities for all. One would hope that they would be delivered in a decentralised manner, so that we won't have the increasing sprawl coming to a few urban centres. One would hope that some of the excellent policies that have been produced will be funded and implemented, like the urbanisation policy, where the focus is very much on decentralising and developing rural urban service centres, and providing services in the rural area, where people own their land and resources. The informal economy policy is another excellent policy designed to see the informal economy as a solution, not a problem. That's what one would hope. One would hope that we would see fewer improper dealings with land and all of those things.

CS   Is there anything further that you'd like to say on the subject of Australia/PNG relations? Anything we haven't covered?

CK   I think Australia, as a former colonial country, is going to have to realise that there are other geopolitical forces that are playing in their backyard. One Australian politician said that the Pacific is basically our backyard, and I thought it sounded a little dangerous or paternalistic. And I saw all this tweeting going on around the room. It was just a slip of the tongue, but it did ruffle feathers. PNG has got to be able to manage this multiplicity of other interests coming in this direction for the benefit of Papua New Guineans.

I have said, 'In fact, PNG can be better than the United States of America.' I said it deliberately and I looked at the ambassador and the audience – Papua New

Guineans mainly – and they were looking at me with horror. How can she say such a thing? And then I went on to say, 'I didn't say the most wealthy or the most powerful. I said that we could be the best country in the world, if we could take the best of the past and the best of what has come in and put them together. My God, what a great country this is.' And there is so much that PNG, the Pacific in general, can teach the world, the Western world. Do they realise that themselves or are they in such a hurry to be part of the Western world? I guess it's not nostalgic, it's realism in many ways: dealing with change, constantly trying to manage change, in a country where you've got an interface between modernity and semi-traditional and traditional time warps.

So I think we can't constantly use our complexity as an excuse, but it certainly is a factor that comes into the development process. There is no 'one size fits all' for PNG. I think we, as a nation, are not dealing enough with the issues of complex social breakdown. I think we're so obsessed with our resources and our money that we have to be very careful that the base doesn't suck us under.

I think that's going to be the biggest challenge for us. How can we translate the enormous boom in wealth that we're going to have into equitable development, or as close to equitable and just development as possible, with the present breakdown that we are facing? I think every politician and every person would admit that we are facing a fairly large social breakdown. So we've really got to focus on that and that means long-term generational planning, as well as for the immediacy. So we've got to deal with the immediate issues, but we've got to be able to plan through for generational change. We haven't done that very well. It's something that PNG has to do.

References

Kidu, Carol, *A Remarkable Journey*, (Melbourne: Pearson Education, 2002).

CONCLUSION

16

AUSTRALIANS AND PAPUA NEW GUINEA: A REFLECTION

Jonathan Ritchie

Like the contributors to this book, I spent a large part of the years from 1960 to 1975 in Papua New Guinea. Unlike most, though, I hadn't made the choice to go there. My parents lived in PNG – my father since just after the Second World War, my mother from a year or two later – so I was a PNG baby, born at the newly opened Port Moresby General Hospital at Taurama, in 1961. Ten years later, we departed for Australia, 'going finish' in the expression of the day.

In many ways, mine was an idyllic childhood, nestled amid the privileged life of the Australian expatriate community, yet with freedom to explore what was, for a child, the peaceful, exciting town of Port Moresby. Memories of days spent swimming in the tepid sea at Ela Beach, of hikes to the war-era gun emplacements and air-raid shelters atop Touaguba and

Paga Hills, nights in the back of the family station wagon at the Skyline Drive-In, and drives into the mountains to escape the heat of Moresby. We went to cool off at Crystal Rapids, on the way to Sogeri and the start of the Kokoda trail. Even as a child I was conscious of those Australian soldiers who had trod this path only 20 years earlier, something my parents took care to remind me of during the obligatory stop along the way at Bomana War Cemetery.

With the hindsight of middle age in noisy, busy and over-populated Melbourne, my childhood in PNG has acquired an almost magical quality. The last years before Independence proved a special time in the lives of the children of the white colonists. It was a period on the other side of the looking-glass, a *fin de siècle* moment ended by our parents' decisions to depart and so create opportunities for Papua New Guineans to take over. It ended abruptly, and for us children, often traumatically. We can never go back.

But really, we don't want to. Maybe, sometimes, we fondly recall the innocence and ease of living in comfortable circum-stances way beyond what would have been the case had we grown up in Australia. Now, understanding that the quality of our lifestyles was built on the backs of many Papua New Guinean men and women, we recognise the illegitimacy of our experience of late colonial life.

My privileged position was due directly to the labours of my family's *haus boi*, Malo, and his *meri*, Eleni, who cleaned, ironed, gardened and shared with me delicious dinners of 'native *kai*' – tinned fish and rice, sweet tea and white bread – which I would scoff down before my 'proper' dinner. Indirectly, our life-style was enabled by the low-paid and often backbreaking work of the men and women who looked after all the menial chores, jobs that no Australian *masta* would even consider performing.

Despite the ending in the early 1960s of much regulated discrimination, its continuing impact was evident still. My fellow students at the Ela Beach Primary 'A' School were all, like me, the children of respectable expatriates. At home, our neighbours in the big houses and rambling gardens high on the hillside in Port Moresby's exclusive Simpson's Crescent – apart from Malo and Eleni and the other *haus bois* and *meris* in their fibro *boi haus* at the top of the gardens – were Australians like us.

Although I was born in the new and non-discriminating General Hospital, my mother had my two older brothers in the European Hospital, located at the apex of the central saddle that divided the windward, Ela Beach side of downtown Port Moresby from the busy port area fronting Fairfax Harbour. In 1961, with the establishment of the new General Hospital, the European hospital was renovated to become home to the Territory of Papua and New Guinea's Legislative Council. From 1964 it accommodated the first democratically elected House of Assembly, and after Independence in 1975, the National Parliament.

In the renovated building's basement sat the Papua New Guinea Museum, intended to display the Territory's wealth of ethnographic artefacts; those that had not been removed – or was it stolen? – for collections in Europe, America and Australia. Though the museum was small, it was nevertheless large enough to give me nightmares. Walking around the spooky, under-illuminated galleries I was reminded that there was a savage land of cannibals and sorcerers, headhunters and malignant spirits lurking beneath the veneer of suburban 1960s Port Moresby. The masks and carvings adorned with tufts of human hair and embedded with teeth – human, dog or of some other being – were clearly intended to invoke spirits of evil, which, I feared, would supernaturally bring about not only my demise but that of the whole culture and people I represented. This was not just an Australian outpost built on the backs of compliant, underpaid native labour. Nor was it a modern city, notwithstanding the glass, aluminium and rein-forced concrete of the newly built skyscraper just down the road from the museum. Papua New Guinea felt like an alien land, truly a heart of darkness. It was not our land, not our country. What on earth was I doing there? What, in fact, were any of us doing there? Why did Australians choose to live and work in PNG? Has their impact been constructive, or has it hampered PNG as it seeks to grow out of its colonial shell?

Fast-forward nearly three decades to my next encounter with Papua New Guinea. As part of my PhD research into the process by which PNG gained its Constitution in the years from 1972 to 1975, I returned to Port Moresby in 1998 to spend some time in the National Archives in Waigani, the heart of PNG's government.

I hoped that I had matured sufficiently to be able to put aside the fears of my childhood. Indeed – despite the evidence of social, economic and political decline that had deepened over the 'lost decade' (as Governor of PNG's Central Bank Wilson Kamit has described the 1990s (Kamit 2008)) – I found myself feeling at home amidst the chaos. Intangible things – the smell of wood smoke and rotting vegetation, the sounds of singing birds and people too, and even the quality of the light and clouds – combined to create a feeling of homecoming. This came as a surprise, as I considered that I had 'put the ways of childhood behind me', and had moved into adulthood in a quite different landscape. It made me think about my own conflicted feelings regarding the country in which I was born.

Since my family left at the end of 1970, and even more since Independence in 1975, Papua New Guinea had acquired a character and coherence as an independent nation that simply was not present in the turbulent decade and a half before 1975. True, as many people said by the late 1990s (and some still say), it could be seen as on its way to being a 'failed state'; but the shared experience of the hardships encountered along the way seemed, paradoxically, to have contributed to fostering this national character.

How relevant was the time before Independence, the period described by Hank Nelson as *taim bilong masta* (Nelson 1982), in creating modern Papua New Guinea? In gathering the experiences of a selection of Australians and Papua New Guineans who lived through the years prior to Independence, this collection helps to supply some answers to this question. Their accounts show the breadth and depth of the Australian engagement with PNG, which affected, profoundly, the composition of the Papua New Guinean state and the structures that were intended to equip PNG and its peoples with what was needed to survive as a new nation.

The period spanned by this collection, the 15 years from 1960 to 1975, was an exciting time for many, both Papua New Guinean and Australian, living in the Territory (as PNG was known at the time). The women and men whose experiences are recounted here, either as personal essays or in interviews with the book's editors, were caught up in the wave of attention and activity that characterised the period, as the Australian government belatedly recognised its responsibilities to prepare PNG for independence and Papua New Guineans began to exert their own influence on shaping the independent PNG nation. If they had experienced PNG at a different time – the 1890s, for example, or the War years – they would be recalling a life so different that it could well have been on another planet.

But the 1960s and early 1970s were special (as we are often reminded). By that time, the world beyond Papua New Guinean shores – which for most of the preceding century had remained remote, with the years between 1942 and 1945 a glaring exception – had begun to intrude, and all those living in PNG experienced some impact from the intervention. By the opening of the period of this collection, the times were indeed a-changin' and a mood of dynamism pervades all accounts contained in the book. Their narrators experienced PNG in a state of flux, in enormous contrast to the many decades that had gone before.

The 1960s began with an avalanche of new nations as former French and British colonies, mainly in Africa, achieved independence – in 1960, there were no fewer than 17 of these. In February of that year, the British Prime Minister, Harold Macmillan, made his famous speech to the South African parliament in which he referred to the 'wind of change' blowing through the African continent. Later in the year, the United Nations General Assembly adopted Resolution 1514 (XV), the Declaration on the Granting of Independence to Colonial Countries and Peoples. Closer to home, Australian Prime Minister Robert Menzies commented to journalists in the same year:

Whereas at one time many of us might have thought that it was better to go slowly in granting independence so that all the conditions existed for a wise exercise of self-government, I think the prevailing school of thought today is that if in doubt you should go sooner, not later. I belong to that school of thought now, (Menzies in *Papua and New Guinea*. 1960, 13–14)

While hardly revolutionary, Menzies' comments indicated that some effects of the wind of change that Macmillan observed were being felt in Australia's own colonial territory of Papua and New Guinea. They reflected the continually growing momentum since the end of the War of economic, social and political development in PNG. The effects of this were beginning to be seen, in health and education, roads and business. They were also increasingly evident in society and politics. Some towns grew dramatically: Port Moresby's population nearly doubled between 1954 and 1961, from 15,600 indigenous and non-indigenous people to 29,000 (Oram 1976, 85). Such rapid growth brought mounting disparity of living standards as rural Papuans and New Guineans began to move into the towns. It also created opportunities to bring people together in a range of creative ways and, for some at least, this involved political activism, motivated by the inequalities exposed by the concentration into urban centres. Groups such as the Port Moresby Workers' Association and the Kerema Welfare Society provided the training for Papua New Guineans like Oala Oala-Rarua, Michael Somare and Albert Maori Kiki who one day would lead the new nation.

As might be deduced from Menzies's comments, there was a strong focus on political development from the top down. A Legislative Council had been set up in 1951, with spaces reserved for three Papuans and New Guineans to be appointed. By 1961 ten years later, it had expanded to include 12 elected Papua New Guineans. But with the rapidly building momentum around the world for decolonisation, this was not considered enough, especially by the large number of new UN members and the Soviet bloc. The United Nations Trusteeship Council, which supervised political and economic development in territories such as New Guinea that were administered in trust on behalf of the UN, regularly sent Visiting Missions to report on progress. Its 1962 Mission, led by the British diplomat Sir Hugh Foot, made radical recommendations on constitutional development that were intended to shake things up; as Foot said to the Australian Administrator, Donald Cleland, 'We've come to put you chaps into a gallop' (Cleland 1983, 264). Around the same time, the Australian government had set up a Committee of the Legislative Council which, more or less independently, made several recommendations that paralleled those of Foot's Mission. Among these was one for an elected, Territory-wide parliament, which became the House of Assembly, a 54-seat body that sat in the building previously occupied by the European Hospital.

Both the Foot Mission and the Australian Administration also saw the need for a dramatic expansion in the educational opportunities available to Papua New Guineans. One outcome was the increased number of government schools, both primary and secondary. Another was the establishment of post-secondary colleges such as the Port Moresby and Goroka Teachers' Colleges, the Papuan Medical College, the Posts and Telegraphs Training College, and the Administrative College.

In 1964 a commission of inquiry into the Territory's higher education needs recommended that a university be established, and in 1966 the University of Papua New Guinea began, with an initial intake of 58 Preliminary Year students.

The colleges and, from 1966, the university, quickly became sites for political discussions which brought together Papua New Guineans and Australians who were committed to ending the colonial era and building for coming independence. The most well known of these was the 'Bully Beef Club', formed by students of the Administrative and Teachers' Colleges and joined at times by Members of the House of Assembly. They would debate, over dinner comprising the eponymous meal of bully beef (tinned meat), the wrongs of racism and colonialism – an activity they shared with other nationalists in many other parts of the world. They were inspired by the examples of anti-colonialist resistance figures such as Frantz Fanon (although in the case of PNG they eschewed violence, something that a nervous Australian government failed to appreciate at the time). In 1967, Bully Beef Club members publicly declared their support for early independence in their submission to a House of Assembly committee on constitutional development, and shortly afterwards they combined to form the first pro-nationalist political party, the Pangu Pati.

The 1968 elections for the House of Assembly provided an opportunity for nationalist Papua New Guineans such as Michael Somare, Ebia Olewale, Paulus Arek and Oala Oala-Rarua to enter the political arena. With others they formed an alliance in the House that maintained a rigid opposition to the Australian Administration and support for self-government at the earliest opportunity. The Australian government kept up its stance that independence would come at a time when the Papua New Guinean people considered themselves ready for it – a handy response to the frequent calls for action coming from the United Nations (particularly the Soviet bloc). The Papua New Guineans in Pangu and other political parties agreed with the sentiment, but disagreed on when such a time would arrive. Conservative Papua New Guineans, often but not only in the Highlands, argued that the emphasis should remain on economic development. The nationalists disagreed, concurring with the Kenyan leader, Tom Mboya (who had visited PNG in 1964 and met several of them), that this approach might result in independence never coming, and that independence should precede economic and social development.

Eventually, the Australians were brought around to the view that independence should come no later than during the 1972–6 term of the House of Assembly. From 1971 they began work on transferring powers and authorities in readiness for the anticipated arrival of self-government (despite official adherence to the policy that Papua New Guineans should determine when self-government and subsequent independence should be achieved). In 1972 the House of Assembly, by this time dominated by Papua New Guineans, saw Michael Somare lead a coalition of various political parties as the Territory's first Chief Minister, a precursor to becoming Prime Minister of an independent PNG. Three years later, on 16 September 1975, independence was finally achieved and the colonial era consigned to history.

The political and social developments that resulted in a Papua New Guinean-led government in place by 1972 and independence in 1975, demonstrate the tremendous changes that took place over the span covered in this collection. They were paralleled by advancements in the fields of commerce, in medical and other sciences, in education and in the arts.

In terms of economic development, the period covered in this collection saw expansion and diversification in an effort to provide PNG with export income in the years to come. For most of the Australian era, PNG's plantation-based economy had remained small-scale, dependent on highly variable world markets, and while at times mining appeared promising, there had been many false starts. The 1960s witnessed an expansion in business opportunities, encouraging diversity and experimentation in agriculture and in ventures such as tourism and small-scale manufacturing. There was renewed attention to mining and resources, seen most prominently in the copper mine at Panguna on the island of Bougainville.

Great advances were made in the sciences, and at times PNG appeared to be a gigantic laboratory that attracted researchers from around the world. Its biodiversity held much promise for medical and life sciences researchers, as inroads were made into malaria and a host of other tropical diseases. Many PhDs were gained and, in some cases, research in PNG was rewarded with the highest honours, including in one case, a Nobel Prize. Students of human society had already 'discovered' PNG, from the earliest days of contact in the cases of Seligman, Rivers, Malinowski and other world-renowned anthropologists, and in the 1960s there were few signs of this interest abating. Scientists found support in the newly established colleges and the university, which in turn helped to train Papua New Guineans as doctors and scientists, again in preparation for a post-independence future.

From the late 1960s, and especially following the arrival of Ulli and Georgina Beier in 1967, characteristically 'Papua New Guinean' arts and literature began flourishing. The Beiers had come from Nigeria where they had been associated with a similar flowering of indigenous – in this case, distinctively African – culture, and Ulli had been invited to join UPNG to teach literature. As he wrote in his own recollection of those years, *Decolonising the Mind: the Impact of the University on Culture and Identity in Papua New Guinea, 1971–74*, he was able to bring together a group of Papua New Guinean writers, poets and playwrights, like Vincent Eri, Russell Soaba and Nora Vagi, whose work helped to build the concept of Papua New Guinean national identity. In the visual arts, Georgina Beier promoted a similar approach, helping to launch the careers of artists like Mathias Kauage and Akis whose contemporary inter-pretations of the transitions being experienced by Papua New Guineans found audiences far beyond PNG itself.

Most of the non-Papua New Guinean contributors to this book had their first experience of PNG during the 1960s, or if they had visited earlier, they returned to make their mark in this time. They joined the influx of Australians and others who came to PNG in the same period, participants in the project of making the Territory ready to stand on its own feet once independence arrived (whenever that would be). The adventure began for many once they had decided to go there, leaving their families, friends and (usually mundane) jobs behind them. However, on first arriving in Port Moresby, many were confronted by the barriers of colonial life and the sleepy primness of the European society that they encountered. Nevertheless, despite the apparent banality of the towns, it did not take long for them to appreciate the opportunities that living and working in PNG provided, to break out from the boredom of urban, middle-class Australia, to feel that they were making a difference and at the same time satisfying their wanderlust.

Not all Australians came to PNG to make a difference, apart from benefiting themselves, however. Many saw the Territory as a place to build their careers, with a lifestyle that would have been out of reach back home, with *haus bois*, sports and a ready-made (and often alcohol-fuelled) social life; and when it came to 'going finish' there was the promise of a generous superannuation scheme. For many, maybe the majority, of Australians the changes going on around them caused considerable alarm, as they feared the coming independence would lead to a rapid descent into violence and anarchy in the manner of the worst post-colonial circumstances seen in places like Nigeria and the Congo. While not all Australians brought with them views about racial stereotyping, some did, and their bigotry was evident in the satirical and frequently racist magazine *Black and White* (published from 1966 to 1969).

As in similarly segregated communities in America and Australia around the same time, the early part of the decade witnessed efforts to bring an official end to discriminatory and racially motivated practices. The Native Regulations introduced at the beginning of the colonial administration that were intended to exert a paternalistic control over Papua New Guineans' behaviour began to be removed, including the ban on Papua New Guineans buying or consuming alcohol, repealed in 1962. As occurred elsewhere, however, removing the legal barriers did not mean that society at large would change its ways, at least not quickly. Even after the Liquor

Ordinance was repealed, the practice of Papua New Guineans being given access to alcohol was frowned on by a conservative colonial society, and only the bravest Papua New Guineans were prepared to challenge the conventions. The more adventurous of the Australians and other expatriates saw shouting a Papua New Guinean colleague a beer in one of the hotels as a mark of distinction, a small act of defiance against the repressive status quo.

Papua New Guinea was a country in the process of a great and rapid transition during the 1960s and early 1970s, the period covered by this collection. Many of the contributors to the book were deeply engaged in facilitating this transition, and responding to the impacts that were being felt by Papua New Guinean society. They were doctors, lawyers, public servants and educationalists – all in roles that enabled them to influence outcomes in what they considered were positive ways. Ken Inglis and Bill Gammage had the opportunity to mark their mark, indelibly, on the structures of higher education in PNG, to the extent that even now, nearly five decades later, they are accorded the highest respect. A similar assessment can be made about the medical fraternity that includes, among the contributors, Michael Alpers, Ian Maddocks, Ken Clezy, Margaret Smith and Anthony Radford: they all have left their mark on medical science and the overall health of the Papua New Guinean people. John Langmore and John Ley's contributions pertained more to Papua New Guinean public affairs, with one an active participant in policy formation in the Administration and the other, *inter alia*, advising the Constitutional Planning Committee from 1972, working on that most essential of components for independence, PNG's Constitution.

An important aspect of the Australian engagement in PNG involved the women (and sometimes men) who went there because their partners did. It is practically impossible to generalise about their experiences, as some chose to follow lives that differed little from what they would have looked like back in Australia, others decided to emulate the worst excesses of white colonial behaviour from examples in Africa, while others seized the opportunities to become actively involved, sometimes in quite different directions from their partners. The self-effacing Christine Stewart – who, as she writes, 'went to PNG to get married. Simple as that' – had an influence far greater than she would admit to, in her willingness to rock the boat of colonial propriety and make strong friendships with Papua New Guineans. Her example of Australian egalitarianism is still remembered fondly in PNG (something I witnessed when I met Christine at a recent conference in Port Moresby). Carol Kidu – who had a similar reason for going to PNG – went even further in her willingness to identify with her husband's people and what soon became her adopted country. Of all the Australians (or former Australians) included in the collection she has exhibited the greatest level of engagement with PNG, something that continues to this day. Robin Radford, whose recollections are included with those of her husband, Anthony, approached the prospect of living and working in PNG with determination, and the couple set out to 'immerse [them]selves in PNG, the land and its cultures, and expected to both give and receive'.

Bill Brown represents the group that many Australians might most often identify with PNG. He was a *kiap*, a member of the patrol service, one of the young men whose job it was to undertake patrols throughout Papua New Guinea and bring with them the benefits of civilisation: delivering law and order, dispensing medicines, and maintaining census records, to ensure that the people in the villages that were visited were aware of the wider world. Bill's experiences in Bougainville at the time of the negotiations of the agreement to commence mining operations, however, went far beyond what might be considered 'normal' for many *kiaps* (a profession accustomed to anything *but* what we would call 'normal').

And then there are the Papua New Guineans: Isi Kevau, Charles Lepani and Meg Taylor (not including in this case, despite her PNG citizenship, Carol Kidu). All three have experienced stellar careers and have made – and continue to make – extraordinary contributions to PNG public life. As they acknowledge, their talents were nurtured by the opportunities they encountered as a result of their own, and their families', engagement with Australians. While they themselves benefited from this, through the examples of their lives and achievements they have inspired and motivated generations of Papua New Guineans. All three of them were (and are) contributors to creating modern PNG.

The men and women whose recollections are recorded in this book lived and worked in Papua New Guinea at the same time as I spent my childhood there. Being there during the 1960s is one thing we have in common. Perhaps we also share a similar awareness of the wonder and excitement that PNG in the 1960s and early 1970s held for many, both Australian and Papua New Guinean. We would agree about the freedom that life there provided for many of us, and the optimism, despite the fearmongering by some Australians, that was in the air as

Independence approached. We would definitely feel the same sense of nostalgia for that time, the *taim bipo* as it is called nowadays.

Where we differ, however, is that while as a child I feared a heart of darkness in PNG, they saw a pressing need to get on and make a difference. The masks and carvings in the museum that so terrified me fascinated and enlivened them, just as they were excited by the prospects of working, Australian with Papua New Guinean, on the shared enterprise of PNG's independence. With hindsight, I have come to appreciate just how special an opportunity it was for this generation. The recollections included in this book show how valuable they understood their encounters were for them.

Regarding the impact they had on PNG on its path to nationhood, I suspect it is still too early to judge. As some of the contributors have acknowledged, Papua New Guinea has not experienced a smooth and upward trajectory since Independence in 1975, and this is an assessment that many contemporary commentators share. Whether the path would have been less bumpy had the nature of Australian engagement been different – whether independence came too soon, or perhaps too late – will probably remain a perennial subject for debate. It is also meaningless. PNG achieved its independence in 1975 after a period of increasingly intense activity from 1960, in which Australians and Papua New Guineans, including the men and women who have contributed to this book, worked together to prepare its people for nationhood. Their work has left a legacy of cooperation and mutual respect among those who know PNG and it is right that their role in helping Papua New Guinea along its path should be remembered, as it is in this book.

References

Cleland, Dame Rachel, *Papua New Guinea, Pathways to Independence: Official and Family Life 1951–1975*, (Perth: Artlook Books, 1983).

Kamit, L. Wilson, 'Central Bank Independence – The First Seven Years', Paper presented by Mr L. Wilson Kamit, CBE, Governor of the Bank of Papua New Guinea, at the 2008 Waigani Seminar, UPNG, Port Moresby, 14 August 2008. www.bis.org/review/r080819b.pdf, accessed 22 January 2014.

Nelson, Hank, *Taim Bilong Masta: The Australian Involvement with Papua New Guinea*, (Sydney: Australian Broadcasting Commission, 1982).

Oram, N. D., *Colonial Town to Melanesian City: Port Moresby, 1884–1974*, (Canberra: Australian National University Press, 1976).

Papua and New Guinea: Some Recent Statements of Australian Policy on Political Advancement, (Canberra: Australian Government Publishing Service, 1960).

 **Michael Philip Alpers** is John Curtin Distinguished Professor of International Health at Curtin University in Perth, Western Australia. He has degrees in science and medicine from the Universities of Adelaide and Cambridge. He is a Fellow of the Australasian College of Tropical Medicine and the Faculty of Public Health Medicine, Royal Australasian College of Physicians. He is a Fellow of the Royal Society, the Australian Academy of Science and the Third World Academy of Sciences.

Since 1961 he has worked on kuru, a neurodegenerative disease found in the Highlands of Papua New Guinea. He spent four years at the National Institutes of Health in Bethesda, Maryland, and nine years in the Department of Microbiology of the University of Western Australia. For 23 years he was Director of the PNG Institute of Medical Research, where he conducted research on major tropical diseases, including pneumonia, malaria and filariasis, and built up the national capacity of the Institute. His research studies have been based in the community, with strong local participation, and enhanced by the collaboration of national and international colleagues. He has been Editor or Emeritus Editor of the *Papua New Guinea Medical Journal* since 1984.

He received the Macdonald Medal from the Royal Society of Tropical Medicine and Hygiene and a Lifetime Achievement

Award from Monash University. He is Fellow of the PNG Institute of Medical Research and Honorary Fellow of the Queensland Institute of Medical Research. He is an honorary life member of the American Society of Tropical Medicine and Hygiene, the Medical Society of Papua New Guinea, the Australasian Society for Infectious Diseases and the Australasian Epidemiological Association. For his contribution to health and development in PNG he was made an Officer of the Order of Australia (AO) and Companion of the Papua New Guinean Order of the Star of Melanesia.

 **William Thomas Brown** was born on 6 December 1929. Educated at Sydney Technical High School, he attended the Australian School of Pacific Administration for five months before proceeding to Papua and New Guinea in December 1949. He completed a Commerce Degree by external study at the University of Queensland between 1966 and 1973.

In 1950 Bill was posted to Kairuku, Yule Island, 160 kilometres west of Port Moresby, and in 1951 became officer-in-charge of Urun Patrol Post – a one-man station in the Goilala – three days walk from Tapini. A term at Kainantu in the Eastern Highlands, leading patrols into the uncontrolled Lamari and Aziana River areas and administering the Sub-District from August 1954 until April 1955, preceded an 11-year stint in the Sepik District, where he was in charge of Patrol Posts Vanimo and Dreikirkir, and of Sub-Districts Aitape, Ambunti, Telefomin, Wewak and Maprik.

In June 1966 Bill was transferred to Bougainville for field duties associated with CRA's prospecting problems, and 'in the

1968 New Year's honours list he was made a Member of the Order of the British Empire … a rare honour never before granted to a DDA [Department of District Administration] officer of Brown's rank' (*KIAP: Australia's patrol officers in Papua New Guinea*, Sinclair 1981). He was appointed District Commissioner for the CRA project area in November 1969, and was District Commissioner, Bougainville District, from 1971 to 1973.

Bill resigned as Head of Administration of the Australian Film and Television School to become Director of Programmes, and sometime acting Secretary-General, of the New Caledonia-based South Pacific Commission from 1978 to 1984. A Fellow of the Australian Institute of Management since 1978, Bill, now retired, and wife Pamela live at Bilgola Beach, NSW, where he continues to pursue his interest in Bougainville affairs.

John Kenneth Albert Clezy, AM, OBE, MBBS, FRCS, FRACS, forsook his South Australian farming heritage for medicine, graduating from the University of Adelaide Medical School, class of 1953. After surgical training in Adelaide and the UK he was appointed Surgical Specialist at Nonga Base Hospital, Rabaul, in 1961. He spent 1964 in India studying the reconstructive surgery of leprosy at the fountainhead: at Vellore with Paul Brand. Although Ken was a general surgeon at heart, from then on leprosy work dominated his career at Madang, Port Moresby and Goroka, and took him to Indonesia, the Solomon Islands, New Hebrides and Western Samoa as a consultant. He is known internationally as a pioneering surgeon and expert on leprosy.

In the mid-1970s, at a difficult time for the University of

Papua New Guinea, Ken was briefly Dean of the Faculty of Medicine and Professor of Surgery, positions he says he occupied more or less by default rather than exceptional merit. In 1984 he became Senior Surgical Specialist at Goroka Base Hospital, where he expanded his longstanding interest in neurosurgery, developed safe surgical treatment for advanced gallstone disease, and helped pioneer non-operative management of the ruptured spleen in adults. He left the PNG Health Department in 1988 for Burnie, Tasmania, where he was a surgeon, Baptist Church organist and lay preacher. The Clezys spent 1999 to 2005 at a mission hospital in Yemen during a hectic time in that country's history. They now live in Adelaide.

Ken married Gwen Burrow in 1953. Of their five children Meredith and Kate studied medicine, but so far none of their 17 grandchildren has followed this path. Ken's memoir *Now in Remission* is in its second printing, and is in e-book format. His first published novel should appear in 2014.

Ken was awarded the OBE by the PNG government in 1988, and was made a Member of the Order of Australia (AM) in 2001. In 1997 he was granted honorary membership of the Neurosurgical Society of Australasia, and in 2001 he received the International Medal from the Royal Australasian College of Surgeons.

 **Bill Gammage** is an adjunct professor in the Humanities Research Centre at the Australian National University (ANU), researching Aboriginal land management. He grew up in Wagga, and was an ANU undergraduate and postgraduate before teaching history at the

Universities of Papua New Guinea (1966, 1972–6) and Adelaide (1977–98). He wrote *The Broken Years* on Australian soldiers in the Great War (1974), *Narrandera Shire* (1986), *The Sky Travellers* on the 1938–9 Hagen-Sepik Patrol in New Guinea (1998), and *The Biggest Estate on Earth: How Aborigines made Australia* (2011).

Bill was historical adviser to Peter Weir's film 'Gallipoli' (1981). He served the National Museum of Australia for three years as Council member, deputy chair and acting chair. He was made a Freeman of the Shire of Narrandera in 1987, a Fellow of the Australian Academy of Social Sciences in 1991, and a Member of the Order of Australia (AM) in 2005.

 **Ken Inglis** was born in Melbourne in 1929 and educated at North Preston state school, Northcote and Melbourne High schools, and Melbourne and Oxford Universities. He has taught at Adelaide University, the Australian National University, Brown and Harvard Universities, the University of Hawaii, and at the University of Papua New Guinea, where he was Professor of History from 1967 to 1972 and vice-chancellor from 1972 to 1975. His books include *Churches and the Working Classes in Victorian England*; *The Stuart Case*; *This is the ABC: The Australian Broadcasting Commission 1932–1983*; *Whose ABC?: The Australian Broadcasting Corporation, 1983–2006*; and *Sacred Places: War Memorials in the Australian Landscape*, which was *The Age* Book of the Year for 1998. He is Professor Emeritus at the Australian National University.

Ken is a Fellow of the Australian Academy of Social

Sciences and the Australian Academy of the Humanities. He holds an honorary Doctorate of Letters from the University of Melbourne. In 2003 he was made an Officer of the Order of Australia (AO). He lives in Melbourne with his wife Amirah, nee Gust. They have six children, all of whom cherish memories of living in PNG.

 **Sir Isi Henao Kevau** was born in Pari village in 1950. He was educated at the University of Papua New Guinea, Royal Prince Alfred Hospital in Sydney, Flinders Medical Centre in Adelaide and the University of Sydney. He was the first graduate of the medical program at the University of Papua New Guinea and the first PNG physician to earn a PhD (University of Sydney).

Sir Isi has served as Dean of Medicine and Executive Dean of the School of Medicine and Health Sciences at the University of Papua New Guinea, and as President of the Medical Society of PNG. He is Professor of Internal Medicine at the University of Papua New Guinea and a consultant physician and cardiologist at Port Moresby General Hospital. He was the first PNG physician to become Professor of Medicine. In 1995 he and Dame Carol Kidu established the Sir Buri Kidu Heart Institute in Port Moresby. Sir Isi has served as Director of the Institute since its foundation.

Sir Isi was the first Papua New Guinean or Pacific Islander to gain fellowship of the Royal Australasian College of Physicians. He was made a Commander of the British Empire (CBE) in 1988, and knighted in 2004 for services to medical education and health.

Sir Isi is an active member of the United Church in PNG. He has served the Church in various roles, particularly through his involvement with the congregation in Pari. He was a keen cricketer and rugby player, and remains an enthusiastic fisherman, using skills he learnt as a boy in Pari. He and Koriki have four children and ten grandchildren.

Dame Carol Kidu was first elected to the PNG parliament in 1997, retiring at the 2012 election. Between 2002 and 2012 she was the only woman in the 109-member parliament. She was Minister for Community Development from 2002 until August 2011. Dame Carol has been described as a 'visionary reformer' because of her commitment to transform legislative and policy frameworks for social development in PNG communities as they interact with Western society. In addition to her ministerial work, she established the Parliamentary Committee on HIV in 2003 and the PNG Parliamentary Group on Population and Development in 2008. A Dame of the British Empire, she was Pacific Person of the Year in 2007.

Dame Carol has been awarded three honorary doctorates; the PNG International Woman of Courage Award by the Secretary of State of the United States of America; the Regional Rights Resource Team Pacific Human Rights Award for her contribution to promoting the rights of Pacific Islanders; and the Cross of Knight in the Order of the Legion d'Honneur of the Republic of France. She sits on various international boards, is a member of numerous associations and committees, and has recently been appointed Asia/Pacific Patron of the Australian Centre for Leadership for Women and a patron of Australian Volunteers International.

John Langmore, after appointment as a base grade clerk, became a research officer in the PNG Department of Labour, a lecturer in economics at the University of Papua New Guinea, and Assistant Director in the Central Planning Office. Following employment in PNG, he joined Gough Whitlam's staff in May 1976 as economic advisor. John continued in that type of role for the following five years, working mainly with Ralph Willis, the Opposition Treasury Spokesman. During that time they proposed and negotiated the Accord, which successfully facilitated growth of employment and declining inflation between 1983 and 1989. In early 1983 John was requested to join Paul Keating's staff and continued as his economic advisor for several months after Labor won the March election. At the start of Labor's term he was Prime Minister Bob Hawke's representative on the organising committee for the National Economic Summit Conference. After several months he returned to Ralph Willis, who was Minister for Employment and Industrial Relations, as his chief of staff.

In 1984 John was elected as Member for Fraser and retained his seat with substantial margins in each of the following four federal elections. Substantial achievements while an MP included chairing parliamentary inquiries on trade, the international financial institutions, Third World debt, and Australia's balance of payments and overseas debt; and co-authoring a book entitled *Work For All: Full Employment in the Nineties* with John Quiggin. He also chaired a Labor Caucus committee which successfully recommended establishment of a comprehensive committee system for the House of Representatives.

John resigned from parliament at the end of 1996 to join the United Nations Secretariat as Director of the Division for Social Policy and Development in New York, a position he held for five years, after which he was Representative of the International Labour Organization to the United Nations for two years. One of his major tasks at the UN was leading the organisation of the twenty-fourth special session of the General Assembly held in Geneva in June 2000 on social development.

John returned to Australia in 2004 and was appointed Professorial Fellow in the Melbourne University School of Social and Political Sciences. As a member of the Melbourne School of Government, where he is Assistant Director Research, he teaches graduate subjects entitled 'The United Nations: Review and Reform', and 'Socio-Economic Development'. He has published extensively in books, journals and in the media.

His Excellency Charles Watson Lepani is from the Trobriand

Islands in PNG. In the 1960s he was one of a number of Papua New Guineans to be awarded an Australian secondary school scholarship, and from 1961–6 attended Thornburgh College in Charters Towers, Queensland.

Upon completing his undergraduate studies at the University of New South Wales and the University of Papua New Guinea, Charles worked as Industrial Advocate for the PNG Public Service Association, where he was successful in securing an increase in the PNG minimum wage for private sector employees. Later he headed the Bureau of Industrial Organisations and chaired the Minimum Wages Board. From 1975–80, as the first Papua New Guinean Director of the PNG National Planning Office, he provided leadership in the formulation of PNG's post-Independence public sector planning system, and in aid coordination. From 1980–81, he was a Mason Fellow at the John F. Kennedy School of Government at Harvard University, where he was awarded a Master of Public Administration. From 1986–90 he was Director of the Pacific Islands Development Program at the East-West Center in Honolulu.

Charles's first diplomatic posting was from 1991–4, when he served as PNG ambassador to the European Union, with accreditation to Belgium, Netherlands, Luxembourg, Italy, Greece, and United Nations agencies in Geneva and Vienna. He returned to PNG to take up the position of Managing Director of PNG's newly formed Minerals Resources Development Company. He served in this role from 1994–6, overseeing the partial privatisation of the nation's mining and petroleum assets, and the successful public listing of Oregon Minerals Limited, of which he was appointed CEO. He has served as an economic and public policy adviser on numerous consultancies, including in 1985 as a member of a team to review PNG's economy, and in 2004 when he was engaged as a member of the Aid Review team by the PNG and Australian governments. Since July 2005 he has served as PNG High Commissioner to Australia. He and his wife Katherine have five children and six grandchildren.

Charles was awarded the Order of the British Empire (OBE) in 1991 and made a Commander of the British Empire (CBE) in 2011 for public and diplomatic service.

 **John Ley** was born in 1938 and educated at Wesley College in Melbourne, Victoria. He took a law degree at the University of Melbourne, then worked in Melbourne law firms for several years before going to Port Moresby as a legal officer in the Australian Administration's Department of Law. After six months in the Crown Law Office, in 1966 he transferred to the Public Solicitor's Office. This role involved appearing in criminal cases for indigent Papua New Guineans in the Supreme Court of the Territory of Papua and New Guinea. In 1966 John was appointed Deputy Public Solicitor in Rabaul, East New Britain. He advised, and appeared for, indigenous clients in a range of civil, criminal and land title restoration cases.

In 1969–70 John took a masters degree in law at the University of London, focusing on African law, comparative criminal law, jurisprudence and comparative constitutional law of the Commonwealth. Upon returning to the Territory he was appointed Counsel to the Speaker and private members of the House of Assembly, remaining in this role until 1976. From 1972–4 he was seconded to the Constitutional Planning Committee, appointed by the PNG coalition government, as its legal officer.

On returning to Australia in 1976, John worked as a senior officer in the Commonwealth Attorney-General's department in a variety of policy advisory roles to do with legal aid, constitutional review, administrative law reform, criminal law, legal policy coordination, protection of movable cultural and heritage property (exports and imports), wildlife protection (exports and imports), and road and air transport legislative reform. As a consultant to the Attorney-General's department, he worked on administrative reform of the provision of grants to Aboriginal and Torres Strait Islander organisations. In the late 1990s he took a postgraduate diploma in environmental law at the Australian National University.

 **Ian Maddocks**, AM, MD, FRACP, FAFPHM, FAChPM, DTM&H, graduated in medicine from the University of Melbourne in 1955. He was appointed to the Papuan Medical College in 1961, and in 1970 became Foundation Dean and Professor of Clinical Sciences at the University of Papua New Guinea. During their last six years in Papua, the Maddocks family lived in Pari Village, close to Port Moresby. In recent years he has written about Pari; *Pari Hanua* was published in 2012.

After returning to Australia at the end of 1974, Ian was appointed Associate Professor at Flinders Medical University. For some years in southern Adelaide he promoted the development of palliative care and, in 1988, was appointed Foundation Professor of Palliative Care at Flinders University. In 1990 he introduced multidisciplinary postgraduate distance awards in palliative care. For over a decade he conducted teaching workshops, introducing palliative care in southeast Asian countries. After retirement from Flinders University in 1999, Ian continued in practice as a consultant in palliative care at the Adelaide Cancer Centre. He supported persons with terminal illness, both in hospitals and their homes.

Ian was inaugural President of the Australian Association for Hospice and Palliative Care and first President of the

Australian and New Zealand Society for Palliative Medicine. He received the inaugural Bethlehem Griffiths Medal for research in Palliative Care and Aged Care, and from 1998 to 2004 was Editor of the international journal *Progress in Palliative Care.*

From 1998 to 2004 Ian was Chairman of the Board of Directors of International Physicians for Prevention of Nuclear War (awarded the Nobel Prize for Peace in 1985), and from 1990 to 2007 was Chairman of the National Consultative Committee for Peace and Disarmament established by Australia's Minister for Foreign Affairs and Trade. In 2003 he was made a Member of the Order of Australia (AM). In 2013 he was made Senior Australian of the Year for services to palliative care and for the promotion of world peace.

Anthony James Radford was born in Melbourne in 1937 to school teacher parents. He graduated in medicine in 1960 in Adelaide, played rugby union for South Australia, and was a decathlete. He undertook postgraduate training at Liverpool, Edinburgh and Harvard universities. After a summer attachment in PNG as a *pikinini dokta* (cadet medical officer), he returned with his family in 1963, spending the next decade working as a lecturer at the Papuan Medical College and as a district medical officer. He developed a unique undergraduate and intern program in rural medicine, and researched infectious and chronic diseases, health services, medical education, archaeology and anthropology. Since PNG Independence in 1975, he has returned to the country many times to work as a consultant. His PNG experiences are described in *Singsings, Sutures and Sorcery* (Mosaic Press, 2012).

After leaving PNG, Anthony moved to the Liverpool School of Tropical Medicine, where he established the first multi-disciplinary masters program in public health in Europe. Subsequently he was appointed Foundation Professor in Primary Care and Community Medicine at Flinders University in Adelaide, a post he held for 20 years. He is Professor Emeritus at the same institution.

Anthony's research interests include Aboriginal health, aged care, medical education, health services and medical history. He has worked as a consultant in international health for national governments, WHO, UNICEF, the World Bank, World Vision and other NGOs. He has served as foundation vice-president of the Australian Faculty of Public Health Medicine, as deputy chair of Save the Children Australia, and on the boards of several professional and social institutions. He has held several visiting professorships, and in 2003 received the Fred Katz Memorial Medal for outstanding contributions to medical education. For the past 15 years he has worked as a locum general practitioner in remote and rural South Australia. He enjoys natural history, gardening and reading.

 **Robin Radford** was born in Melbourne in 1937. Her childhood was spent in the gold mining town of Ararat in western Victoria, and then in Adelaide. The eldest of four girls, her mother gave her a love of books, poetry and prose, of stories of faraway places and times, travel and adventure. Her father taught her about the Australian

bush and gave her a love of gardens. She graduated in Arts from the University of Adelaide in 1960, majoring in history and sociology combined with a diploma in social studies. At university she was active on the Students' Representative Council and in the International Club and Student Christian Movement. She obtained a blue in hockey and played in the Australian combined universities side. She and Anthony were selected for the first Australian universities student delegation to tour India in 1958–9. This experience, and joining the South Australian Anthropological Society, prepared them for their move to PNG.

In PNG Robin pursued her interest in history, particularly of the Kainantu sub-district, and she completed an MA at the University of Papua New Guinea. Several articles and a book – *Highlanders and Foreigners in the Upper Ramu* (MUP, 1987) – resulted from this work. She worked as subeditor of the *Papua New Guinea Medical Journal* and as a research assistant in the Prehistory Department at the University of Papua New Guinea. She became the local reporter for the ABC, played squash, climbed Mt Lamington, taught basic life skills to medical orderlies and their wives, established a Junior Red Cross group for village girls, and acted as research assistant to her husband, who reciprocated by fulfilling a similar role for her. Together they traced pre-contact traditional trade routes.

Back in Australia, and in addition to watching over her family, Robin has worked as a professional historian, social worker and board member of Anglicare. She established the Diocese of Adelaide Archives and is still its archivist. Robin and Anthony have three graduate children, nine grandchildren and one great-granddaughter.

 Jonathan Ritchie is a Senior Research Fellow with the Alfred Deakin Research Institute at Deakin University in Geelong, Victoria. Born and raised in PNG, he is a historian who is most interested in PNG's journey from colonial territory to independent nation, especially as experienced by Papua New Guineans themselves. His PhD addressed the Papua New Guinean people's contributions to the Constitution, and more recently he has conducted a large oral history exercise for the National Library of Australia, interviewing more than 50 Australians who lived and worked in PNG from 1940 to 1975. Following the publication in 2012 of his biography of one of PNG's 'founding fathers', the late Sir Ebia Olewale, Jonathan is pursuing ways for the life experiences of other important Papua New Guineans to be recorded and retold, for the benefit of all Papua New Guineans. These stories contain lessons for future generations about how the task of bringing PNG's diverse peoples and cultures together into an independent nation was achieved.

 Margaret Smith, AM, MBBS, FRCOG, FRANZCOG, was born on 14 July 1932. She graduated in medicine from the University of Adelaide in 1956. Most of her postgraduate training in obstetrics and gynaecology was undertaken in Edinburgh. She was made a Member of the Royal College of Obstetricians and Gynaecologists (MRCOG) in 1963, a Fellow of the Royal College of Obstetricians and Gynaecologists (FRCOG) in 1971, and a Foundation Fellow of the Australian College of Obstetricians and Gynaecologists (FRANZCOG) in 1978.

Margaret moved to Perth in 1972 after seven years in the PNG Highlands. For 15 years she was Senior Lecturer in Obstetrics and Gynaecology (University of Western Australia), based at King Edward Memorial Hospital. In 1978 she founded the first menopause clinic in Western Australia at this hospital. This clinic is named after her.

Margaret is a foundation member and past president of the Australasian Menopause Society. She co-founded the Centre for Attitudinal Healing in 1986. In 1994 she was named Citizen of the Year in the Professions (Western Australia) for her public teaching role and work with the Centre for Attitudinal Healing. In 1996 she was made a member of the Order of Australia (AM). In 2011 she was inducted into the Women's Hall of Fame in Western Australia.

Although retired from active practice, Margaret still teaches medical students part-time at the University of Notre Dame Australia (Fremantle). She is also a student and teacher at the School of Philosophy in Perth (affiliated with the London School of Economic Science). She works as a volunteer at the Ostomy Association of Western Australia (WAOA).

Margaret has written three books: *Midlife Assessment* (1998); *Is it me or my hormones?* (with Patricia Michalka, 2005); and *Now and Then: A Gynaecologist's Journey* (2010).

Christine Stewart graduated BA (First Class Honours) from the University of Sydney in 1966, where she studied Indonesian and Malayan Studies and Anthropology. She first went to PNG in 1968, and gained an LLB from the University of PNG in 1976. She 'studied' beef farming in the Bega Valley of NSW during the 1980s, and then returned to PNG to work, first with the Law Reform Commission and then with the Department of the Attorney General. She spent more than two years in Nauru, drafting legislation there, and subsequently took up consultancy work, working in PNG and the Pacific. In 2012 she was awarded a PhD by the Australian National University, Canberra, for a thesis entitled '*Pamuk na Poofta*: Criminalising Consensual Sex in Papua New Guinea'. She continues her work in law reform and drafting.

 **Dame Meg Taylor** is a citizen of PNG. She received her LLB from the University of Melbourne, and her LLM from Harvard University. She practised law in PNG and served as a member of the Law Reform Commission. From 1989–94 she lived in Washington, DC, where she served as PNG ambassador to the United States, Mexico and Canada.

Dame Meg is co-founder of Conservation Melanesia and has served on the boards of international conservation and research organisations. In addition, she has served as a board member of a number of companies in PNG in the natural resources, financial and agricultural sectors, and on the boards of companies listed on the Australian Securities Exchange. She was appointed to the post of Vice President and Compliance Advisor Ombudsman of the World Bank Group in 1999, following a selection process led by civil society, industry and academia.

ACKNOWLEDGEMENTS

Our principal acknowledgement is to our contributors. All gave their time to tell of their lives in PNG – without their efforts there would be no book. It was a pleasure and privilege to work with these remarkable Australians and Papua New Guineans. Similarly, we are grateful to Jonathan Ritchie, a PNG resident in *taim bipo*, for writing the conclusion, and to Lara Giddings, Premier of Tasmania from 2011 to 2014, for providing the foreword. University of Queensland ePress is a most efficient and professional publisher. Our thanks to Clive Moore, Dean Mason, Simon Stack, Beth Barber and all the staff who worked with us on the book. Thanks also to Ray and Helen Spark, who supported this project from the outset. We drew constantly on their memories of PNG and benefited greatly from their knowledge and suggestions. Other early supporters were Ken Inglis, Bill Gammage and the late Hank Nelson. Together they formed an unofficial publishing board when this book was no more than a vague idea. Asked for his thoughts on whether the idea was worth pursuing, Hank replied, 'Yeah, why not. I'll read anything.' His voice would have enriched this book.

INDEX

Wake, Anarai'i 104–5
Wakeford, John 176
Warren, Robin 56
Warrilow, Chris 174, 175
Watson, Lepani 196
Wellington, Jim 175
Whitlam, Gough 4, 37, 78, 108, 133,
150, 189, 195, 199
Wigley, Stan 67
Willis, Ralph 134

Wohlers, Peter 175
Wolfers, Edward (Ted) 152, 192
Wright, Eric 68

Yancey, Philip 40
Yocklunn, John 192

Zigas, Vincent 25-6
Zylstra, William 94
Zzefirio, Banare 96

Printed in Australia
AUOC02n0839140714
262121AU00007B/13/P

9 781921 902437